A TOUCH OF
COLLINS

A TOUCH OF COLLINS

The story of a
show-business dynasty

*

JOE COLLINS

WITH

JUDITH SIMONS

COLUMBUS BOOKS
LONDON

Jacket photographs
Front cover: Joe with (left to right)
Joan, Natasha and Jackie.

Back cover: (top) Will Collins,
sisters Bessie Pacey (real name
Assenheim) and Hettie Collins in
'black face', young Joe with sisters
Lalla (left) and Pauline, young Joan
with baby Jackie and Joe today with
dog Max.

First published in Great Britain in 1986 by
Columbus Books Limited
19-23 Ludgate Hill, London EC4M 7PD

Designed by Fred Price

British Library Cataloguing in Publication Data
Collins, Joe
A touch of Collins: the story of a showbusiness dynasty.
1. Performing arts—Great Britain—History—20th century
I. Title
791'.092'4   PN2595

ISBN 0–86287–308–8

Phototypeset by Falcon Graphic Art Ltd
Wallington, Surrey
Printed and bound by
Mackays of Chatham Ltd, Kent

CONTENTS

1

Overture and Beginners

I am a showman, so I am not going to be modest about the truth. We Collins are a remarkable family. The exceptional stamina, drive and flair of our forebears has manifested itself through the generations and made us what we are today.

My cockney maternal grandmother, Leah Assenheim, bore 19 healthy children and lived well into her nineties. My father, Will Collins, who came from a line of successful fishmongers, struck out in the 1890s into vaudeville and by his thirties was a top stage impresario. He certainly had drive and flair. It was my father, and my soubrette mother Hettie Collins, who ensured that show business, from his generation on, was the Collins family trade.

Both my late wife Elsa and my present wife Irene stem from roots as solid as my own. Elsa, mother of my three eldest children – Joan, Jackie and Bill – was the daughter of William Bessant, a South Londoner who started working life as a railway porter. He and his wife Ada reared a family of eleven children, all of whom worked hard and did them credit. My second wife, Irene, mother of my youngest child, Natasha, comes from a coal-mining background in Germany.

The Collins story may not reflect the glittering image projected by Joan and Jackie in their work today, but it is about real people, not glamorized fantasy characters.

We all have our own individual characteristics, needs and personalities. Joan and Jackie are both quick-tempered, something inherited from me. My son Bill is rational and calm, more like his mother and her forebears. My youngest daughter, Natasha, is very independent. As she wants to be a soldier, that's a quality she needs.

Sadly, my first wife, Elsa, did not live to see the glamour and fame that Joan and Jackie have brought to the family name today. It is Irene, my second wife, who has supported me against the huge tidal wave of publicity – with its triumphs and tempests – which has threatened to engulf our family.

I can't deny it. The Collins family thrives on excitement and challenge. My two eldest girls, Joan and Jackie, did not reach the top of their competitive fields on a plane of tranquillity. As for Natasha, what she has witnessed in her growing-up years has been excellent preparation for keeping her cool in all circumstances when she goes into the army.

One can hardly blame Bill, who is of a different temperament, for distancing himself from all the turmoil and getting on, determinedly, with his own work.

Not so many years ago it was *I* who was the best-known member of our family, a top theatrical agent and entrepreneur. But today, when I am out and about, people point to me and say, 'You know who that is, don't you? That's Joan and Jackie Collins' father.'

I chuckle. Real fame at last!

But personal fame never was my aim. I have been content to be a 'Mr Ten Per Cent'. While contracting work for stars like Peter Sellers and Shirley Bassey I never sought the limelight for myself. Some of the artistes were simply my clients, others my friends. As agent for the singer Dorothy Squires I was a friend of her former husband Roger Moore when he was just another hopeful young actor. More recently I guided the careers of Mike and Bernie Winters, and helped my wife Irene steer singer Roger Whittaker right to the top.

I have had a good life. From the day I was born I have been in the wings, watching the whole spectrum of show business from the minstrel shows of the Edwardian era to video today. I'm pleased as punch to have passed on the Collins vigour to Joan, Jackie, Bill and Natasha.

In a hundred years from now, another few generations, people may not be watching *Dynasty* or rushing out to buy Jackie's novels. But this book will attempt to show how the Collins line gilded the entertainment industry throughout the twentieth century.

Our family name was not 'Collins' originally. My father, Isaac

Hart, was born on 11 November 1876, son of a fishmonger, Zuesman Hart, and his wife Julia (née Phillips).

Zuesman and Julia were married on 23 February 1875 at the Great Synagogue, Duke's Place, in the City of London. Zuesman's father Zalig, my great-grandfather, was also a fishmonger. Julia's father, Isaac Phillips, is described on my grandparents' marriage certificate simply as a 'dealer'.

Both families bore names famous in Anglo-Jewry. In the eighteenth century Aaron Hart had been rabbi at the Great Synagogue and was, in fact, Chief Rabbi of Great Britain. I do not know if he is one of my ancestors, but his family, like mine, belonged to the tribe of Levy. One of Rabbi Aaron Hart's descendants was Ernest Simpson, the second husband of Wallis, who later became the Duchess of Windsor.

On the Phillips side, Sir Benjamin Phillips was Lord Mayor of London in 1865, and his son Sir George Faudel Phillips was Lord Mayor of London in 1896. Again, I have no proof of family connection.

What I do know is that both families from which I stem – my mother's side too – lived in the Middlesex Street area, better known as Petticoat Lane, a part of the East End with a shifting, cosmopolitan population of native British, Jews, Irish, Chinese, Germans, Dutch, Indians, Poles and Russians. It was an area of smelly alleyways, overcrowded homes and appalling work conditions. But the barrel organs and gin shops brought gaiety to the street atmosphere, and there was always the pleasure of socializing in the shops and stalls of the Sunday market in Petticoat Lane, Sundays being the one day of the week when the overworked East Enders had time to do their shopping.

The people there had a lust for life, good humour, determination and a great sense of kinship. For many of the people born in this area, the very atmosphere gave them vigour and an iron will to better themselves.

By the 1890s the Hart family had achieved that ambition to progress. My great-grandfather Zalig Hart opened a fish shop in Westbourne Terrace, Bayswater, a gracious area of London where the 'nobs' lived. Zalig's son Zuesman, my grandfather, went into the expanding 'fast-food' business and opened two fried-fish shops, one in High Street, Bloomsbury, and the other in Little Andrew Street, between Upper St Martin's Lane and Seven Dials: right in the heart of the theatre district.

The theatres fascinated Zuesman's teenage son, Isaac – my father. He was a handsome lad, and totally stage-struck. In 1891 at the Tivoli in the Strand, a sensational new star made her début. She was a saucy young lady in a big Gainsborough hat, a short red dress over frothy petticoats and high-heeled boots. As she high-kicked and danced through her famous song 'Ta-ra-ra Boom De-ay' she brought a touch of Parisian verve to the London music hall. Her name was Lottie Collins.

Watching from his seat in the pit, my father was enthralled by her. Lottie Collins became his idol, and he decided to change his name to hers.

From that point, when my father stood at stage doors, collecting performers' autographed photographs, he insisted that they wrote 'To Will Collins'. (I don't know where he got the 'Will' from.)

So started my father's show-business ambitions. By the time he reached his twenties he was determined to turn his back on the fish trade and go into what he called 'vor-dor-vil': he savoured every syllable of the word.

My father was supported in his dream of the theatre by his pretty, dark-haired girlfriend, Henrietta Assenheim. She too had stage ambitions, and a natural talent. She won a place in a London stage musical and while still in her teens was Principal Girl in the pantomime *Aladdin* at the Theatre Royal, Bristol. My father insisted that she should use a stage name similar to that of his idol, Lottie Collins, so Henrietta Assenheim became Hettie Collins.

I do not know the circumstances of how my father made his break with his roots; however, I do know that he followed many other adventurous young men to the prospecting mines of South Africa. He worked as a newsagent, and as a court bailiff, until finally he got a job as business manager of a theatre company.

My father had business acumen as well as youthful dreams, and he was soon putting on variety shows and concerts of his own. His companies toured South Africa and Rhodesia. It was at this stage of his life that he ceased to be Isaac Hart and became known officially as Will Collins.

My father was most enterprising. Even when the Boers, uneasy about British dominance in South Africa, invaded Natal and besieged the towns of Mafeking, Kimberley and Ladysmith, my father was not deterred. He would post the bills announcing his entertainments on tree trunks and draw audiences from all the warring factions.

The London show-business newspaper *The Encore* reported in 1900:

Mr Collins is a most obliging gentleman. He will get up a show to suit all the classes in South Africa. He is on friendly terms with both Boers and Britons and also persona grata among the Zulus, the Basutos, the Matabele and other dusky gentry who are now our friends and allies, but were once arrayed in war panoply against us.

The report ended by saying that Mr Collins could be reached in Cape Town, where he would be 'happy to greet any members of the profession coming out from the Old Country'.

When my father had established himself in South Africa he proposed to his sweetheart Hettie Collins by letter, suggesting that she come out with a dancing troupe and they could marry as soon as she arrived in Cape Town.

She readily agreed. Entertainment for the Boer War troops was a patriotic service, for early in 1900 large bodies of Imperial Volunteers, Imperial Yeomanry and – for the first time in British history – huge contingents from the Dominions, had been sent to South Africa to fight the Boers.

My mother and the rest of the company travelled around South Africa by bullock wagon in the wake of the soldiers, putting on entertainments in candelit theatres.

On 17 May 1900 my mother was appearing in Kimberley – no longer under siege – when the company manager rushed on stage, interrupting the performance: 'Although we have had no confirmation of this great and glorious news, Mafeking has at last been relieved,' he cried. 'Let us raise our voices across the world to cheer that gallant cavalry hero Colonel Baden-Powell. God save the Queen!'

11

The audience cheered Baden-Powell (who later founded the Boy Scout movement), and at this historic moment my mother led the singing of the National Anthem.

When my mother's entertainment company finally reached Cape Town, in December 1900, there were considerably fewer girls than had originally set off from Britain. With so many soldiers around, most of the dancers and comediennes had married and left the troupe. But Hettie had remained faithful to Will Collins and they were married in Cape Town, by special licence, on 10 January 1901.

Hettie continued to star in shows, touring in the plays and musicals presented by my father, until the following year, when they had their first child: I was born on 3 November 1902 at Port Elizabeth, six months after the Boer War ended. In features and colouring I resembled my mother, but my temperament came from my father.

After my arrival my mother devised a new stage act: two of her sisters, Hannah and Bessie, came to South Africa to join her as the Three Cape Girls. The sisters blacked their faces, dressed up in a variety of costumes – from shirts and breeches with long dashing cloaks to frilly polka-dot dresses – and performed skilled dance routines on the tips of their long-toed boots.

The girls would do their quick changes in two tents erected on the stage, an arrangement that enabled me, the new baby, to be left within easy reach of my mother, hidden away in one of these shelters. Also concealed in my hideaway was Auntie Bessie's favourite tipple, a bottle of Guinness.

One evening Auntie Bessie, after taking a quick swig in the dark of the tent, accidentally dropped her bottle on my head. I don't know what the audience thought when they heard a baby's howls coming from the tent and saw a trickle of brown liquid oozing across the stage, but my meticulous father was furious. He insisted that his wife stopped working and decided to find some position in London. So back we travelled to England in a ship bursting with war brides, returning soldiers and their offspring. Guess who won first prize in the shipboard baby competition?

Once back in London my father soon found his feet. Musical

comedy and music hall were at the height of their popularity, and there were plenty of openings for shrewd, imaginative, forceful men like Will Collins. He wrote to theatre-owner Oswald Stoll (later Sir Oswald) enclosing his photograph. I still have a copy of that letter, written with my father's usual broad-nibbed pen.

Dear Sir,

Being disengaged for acting, business or stage management, I am taking the liberty of writing to you, should there be a vacancy at any time. I hold the best of references from the leading music hall and theatrical managers. A reply at your convenience will much oblige.

Yours respectfully . . .

Stoll responded immediately, offering my father a post as assistant manager of the Holloway Empire, in North London, where he made such a good impression he was soon asked to open and manage Stoll's latest theatre, the Ardwick Empire in Manchester. This was a palace of a place, all gilt and plush, with – a wonder of the age – large foyers lit by electric light chandeliers instead of the usual gaslight. A forerunner in the effort to clean up the music halls, it was advertised as 'the home of family entertainment'.

I never met my paternal grandparents and, as far as I can recall, my father never mentioned their names to me. However, my mother's parents, Joe and Leah Assenheim, I knew and loved well. Like the Harts, they originated from the East End, from Stoney Lane, which intersects Middlesex Street (Petticoat Lane). The Assenheims were proud to be true East Enders, revelling in the rumbustious atmosphere, the community spirit.

Grandpa Joe had started in business selling lobsters at racetracks where he was known as 'Lobster Joe', until he found a more lucrative living as a 'hokey pokey' man, with a stall in Petticoat Lane market. The Assenheim hokey pokey (it means cheap ice cream sold in the street) was vanilla flavour, with a streak of raspberry through the middle.

'Hokey pokey, penny a lump, that's the stuff to make you jump!' was my grandfather's street cry.

Grandma Leah Assenheim, a gentile girl who had converted

Will Collins, Business and General Manager.

Nov 8th 1903

Has represented the following Companies:

Mr. George Edwardes' London Gaiety Company.

Miss Nance O'Neil and Company.

Mr. Willie Edouin and London Company.

Mr. George Edwardes' Repertoire Comedy Company.

Mr. Edward Terry and London Company.

Australian Opera Company.

...land's Dramatic Co.

...o. Walton's Musical Comedy Company.

...erican Company.

...Vaudeville Co.

...le's Opera Company.

...le's Vaudeville Co.

...d's Entertainers.

Terry's Theatre Strand.

Oswald Stoll Esq.

Dear Sir

Being disengaged for acting, business or stage management, I am taking the liberty of writing in to you, should there be a vacancy at any time. I hold the best of references from the leading music hall & theatrical managers. A reply at your convenience will much oblige.

Yours respectfully
Will Collins

Will Collins' letter announcing his availability for work.

14

to Judaism, bore my grandfather 19 children, and Grandfather Joe was proud of her. They would drive in style to the races in a horse-drawn carriage, my grandmother with her latest baby in her arms and heavily pregnant with the next.

Despite the demands of producing and rearing a huge family, my Grandma Leah still had energy to spare. She was a first-class milliner, and she made a handsome contribution to the family coffers. For the East End girls, no matter how shabby their clothes, loved magnificent hats with huge gaudy feathers. Their dresses might be torn, their faces dirty, but even when they got into fights the girls' hats would always, miraculously, escape damage.

My mother, Hettie, was the seventh of the Assenheim children. She never had any training for the stage, but she had style and charisma. When she appeared in shows the critics' notices were fulsome: 'Miss Hettie Collins is a thumping favourite . . .'; 'Most charming little lady. . .'; 'Miss Hettie Collins takes the bun for dancing and singing and in fact everything she does.'

With my father's future now assured, our family expanded. My sister Lalla was born in Manchester in 1905, in our home behind the Ardwick Empire. My parents named her after Lalla Selbini, constant companion and assistant to The Great Lafayette.

The Great Lafayette is the first top star I remember meeting within the family circle. Born Siegmund Neuburger in Munich, Germany in 1872, but a naturalized American, he is still regarded as having been the greatest illusionist of all time. His death is another piece of theatrical history. He was killed in a backstage fire at the Empire Palace in Edinburgh in 1911, together with members of his company and several of his 'live' prop animals, including a lion.

After Manchester, Sir Oswald Stoll promoted my father to circuit manager of all his London theatres. The one which he made his headquarters was the Shepherd's Bush Empire in West London, and it was in 1907 in our new house in Pennard Road – behind the theatre – that my sister Pauline was born.

My sisters' arrival did not oust me from my special status in the family. I was the son, the beauty, the most cherished of children. My own offspring now claim that I was 'spoiled rotten'.

My father made sure that I would grow up feeling the music hall was my second home. He would take me with him through the alleyway to the theatre in the mornings where, to the amusement of the cleaners, I would sit in the orchestra pit, baton in hand, pretending I was the conductor.

Harry, the stage-doorkeeper, made me a whip from plaited string, and I would race around the Shepherd's Bush streets imagining I was driving one of the horse-drawn buses which stopped outside the Empire.

I found horse-drawn transport altogether fascinating. I would gasp when a horse fell down and had to be assisted to its feet by volunteers. I was excited by the galloping horses which drew the fire engines, kicking up clouds of dust as they raced to do their duty. I envied the boys, not much older than I was, who were employed to sweep up the horse dung, darting amidst the traffic with their brushes and pails.

I loved all the London street life of Edwardian times . . . the men selling crumpets and muffins, ringing their bells and shouting their wares as they came along our road, the men with their horses and drays shouting 'Any old iron!'

I realized the gulf between the poor and the comfortably off through watching the little chimney-sweeps. Due to the high and horrible accident rate these boys were no longer forced to climb up inside the chimneys, but it was still a filthy dirty job.

My own life was so much more protected.

Every day after lunch, and our afternoon rest, my father would change into full evening dress, I would be put into a velvet suit – the model Edwardian child – and we would go to the theatre for the evening performance.

One artiste made a mistake my father could not forgive. This was bill-topper G.H. Chirgwin, known as the White-eyed Kaffir because he drew a large, white, diamond-shaped patch on his black minstrel make-up. Chirgwin was once foolish enough to pick up Will Collins' precious little Joe and carry him on to the stage!

He introduced me to the public. 'Look at this dear little fellow I found in the wings!'

Unlike the ladies of my family, I had never liked facing an audience. I hid my face from the applause, and in the confusion some of Chirgwin's black make-up smeared my pristine white silk collar.

'Look what you've done to the child!' my father cried angrily. He never booked Chirgwin again.

Actually, I was sorry when Chirgwin disappeared from my life. His songs 'The Little Blind Boy' and 'My Fiddle is My Sweetheart' would bring tears to my eyes.

My father eventually left Stoll and began staging his own productions. One of his coups was engaging monocled comedian Ralph Lynn – a bit of a silly-ass type – who later became a star of screen farce, teamed with Tom Walls.

My father sailed to America specially to see Lynn, where he was appearing in Cincinatti, and booked him to play the lead in a musical comedy called *Peaches*.

During the pre-London provincial tour, when the show was playing in Liverpool, two American banjoists in the cast asked Lynn's advice about London accommodation.

'I know an excellent place,' Lynn said, 'better than any hotel. The landlady is usually booked up, but I'll give you the address and you can write to her. She's a Mrs George of no. 11 Downing Street. Very convenient for the West End.'

The banjoists duly wrote off, requesting two adjoining rooms, but received no reply.

My father entered the spirit of the joke. 'Mrs George is like that,' he said. 'Bad at letter-writing. But just go straight to no. 11 when you arrive in London. Any policeman will direct you.'

The two fall guys duly arrived with their luggage at the residence of the Chancellor of the Exchequer (later to be the Prime Minister), then took the same cab on to our own new pretentious house and garden in Goldhawk Road, West London. My mother, resplendent in one of her new hobble-skirted dresses, greeted them.

'We've decided to stay here instead,' the banjoists informed

17

my parents. 'Mr and Mrs Lloyd George wouldn't even come to the door. They sent their butler.'

The show I remember most vividly from that time, however, was not *Peaches* but an entertainment called *Redheads* in which my Aunt Hannah Assenheim (who used the stage name Hannah Hart, my father's original surname) was principal dancer. *Redheads*, not dissimiliar to the modern musical *A Chorus Line*, was about a fashion house auditioning red-headed girls for a dress show. The applicants included a girl from the Fire Service, a runaway heiress, a girl always dissolving into tears and so on. My father and I were so sold on this show we would recite the entire script word for word. My father even taught it to Polly, our pet parrot.

Though I shared so much with my father he did exclude me from one of his pleasures: I was not allowed to go near his pianola. On Sundays, his one free day of the week, he would sit alone in the lace-curtained parlour playing this mechanical piano, as up-to-date then as stereo and video today. Light classical pieces, the latest Gilbert and Sullivan comic opera songs, would trip invitingly off the music roll with my father using foot-operated bellows to operate it. But my sisters and I were not allowed to turn my father's pianola-playing into a sing-song.

By the time I was eight years old my father was really prosperous. 'You've got to have push and go to get ahead!' he would tell me. He certainly had plenty of it himself. He was one of the first men in the British theatre to realize the value of publicity and employ a press agent for his shows, and one of the first to bring American vaudeville artistes to Britain on a large scale.

Each morning, dressed in immaculate frock coat, shirt with winged collar and top hat, my father would catch the white steam-powered National Bus (faster and more expensive than the horse-drawn kind) to his West End offices in Panton Street. The telephone, a fairly new invention, was still not used on a large scale for doing business and my father did long-distance deals by telegraph. His telegraphic address was a rather whimsical one: Snillo Willo.

As a modern man, my father stopped playing the pianola on Sundays when he found a new hobby: motoring. He did not learn to drive himself but instead hired a motor car complete with a uniformed chauffeur, either a chain-driven Daimler or a French car, a Charron.

This latter vehicle was not exactly reliable. When we came to Hand Cross, a steep hill on the road to the Sussex coast, we would all have to get out and push.

The whole family took part in these Sunday outings and we always went 50 miles south of London to Brighton. This was the start of my life-long affection for this seaside resort. When I took my own children there – Joan, Jackie, Bill and Natasha – I was happy to see the reflection of my own early pleasure.

When I first went to Brighton it was a fashionable watering-place, with elegant Regency houses and a three-mile-long promenade, the finest in Europe. We would visit the fantastic Pavilion, built by the Prince Regent, stroll among the shops in The Lanes, dating back to the days when the place was a fishing village, and ride on the Volks Electric Railway, the first electric railway in Britain, that ran along the beach.

My father, who wanted only the best for me, put my name down for Charterhouse, the famous public school, and in the meantime I was sent away to prep school at Rottingdean, Sussex, a picturesque village just down the road from Brighton, where distinguished 'old boys' included Lord Jellicoe, Admiral of the Fleet and later Governor-General of New Zealand.

Going away to school was a culture shock. After three miserable weeks I felt I could stand it no longer. I wrote a threatening letter to my parents that said: 'If you do not bring me home at once I will kill myself. I intend to throw myself off a cliff.'

Well, spoiled child I may have been, but my parents knew it was now time for me to start growing up. They simply wrote to the headmaster and his wife, who gave me a reassuring pep talk. The crisis passed, and I adjusted to my new life away from home and among other boys.

I learned to be self-reliant, and to control my inner emotions – perhaps too well. My daughter Joan has always complained that while I am a 'loving father' I am also 'remote', a sentiment shared by others close to me. I am, I suppose, a product of the British boarding-school system.

I cannot claim, however, to be a highly educated man. At school I was more interested in sport than studying. On the field I was a good all-rounder. I captained the school soccer team, played scrum half with the rugby team, was long-stop in the cricket team and one memorable sports day won the Silver Cup, presented by Colonel B.R. James, father of a fellow pupil, for the 100 yards' sprint. I am still very proud of that trophy.

I also have memories of less worthy pastimes, like sitting in the clock tower with two chums rolling improvised cigarettes made of brown paper. Though the big bell striking the hour and half-hour almost deafened us it did not put us off our smoking. To conclude our interlude of forbidden pleasure we would raid the apple trees near the school grounds, out of bounds to us boys.

On Sundays I became virtuous and sang in the choir at Rottingdean Church. I presume I was chosen as a chorister because I looked so angelic and handsome in my white surplice. Obviously the choirmaster was not deterred by the fact that I was Jewish – nor that I couldn't sing.

Cocooned in the happy world of Rottingdean Preparatory School, I have no recollection of that day in August 1914 when war was declared in Europe. It made no deep impression on me.

This cherished period of my life came to a sudden end, owing to an incident during one of my father's shows at the Shepherd's Bush Empire. One evening, while I was dreaming of glory on the sports field, my father was keeping a keen eye on one of his productions. A girl dancer was being swirled around the stage in the arms of her partner when the belt fell off her dress. Instead of ignoring what had happened she instinctively stopped dancing and bent to pick it up, while the orchestra played on and her partner (also her husband, an American named Larry Sebellas) waited at her side.

My father – always a perfectionist, and with the hasty temper which each of our line has inherited from him – was watching from his usual place at the back of the circle. Unable to contain his anger, he stormed backstage and ranted at the girl as she stepped into the wings.

'You idiot!' he shouted. 'You spoilt the whole performance. Theatre is supposed to be magic. You broke the spell, brought the whole thing down to a mundane level. You don't deserve to be in a professional show. You're nothing but an amateur!'

'Don't you dare speak to my wife like that!' retorted the partner-husband, rushing to his wife's side. 'Shut up bawling at her or I'll. . .'

Sebellas raised his fists.

My father retaliated and struck the first blow.

Sebellas aimed a sharp kick at my father's ankle.

As my father hopped in pain, that should have been the end of the nasty little incident. But the kick caused a blood clot to form in my father's leg. The doctor advised him to rest in bed for a couple of weeks. During his convalescence S.W. Wyndham, the music-hall comedian, came round to cheer him up. After my mother had ushered him into the bedroom, she went to fetch the two men some strawberries and cream while they had a good chat.

Wyndham knew how to tell a joke. My father shook with laughter . . . until the blood clot reached his heart. He literally laughed himself to death. He died on 17 June 1915, aged 39.

When the headmaster called me to his study to break the news I was still in a state of euphoria following my triumphs in the school sports day. After the first shock of grief I grasped very quickly that from now on my path to manhood would not be what my father had intended for me.

As I travelled back to London to be with my mother and sisters my attitude changed forever. I knew I could no longer expect the privileged start of a rich man's son. I was now the man of the family, and would have to do my best to step into my father's shoes, to make my own way, as he had done.

I read the obituary in *The Encore*:

Mr Collins was a man who made many friends and few enemies. His influence upon the music hall business was a wholly good one. He had an agile mind and keen insight into the conditions of our business.

I hoped that I too would be a credit to the Collins name.

My father had been well insured, but due to the circumstances of his death my mother did not get the insurance money. However, my parents were well liked and friends rallied round. One of my father's partners, Sam Gething, carried on the business for a little while, providing my mother with an income.

Our finances still permitted me to fulfil my father's wish that I should go to a public school. My mother chose St Paul's in London, not the more expensive Charterhouse, as Father had intended, but still an excellent school.

Mother moved away from London to a house on the seafront at Brighton – 102 King's Road, right next to the Grand Hotel (which was blown up by the IRA, with loss of life, during the 1984 Conservative Party Conference).

Having to pay for my education, and dancing and elocution lessons for my two sisters whom she was having trained for the stage, Mother's resources were strained. To help matters, she took in paying guests, theatricals who came to play a week's engagement at the local Hippodrome. They were top names in vaudeville.

Among our lodgers was the earthy comedienne Marie Lloyd, the 'Queen of British Music Hall', ranking in celebrity with Queen Victoria and Florence Nightingale, who had been with my mother in the first British company to perform in the Rand after the Boer War.

Marie Lloyd stayed at our house with her third husband, the jockey Bernard Dillon, 18 years her junior. Now in her forties, Marie was apprehensive about losing her youthful appearance.

'Bring me a hot iron, Het!' I heard her shout to my mother one day. 'I want to try to smooth out the wrinkles on my belly!'

I felt sad for Mother as she rushed around fulfilling her celebrated guests' demands. Had she not given up her career to care for her husband and family, Mother might well have been a star herself.

Pasted carefully in a book were her reviews for the musical comedies in which she had appeared: *The Telephone Girl, The Showman's Sweetheart* and – a huge hit in its day – *The Chinese Honeymoon*.

The ALHAMBRA PALACE OF VARIETIES,
ST. JOHN STREET.

THE ONLY MUSIC HALL IN CAPE TOWN

TO-NIGHT,
Miss HETTIE COLLINS,
Comedienne and Dancer.

THE TWO GRACES,
MISS LILY ADAIR

12 STAR A...

Business M...

ALHAMBRA PALACE (business manager, Mr. G. H. Clother).—A strong bill of ample dimensions and good quality is under treatment at this hall, whose operations are well looked after by Mr. Geo. Clother. Miss Hettie Collins, a charming comedienne and expert dancer, opened here last Saturday night to a big audience, and what a grand reception they gave her! She sang four songs, and then gave two very clever dances. Miss Collins fairly captivated the audience on Saturday, and should be a big draw for the present management of the Alhambra.

THE ALHAMBRA,
ST. JOHN-STREET.

TO-NIGHT,
Starring and Expensive Engagement of

Miss HETTIE COLLINS

The Dashing Comedienne and Dancer, from the Principal London Music Halls.

Kitty Cunningham,
George Mason,
Leah Ballard,
Arthur Kennedy,
Bradfaugh,
Hetty Heywood,
Bonnie Goo...
The Selvey...
The Great...

Conclu...

"DON'T...

Popular P...
Private Bo...
Business M...

WANTED KNOWN.
THAT
Miss Hettie Collins
HAS
DISTINCTLY REFUSED TO APPEAR AT THE
Alhambra Music Hall.
(Sgd.) HETTIE COLLINS.
January 22th, 1901.
1077

Empire Theatre.

Sole Lessee · ... JULIUS PHILLIPS.

Saturday · and · Monday,
JUNE 8 and 10,

"A CHINESE HONEYMOON."

A new and original Musical Comedy by GEORGE DANCE. Music by HOWARD TALBOT.

Characters.

Mr. Pineapple ⎫	...	Mr. GEO. WALTON
Mrs. Pineapple ⎬	On their Honeymoon Trip	... Miss MARIE CAMPBELL
Florrie ⎭	...	Miss BESSIE PAYNE
The Emperor Hang Chow		Mr. CECIL CROFT
The Lord Chancellor Chipe Chop		Mr. ARTHUR SOUTTEN
The Lord High Admiral Li Hung		Mr. HARRY LAMBART
Tom Hatherton	...	Mr. TOM KINNARD
Soo Soo	...	Miss VIOLET WARD
Fi Fi	...	Miss HETTIE COLLINS
Yen Yen	...	Miss LOTTIE ASHFORD
Len	...	Mr. ROBB. TEES
Chifoo	...	Mr. T. WARDROP
Mrs. Brown	...	Miss ALICE ALEXANDER

Hettie Collins' show-business career in South Africa was much in evidence in the local press, as these cuttings show.

My father had been so proud of what the critics had written: 'Hettie Collins is a dashing comedienne and dancer'; 'Miss Hettie Collins is a dashing, dauntless, daring dancer and a comely, cooing, kicking comedienne.' And she was praised for her renditions of the Cockney songs 'I Want to Be a Lady' and 'The Bloke That I'd Like To Go Out With'. I don't remember her ever singing them once she gave up the stage.

By now I was very much aware of life outside the school environment, of the devastating war being fought in Europe, and the huge death toll it was producing. My beloved Uncle Phil, youngest of the 19 Assenheim children, was killed at the Front in France. As I went through my paces with the Officers' Training Corps, under canvas at Marlborough, Wiltshire, I envisaged that soon I would be in the trenches, answering Lord Kitchener's call 'Your Country Needs You!'

It seemed no time to be sitting in a classroom, learning subjects I believed would be no use to me. Shortly before my fourteenth birthday I decided to leave school and get a few years' work experience before I joined up.

I wrote to Mr Nicholas Pallister, business manager of the thriving Moss Empires theatre circuit, telling him I was Will Collins' son and asking him for a job. Mr Pallister, who had known my father well, asked me to come for an interview, and offered me a position in the Moss Empire offices in London.

My mother had mixed feelings about the matter. She was uneasy that I was not completing my education, but she was pleased that I had chosen to work in show business.

She saw the logic of my argument: 'I'm not very academic, and it's better for me to go out and earn some money. I'll get basic knowledge of the Moss Empires business and then may even work my way up to managing one of their theatres.' This was the height of my ambitions.

I drew myself up to my full 5-foot 10-inch height. 'You don't have to worry about me. I know how to conduct myself; I'm a man of the world.'

Yes, at 13¾ this was exactly how I saw myself. Joseph William Collins was now set to take his place in the adult world . . . at 7s 6d per week.

2

My Apprenticeship

When I accepted my position of office junior with Moss Empires my mother took me immediately to an East End tailor, He put me in the hands of his son Sammy, a lad of about my own age, who was his apprentice in the trade. Sammy made me a dark navy blue suit in best worsted, complete with waistcoat, costing £10. I felt proud as a peacock: I was so impressed with Sammy Stewart's workmanship that he is my tailor to this day (he is now a partner in the top West End firm Lord & Stewart).

In my new finery I felt completely grown up. But my mother suddenly had misgivings about my encountering 'bad company' while commuting to London. I reassured her, secretly looking forward to such fast living.

That first day as a wage-earner I walked to Brighton Station, arriving at the platform about 20 minutes before the train was due to leave. Finding a third-class compartment all to myself, I waited for the adventure to start.

Two portly men in the 'city gentleman' uniform of bowler hat, rolled umbrella and briefcase flung open the door.

'There's only this lad in here!' one of them called. 'If we can manage to keep everyone else out we can get a game going.'

Two more men arrived and greeted my companions, giving me glances which indicated I was of no account at all. As the train started moving one of the men opened his briefcase, produced a blanket and spread it over the knees of the conspiratorial quartet.

Another placed his leather attaché case on top of the blanketed knees to form an improvised table. A third gave me a clue what was about to happen: he pulled out a pack of cards. Soon the men were engrossed in a card game I later learned was called 'faro'. As money changed hands I watched, fascinated. This was obviously the 'bad company' Mother had warned me about.

An hour later, as the train neared Victoria Station, one of my companions condescended to speak to me.

'Haven't seen you on the train before,' he remarked, eyeing my new office clothes. 'Just started work in town, have you?'

I nodded.

'Well, if you'd like to make yourself a copper or two, get to Brighton Station early tomorrow and save a compartment for us. Keep it empty till we get there.'

'How do I do that?'

'Sit there laughing your head off, so other people will think you've got a screw loose. No one will get in with you if they think you're barmy.'

Next day I was again early on the train, but I was too inhibited to stage the suggested 'loony' act. I found it more dignified simply to hang out of the window, pretending I was reserving seats for the rest of a family party. Soon I had earned myself quite a bit of pocket money by keeping seats for the card-players.

My new job at Moss Empires consisted of routine beginner's duties – running errands for my superiors and distributing the mail after it had been opened and sorted out in the post room.

Occasionally on my rounds I'd pinch a delectable Turkish cigarette from the silver cigarette-box on Albert de Courville's desk. He was the producer of the big shows at the new London Hippodrome, Moss Empires' top theatre. Occasionally, out of curiosity, I'd read some of the letters I was distributing.

On my first day I was intrigued by a letter on notepaper headed 'Canterbury Cathedral'. Apparently a clergyman had complained to Moss Empires about the religious songs 'Star of Bethlehem' and 'A Holy City' being performed in music halls. My company had asked a Church of England dignitary to check the situation, and now he was offering reassurance: 'When these songs are performed the reception is of a subdued and attentive kind fitting to the subject. I had found this even in some of our lower-class halls, patronized by ill-educated people,' he wrote solemnly.

Another letter complained about the 'low quality' of music-hall jokes. 'The mother-in-law, the lodger and a certain parasitic pest are drawn upon much too largely in order to obtain a cheap laugh,' wrote the pompous correspondent. (Comics still joke about lodgers and mothers-in-law, but that third source of mirth, the 'parasitic pest', namely the human flea, no longer seems to trouble us.)

In my days of delivering the post there was always correspondence about whether smoking should be permitted in theatres and whether people dropping lighted matches on the floor should be prosecuted. The anti-smoking lobby was, even then, a powerful force.

Requests from Moss Empires artistes to recommend London accommodation were a regular part of the mailbag. Where, I wonder, did Moss Empires manage to accommodate that visting troupe of ten performing dogs, described by their owners as the 'highly trained and cute chihuahuas of Mexico, the smallest and rarest canine race in the world'? They were coming to London from Middlesborough, Yorkshire where – according to their owners – 'they were a terrific hit at the Empire and the talk of the entire town'.

I used to speculate about what went on in some of the boarding houses we suggested. Imagine this lot sitting round one table: Ahrensmeyer, the Cowboy Hypnotist; La Tostia, the Mandoline Girl; Harry Houdini, the Famous Jailbreaker; and The Gay Gondoliers, 'the gayest of the gay' (the word 'gay' in those innocent days simply meant 'merry').

The 7s 6d a week I was paid for my role in the smooth running of a theatre empire covered the cost of my Brighton-to-London season ticket on the Southern Railway. On top of this my mother gave me a shilling a day to pay for my lunch and bus fare from Victoria Station to my office, off Leicester Square. Any extra money I made, such as tips for running errands or reserving seats for the card-players, I could spend as I liked.

I needed this additional income as I was now beginning to go out on dates with the local girls.

In a basement café on the Brighton seafront I had met a young lady called Jeddy, five years older than me, who served in a sweetshop. We started going out together regularly. I'd take her to the pictures (the 'flickers'), then for coffee and cakes, and we'd end our evening with a walk on the shingle beach, making for the dark shelter beneath the iron supports of the pier, the local 'lovers' lane'.

I felt I was being very bold, but one night my kisses and gropings were not enough for my Jeddy. 'Why don't we do it properly?' she whispered urgently.

'Do it?'

'Come on . . . don't you know what "it" is?'

My heart was thumping madly. I felt the whole secret of life was about to be revealed to me. Of course I knew what 'it' was. Every pre-pubescent schoolboy knew that. But there was a snag. I did not know *how*!

Through my clumsy efforts Jeddy soon realized that I had no practical knowledge of the female anatomy. I did not even know how to penetrate female underwear: in those days girls wore a kind of one-piece garment called 'combinations'.

'Come on,' said Jeddy determinedly, 'I'll have to show you.'

Somehow we managed it. At the age of 14, on a hard bed of sharp, sea-washed stones, I lost my innocence and began to live.

After the first experience with Jeddy I met many other young ladies in Brighton who fell for my charms. I'm afraid I was a great worry to my mother, who wondered if I'd get some girl 'into trouble' – but fortunately that did not happen.

For all my newly discovered manhood, I still had my childish moments. One day a friend and I decided to have fun with some fireworks we found in our attic. Our intended strategy was to fire rockets out to sea from my bedroom window.

We were not very good at it. A woman walking along the promenade moved into our firing line and our rocket set her dress alight.

The poor lady was not injured. She quickly smothered the flames. But her dress was ruined, and to our chagrin she came marching up to our front door and started shouting at my mother.

I have to say this for Mother: she didn't call me down to face the music. She simply offered her apologies, paid the lady a few pounds in compensation, and hit me were it hurt the most – in the pocket. She stopped my lunch allowance for a few weeks, which meant I had no money for going out on the town.

Instead I put my excess energy to worthy use: I volunteered to assist a man who was running concerts for the wounded Canadian soldiers brought to Brighton to recuperate.

The war was now much closer to home. The bombing raids had started. We knew when the planes were coming because policemen and Boy Scouts on bicycles rushed around the streets blowing whistles. Usually by the time the warnings came I was already on the train heading home to Brighton. The train would halt, the glowing coal-fire engine would be dowsed with water, and we'd sit for hours in the darkened train waiting for the 'all clear' signal.

In the summer of 1917 I saw for myself the devastating results of this new form of warfare when a German airship, an L 45, dropped a bomb right in Piccadilly Circus. It exploded outside the big department store, Swan and Edgar's, not far from my office. In that raid 31 people were killed and 47 injured. It was the first time I had witnessed death from the skies.

With the Germans torpedoeing one in every four ships that left British harbours, food rationing had to be introduced. America came into the war and Russia withdrew from it, too occupied with its revolution. In Britain what seemed to be old men – those aged 41 to 50 – were now being accepted for the army.

In the middle of all this, we at Moss Empires were coping with the latest quirk of bureaucracy. With so much else to worry about, someone in Parliament had still found time to introduce new regulations concerning the sale of liquor. We were told that at the London Hippodrome spirits must not be dispensed by a barman but sold in tot bottles. Our entire staff was put to work filling these little containers with the regulation amounts of gin and whisky.

I don't remember much about the day the First World War ended, 11 November 1918. Instead of celebrating, the family spent the day quietly at home, remembering Uncle Phil, who had been killed in action.

At Moss Empires I had been promoted to ledger clerk in the accountancy department, concerned with the cost of scenery and costumes and the purchase and re-sale of liquor in the theatre bars, and I was fully aware of the thriving business in which I was employed. At the time the company owned 31 theatres around the country. Music halls were flourishing: there were 60 in Greater London alone.

I was also aware that music hall had a growing rival – the movie house. My father had been a pioneer in British theatres of the American bioscope – silent films, introduced as a novelty to round off a variety show. Now, a decade later, the full-length movie was drawing big audiences. Even Moss Empires had added two 'picture houses' to their list of theatres, one in Birmingham, the other in Cardiff, South Wales.

I liked going to the flickers, and even had a favourite screen pin-up girl, a lovely, effervescent blonde from St Louis, Missouri called Laura La Plante. I saw her in *Poker Face* with Buster Keaton and in another film called *Beware of Widows*. Her style was rather like that of Doris Day a few decades later.

I never thought of Laura La Plante as a flesh-and-blood being until the summer of 1985, when my daughter Joan appeared in an American television presentation, *Night of 100 Stars*, and there among the guests was my adored Laura, now a little old lady, but still pretty.

In my teens, however, I had no professional interest in the film industry. The height of my ambition was to see myself in white tie and tails, a splendid red sash across my chest, greeting patrons in the foyer of a Moss Empires variety theatre.

At about the time of my 18th birthday I approached my boss, Mr Pallister, and asked for a job in one of the theatres.

Mr Pallister was agreeable. He sent me on my rounds as an assistant relief manager for the Empires in Nottingham, Leeds, Newcastle-on-Tyne and Finsbury Park, North London.

The reports on my relief job being favourable, Mr Pallister called me to his office.

'There's a vacancy at the Empire Theatre, Sheffield, up in Yorkshire. We'll make you resident assistant manager there under our Mr Richard Sidebotham. It's an honour: you'll be the youngest assistant manager on our circuit. We'll pay you £5 a week,' – more than twice what most workers earned in Sheffield at that time – 'and we'll expect good results. Dickie Sidebotham will look after you.'

It was a new adventure; Sheffield, a city of 500,000 inhabitants, famed for its cutlery and steel, was to be my first experience of living in the industrial north.

As I was only 19 years old, Mr Sidebotham, considerate gentleman that he was, took it upon himself to find me 'digs' with people he felt would look after me well. He fixed me up at the home of a Mr and Mrs Joe Johnson, who charged me 30 shillings a week for the rental of an attic bedroom, full meals and laundry.

I arrived in Sheffield, a grimy place in those days, one wintry Saturday lunchtime and made my way to the narrow street where the Johnsons lived. Motherly Mrs Johnson, who had been gossiping with the neighbours in the back courtyard, led me straight into the kitchen of her tiny, terraced house. In that household, I learned, everything happened in the kitchen.

'You must be starved, lad!' (In Sheffield the word 'starved' meant 'very cold'.) 'Just warm yourself up in front of the fire. Then you can have a wash.' She pointed to a corner of the room. 'There you are – the sink's over there. When you've dried down I've got a nice big dinner waiting for you.'

Mrs Johnson duly drew a wooden chair up to the kitchen table, told me to sit down and placed in front of me a huge, golden concoction made of batter and covering the entire dinner-plate.

I felt a shockwave of dismay. I recognized what I had been given as Yorkshire pudding. But at home we ate it just as a little bun-sized accompaniment to roast beef and vegetables. It was never served as an entire meal.

As I picked up my knife and fork a happy thought struck me. Perhaps what I was about to eat was not Yorkshire pudding after all, but that other traditional English dish, toad-in-the-hole. Perhaps there were sausages concealed in the batter. I prodded in vain, searching for them.

So this huge portion of Yorkshire pudding was Mrs Johnson's idea of 'a nice big dinner'. I mentally totted up how much it would cost me to go out and get myself a satisfying meal.

31

No sooner had I finished eating my crisp, light plateful when Mrs Johnson dived into the oven next to the hearth, this time bringing out a dish of roast beef, roast potatoes and greens.

She laughed at my relieved face. 'Did you think the Yorkshire was all you were getting for your dinner? You people from down South don't know nowt about food!' she chuckled. 'Round here we always eat the Yorkshire pudding before the other stuff.

'I'll see you don't go hungry.' She nodded at my brimming plate. 'When you've got through that lot there's a nice apple sponge for you.'

Mrs Johnson was a marvellous cook. That delicious first dinner in Sheffield is a meal I have remembered all my life.

There was a further treat in store for me that day. When I had finished eating, Mrs Johnson asked me what I was planning to do that afternoon.

'I think I'll go into town and take a look at my theatre,' I replied.

'Eeh, you don't want to do that yet!' Mrs Johnson sounded astonished at my limited horizons. 'Plenty of time for that come Monday morning. Now I'll tell you what you'll do this afternoon. You'll go with our Joe to Bramall Lane and watch the Blades.'

'They're playing Liverpool today.' This was Joe Johnson, a quieter person than his wife, speaking up at last.

I stared at them both. 'Bramall Lane? The Blades?'

Mr Johnson then spelled out to me that the Sheffield United football team was called the Blades because of its cutlery-town origins and that Bramall Lane was its home football ground.

This was the last time I ever showed ignorance about a football team. Since Joe Johnson introduced me to Saturday soccer I've been hooked for life, with special sentimental feeling for Sheffield United. To this very day, when I check the football results I always look first for Sheffield United. Although, unfortunately, they have gone down very much in the last few years, I remember when they had some spectacular players whom I hero-worshipped, among them Freddie Tunstall, who played outside left for England, and Billy Gillespie, the inside left who played for Ireland.

I have tried to pass on my passion for soccer to each of my children in turn, but none of them has ever shared my feelings about watching a football game.

Active young Bill preferred playing football himself to being a spectator. Joan came with me once or twice to the Arsenal ground in London. She pretended it was all very exciting, yelling when I yelled, but she didn't fool me. I could see she was bored.

Natasha, my youngest daughter, has rarely been to Arsenal with me. When I watch matches on television she will slip into the room and make her comments on the game. While analytical and quite knowledgeable she does not get carried away.

Jackie came with me to football more often than the others and made a genuine effort to share my enthusiasm and to understand the mystique and fellowship of being in a crowd, cheering on our team. She would wear a scarf in the red and white Arsenal colours, which she had embroidered with the names of the players. For all her efforts, which I appreciated, I realized that at heart she was only doing it to please Daddy.

She did learn something, however, which proved useful to her later on, when she scripted the film *Yesterday's Hero* starring Ian McShane as a star footballer on the slide. Jackie's own vivid memories of soccer matches stood her in good stead, and so did my personal contacts: I arranged for my friend, half back Frank McLintock, the former Arsenal captain, to be adviser on the match sequences.

My children all think I must have been crazy when I tell them that back in my Sheffield days my passion for soccer at times took priority over my job.

In those days, extensive newspaper publicity for shows was practically unknown. We relied instead on huge bill posters. I was being paid an extra ten shillings a week to spend Saturday afternoons touring the outlying districts to check that the bill posters were doing their job properly. My trips out into the Yorkshire and Derbyshire countryside were pleasant; Sheffield in the 'twenties was dubbed 'a dirty picture in a beautiful frame'. I have to confess, however, that despite the lure of fresh air and scenery, as long as the size of our theatre audiences was satisfactory, I neglected the bill-inspection part of my duties, preferring to spend my Saturday afternoons at a football match. That was the highlight of my week.

I found the Yorkshire people true to their reputation for friendliness and sincerity, and I had made good friends in Sheffield. One was Bill Robinson, a scrap-metal dealer I met through helping his two daughters get their start in show business. Iris and Phyllis Robinson, an amateur song-and-dance duo performing at charity concerts, won themselves a last-minute spot on the Empire bill after a professional act had failed to turn up.

Iris later married and gave up stage ambitions, but her sister stayed the course and made her name as vocalist-entertainer Phyllis Robbins. I was often invited to spend Sundays with the Robinsons, who lived in the East End of the city, near the steelworks, where the sky was lit up at night by the glow of furnaces.

Other friends were Moses and Annie Newman, a charming elderly couple who welcomed me into their house behind their plumbing and glazing business opposite the Empire's stage door. I got acquainted with them through their eldest daughter, Raie, who would come over to the theatre with tea and home-made cakes for Mr Sidebotham and me. I offered to help the Newman son, Joe, when he stood as a candidate for the city council. While I willingly drove his motor car during the election campaign I declined his suggestion to take my turn pushing his beautiful baby Lawrence in a pram bearing the notice 'Please Vote for My Daddy'.

Despite baby Lawrence's appeal, Joe Newman did not win a seat on the council, but he prospered in the family business, eventually became a Justice of the Peace and his wife Rose and daughter Audrey were presented at Court.

The Newmans and the Robinsons were the people I mentioned in my letters home to Mother. What I did not mention was my other social life, taking turns to date each of the six programme-sellers at my theatre. They were not all beauties, I have to admit, and some of them were no doubt grateful for my advances, but I didn't want to neglect any of them in case she felt hurt! We'd take our fish-and-chip supper back to my current date's apartment, but I was careful never to linger too long before returning to my attic at the Johnson house. Walking through the Sheffield streets in the small hours could be an unpleasant experience, for you were likely to cross paths with a crowd of rats. There would be literally thousands of the shaggy, sharp-toothed creatures, stealing in weird, threatening packs along the main street on their way to a new position on the river Don.

The first time I saw this fearsome procession I was so scared I ran blindly up a side street. When I reported back to Mrs Johnson she laughed at my fright.

'If you don't interfere with them, they won't interfere with you. Next time, just step into a doorway until they've passed.'

Between my extra-curricular activities I was also having a good time learning my job in my thrilling world of music hall.

The busiest weeks of the year were the pantomime season, when people who otherwise never set foot in any variety theatre brought their children along for their special annual treat – the lavish combination of spectacle, comedy, singing, dancing and audience participation set within a fairytale.

Our 1921 Christmas pantomime at the Sheffield Empire was a spectacular production of *Jack and Jill*. We made what was then a daring break with tradition. Instead of the Principal Boy being a leggy, thigh-slapping girl in tights, we had a real boy, the bill-topping singer Fred Barnes, whose theme number was 'I'm the Black, Black Sheep of the Family'. Since Barnes did it the Principal Boy role has frequently been played by men.

In our *Jack and Jill* the comedy role was given to a newcomer from the nearby town of Rotherham, a young chap called Sandy Powell. It was a good start to his career, but his moment of true glory did not come till a few years later, when he made his first radio broadcast.

Powell was overcome with excitement. 'Can you hear me, Mother?' he shouted into the microphone. Those words became his catchphrase.

My own particular interest in the pantomime wasn't the stars but – wouldn't you have guessed! – one of our chorus line-up,

the well-drilled, high-kicking John Tiller Girls. I was particularly smitten with Marian, but our romance didn't last. At the end
of the pantomime season she just packed her wickerwork
costume skip and disappeared from my life.

Those days in Sheffield were among the happiest I have ever
known. I learned the practical side of running a theatre, had
many girlfriends and my first taste of celebrity status, for in the
'twenties the management staff of a big variety theatre were very
important people in the community. In short I had everything
going for me.

I still recall the Johnson kitchen, with its welcoming fire in the
grate, and the smell of freshly baked bread. I remember the
womenfolk of the Johnson street – there was always a crowd of
them gossiping in the communal courtyard – kidding me about
my very active love life and trying to make me blush. Today,
whenever I hear someone with a South Yorkshire accent I feel
instant rapport.

I remember the girls in clogs, clattering past the Empire in
noisy groups on their way to work at the cutlery factory down
the road. These raunchy, hard-working 'buffer' girls, so-called
because they were employed to buff (polish) knives and forks,
would spill out into the street, arm in arm, when the midday bell
rang. They wore protective red head-bands, but the words
coming out of their mouths were deepest blue. Never before or
since have I heard such language! These girls threw out coarse
challenges to any young man crossing their paths, between
screaming to each other about the previous night's activities.
The dialogue in my daughter Jackie's books, now considered
daring, is insipid by comparison with the explicit talk of those
girls from the buffing shop.

I confined my sexual adventures to the Empire programme
girls, and they proved my undoing. In 1923 the blow fell. Mr
Nicholas Pallister, business manager of Moss Empires, came up
from London to confront me.

'It's about the cash discrepancy at the confectionery kiosk,' he
began. 'We know you've been giving boxes of chocolates to the
programme-sellers. And you haven't been making up the
balance.'

I defended myself. 'Mr Pallister, I haven't given them so many chocolates that I deserve to be fired!' I protested.

'No, that's not what I have in mind. But it's time we moved you on. We're transferring you to our Olympia Theatre in Liverpool. The manager, Pierre Cohen, is the strictest manager on the circuit. He'll keep an eye on you. You'll be second assistant manager under assistant manager Don Fraser.'

I was relieved. The Olympia, in West Derby Road, was the biggest provincial theatre in the country, twice the size of the Sheffield Empire.

Though I was to be only no. 3 instead of no. 2 on the staff I was not really being demoted, only moved sideways.

I had visions of bigger shows, new girls to meet, fresh fields to conquer.

Mr Pallister read my mind. 'Now take my advice, Joe Collins, and don't try your hanky-panky with the programme girls at the Olympia. I'll tell you before you start that they're all engaged to be married and they're not waiting for *you*!'

3

Hard Times

My accommodation in Liverpool, at the home of a classical musician, was less warmly memorable but more up-market than the Johnsons' home. There was even a bathroom and a lavatory in the house.

I arrived in the city on one of the Sunday trains with special carriages for theatrical traffic. Before road haulage became general entire shows – the artistes, band, scenery – were moved by rail. In those days, it you wanted to stare at the stars in their off-duty hours all you needed to do was stand around on a Sunday at any of the major railway junctions – Crewe, Cheshire, especially – and watch the big music-hall names greeting each other as they changed trains on their way to their next engagements.

The big American show-business attractions in those more leisured pre-air travel days came to Britain by luxury liner. One of my first jobs as second assistant manager of the Olympia Theatre in Liverpool was to go to the docks to welcome Paul Whiteman, 'King of Jazz', and his orchestra, the world's top band, who wedded popular songs to symphonic orchestration. I had bought their smoochy records 'Whispering', 'The Japanese Sandman' and 'Avalon' as gifts for my former girlfriend, the John Tiller girl. Whiteman's show, like all the major revues, was staged at the Olympia prior to opening at the London Hippodrome.

The other striking talent I recall from my Liverpool sojourn was an up-coming new girl, little Gracie Fields. She made her singing entrance on our stage perched on top of a red London bus in the revue *Mr Tower of London*.

'Our Gracie', four years older than me, had been struggling to make a career for herself, sometimes working in the cotton mills of her native Rochdale, Lancashire between stage engagements. Now, encouraged by her new husband and manager, the comedian Archie Pitt, who produced and co-starred with her in *Mr Tower of London*, her brilliance as a performer was becoming recognized.

Gracie was not happy in her marriage. She and Pitt, 18 years her senior, quarrelled constantly and shrilly. But though Gracie said bitterly the marriage was a 'completely professional arrangement', she did agree that at least on that level the partnership worked well. While the *Liverpool Echo* theatre critic said nothing in favour of *Mr Tower of London* as a production, he went wild over Gracie herself, praising her warmth, her comic personality and her operatic singing voice.

Gracie's presence alone turned her husband's show into a major theatrical happening. It was a hit at the London Hippo-drome and toured for a solid nine and a half years.

Later, in the 'thirties when the Lass from Lancashire was a screen star with a £200,000 Hollywood contract (she was reputedly the highest-paid woman in the world), my sister Pauline worked with her in a movie directed by Monty Banks, Gracie's second husband. Pauline's job was to 'double' for Gracie in shots requiring a strong swimmer.

Back in the mid-'twenties, though, when future superstar Gracie was still singing her comedy songs 'The Biggest Aspidistra in the World' and 'The Rochdale Hunt' in the lesser provincial music halls, Pauline was already playing on the London stage in the most lavish productions of the decade. She danced in *Rose Marie* with Edith Day at Drury Lane and was in Noel Coward's first revue, *London Calling*, at the Duke of York's.

Lalla, the elder of my sisters, had made a promising début too. At 16 she danced in *Joy-Bells* at the London Hippodrome with the Original Dixieland Jazz Band, the first time a jazz band was featured on an English stage.

Lalla went on to see her name in lights on Broadway, opening at the Times Square Theatre with *André Charlot's Revue of 1924*, with a team that included two future screen stars, Jessie Matthews and Marjorie Robertson (who later changed her name to Anna Neagle).

The newspapers of the time reported coyly that during the transatlantic sea crossing Lalla had been 'spending time' with the star of the André Charlot company, Jack Buchanan, the debonair, immaculately tailored matinée idol.

All the girls I met in Liverpool showed great interest in my sister Lalla, pressing me for details of her romance, but I always had to plead ignorance. Little did I realize then that this would be the type of answer I'd find myself reciting all my life, whenever strangers asked questions about our family affairs.

It has been my destiny to live in the reflected glory of the Collins girls, first my two sisters, now my daughters. I have learned to be polite . . . but not *too* informative.

Today, when I am taking a peaceful stroll on the seafront in Brighton or Hove with my wife Irene, my youngest daughter Natasha and our schnauzer dog Max, people I barely know will pounce on me to ask about Joan and Jackie. They don't even start with a polite 'How are you, Joe?'

To be truthful, while I am deeply concerned that my daughters should be happy, I am not prepared to discuss their private lives.

I don't think my acquaintances believe me, but it is absolutely true that I don't watch *Dynasty* regularly, nor do I read Jackie's books. Neither, back in the Roaring 'Twenties, did I go to see my sisters' London shows. Nevertheless, I was proud of them, as I was of my daughters years later, for they were lovely girls.

Pauline was a dashing brunette, very devoted to the older Lalla, an exquisite, petite blonde, a girl-about-town, with very grand ideas. She started her day at 11 am, breakfasting on a quarter-bottle of champagne. I don't know where she got her energy from, because she never seemed to eat a square meal.

To the public she was the prototype, sparkling 'flapper', swathed in white furs, living it up at Oddenino's and the Café de Paris.

Lalla worked in several shows with Jack Buchanan and starred opposite him in a tour of the musical *Sunny*, but she did not marry him. Her brief first marriage was to Reggie Levy, youngest of three brothers who owned a chain of pubs. Her second husband was a wealthy businessman, Mark Godfrey. Lalla retired from the stage and remained happily with 'Goddy' until her death, aged 69, in 1974. They had an elegant apartment in Belgravia, London and Lalla was much lauded for her charitable works. During their childhood my children Joan, Jackie and Bill looked up to Lalla as the 'star' of the family.

Right until her final illness Lalla kept her good looks and her trim shape. To this day my other sister, Pauline, is still attractive and vivacious, too, with the slender, supple figure of a young girl. My daughters Joan and Jackie and my son Bill all look younger than their years. As for me, I sometimes feel my age, but I have never been told that I look it!

Back in 1924, when I *was* young – 22 to be precise – I became impatient about living in Liverpool and wanted to get back to London.

My chance came when Moss Empires loaned my services for a most exciting job with H.M. Government at the 1924 British Empire Exhibition at Wembley, the patriotic spectacle of the year.

I was to be assistant manager of a theatre within the government pavilion, where the Admiralty was commemorating a famous British war victory of the 1914–18 war, the attack on Zeebrugge, known as 'The Battle of the Mole'.

In the teeth of German fortifications a British naval force, with novel strategy, had deliberately sunk British ships filled with concrete at the entrance of Zeebrugge Harbour in Belgium, preventing the exit of the enemy German submarines.

To watch our show depicting this event in miniature, the audience was seated in tiers, looking down on a huge water tank, and a model of Zeebrugge Harbour, complete with that massive breakwater, the Mole. Our model fleet was propelled across the 'sea' on electric rails. The production was noisy and rousing, with a 'soundtrack' of men shouting and guns booming.

The show lasted 25 minutes, and it took almost twice as long to set up.

King George V declared the exhibition officially open on St George's Day, 23 April 1924, the sixth anniversary of the historic attack. I duly stood in line and was presented to King George, his wife Queen Mary and their eldest son, the Prince of Wales, later the Duke of Windsor.

Our 'battle' was staged five times a day, and as I was soon promoted to manager I was kept so busy I never had a chance to watch an entire performance. I was too concerned with getting the public in, organizing staff, running the theatre.

In my off-duty hours, though, I did enjoy the other attractions of the exhibition site . . . especially the ballroom.

Dancing is not one of my talents. I could never get the hang of the black-bottom, the foxtrot or even the waltz; the only steps I ever mastered were those of the charleston. I went to the Wembley Exhibition ballroom because I found it a handy place to meet girls. I'd select the partner of my choice, literally walk her round the floor holding her as close as I could, then I'd offer my bait.

'I've got my new car outside. Care for a spin?' My come-on line never failed. The girls soon learned my little Wolseley had a very comfortable back seat.

Life was getting very fast for me. I had a demanding job, I had my girlfriends – and I wanted still more excitement. I decided to try gambling.

A pal and I took a ferry to France, heading for the casino in Le Touquet, where I became so excited about trying to win my fortune at roulette I could not tear myself away from the table and missed my return boat to England.

Being resourceful, I managed to arrange a lift back to London on the mail plane, which was piloted by a Captain A.O. Jones who later became the chief pilot of British Airways.

This was my first flight. There were only four passengers, each of us strapped into our seat, with cotton wool in our ears and our luggage beside us in the gangway.

'Don't move an inch, or you'll upset the balance of the plane!' Captain Jones warned.

I was too scared even to stretch my legs.

I had been so worried about not getting back to Wembley in time for the performance I vowed there and then I would never go near a gaming table. I have kept my vow. Today I visit casinos for a meal with my sister Pauline, who likes a game, but I never join in the play.

Though I had finished with trying my luck at gaming tables, I still had a gambling urge, so I turned to the gee-gees. Clutching my copy of *Racing Specialist* I took my entire week's wage of £7 10s (£7.50) – a lot of money in those days – and set off north to Yorkshire for the Doncaster Races. I had a bad day. I lost every penny – even the price of my rail fare home – and had to hitch-hike back to London.

In the circumstances, this was the finest thing that could have happened to me. For from that day I have confined my gambling to the one field where I know what I'm doing: show business.

In 1925, though, I was still too young to 'play safe' in life. When the Wembley Exhibition ended I left Moss Empires. It was a bad time to leave a job without another to go to, for the post-war trade depression had led to massive unemployment in Britain. But I had never experienced being out of work: so far I had done well, and was self-confident.

At first my optimism was justified. I found a new job almost immediately, managing a touring revue for Grafton Galleries, with whom my sister Pauline had been a dancer. The next job was no problem either: a theatrical firm, Mr and Mrs Elias B. Senor and Family, asked me to manage their show *Cranky*, another revue which was touring the provinces.

This turned out to be an interlude which still gives me nightmares, for it led to one of the most frightening experiences ever, my one and only performance as an actor.

One Monday, when we were due to open at the Theatre Royal in Rochdale, Lancashire, our comedian, Bob Stevens, was taken ill. Despite a quick re-shuffle of the cast, we were left one person short for a military sketch which needed a captain; as bad luck would have it, I was the only man available who fitted the hired uniform and knew the script.

The sketch was about a sergeant bringing a defaulting private before the captain (me) for a ticking-off. I have such a mental block about the whole miserable episode I can't recall any details of the dialogue. All I do remember is my paralysing stage fright.

The curtain went up to reveal me sitting behind a trestle table, wearing officer's uniform and looking absolutely petrified.

By ill chance I had the opening lines.

I started speaking. I could hear a rustle in the stalls as people craned forward.

'Begin again,' hissed the sergeant through clenched teeth. 'They didn't hear you!'

Choking with nerves, I repeated my maiden speech.

'Talk up! Talk up!' the sergeant said, bending towards me. 'They still can't hear you.'

I said my lines, the sergeant spoke his, and the sketch continued. I could hear restive grumblings from the auditorium. I knew that my voice was not projecting across the theatre, but there was nothing I could do about it.

The sergeant began to panic too.

'For Pete's sake, *can't you speak up?*'

My terror turned to temper. At last I found my voice. It came out in an anguished bellow.

'I've had enough of this!' I shouted. 'You can get someone else for the next performance. *I'm* not going through this again!'

The whole house roared. At last I'd made myself audible.

I'm afraid that, unlike others of the Collins family, I was not born to be a star.

My experience in Rochdale had such a traumatic effect that I refused to manage another touring revue in case I was forced to go on stage again.

In fact I felt so badly I decided to leave the theatre altogether and try my chances in some other business while I was still young enough to make a fresh start.

I became a market trader. Taking my entire capital of £30, I bought a mixed stock of unbranded perfumes, cosmetics, toothpaste, shoe polish and other cheap wares from an East End wholesaler and hired a stall in the new Southall indoor market in West London.

Within weeks I knew I had made a mistake. Standing in markets was no life for me. I had the same handicap as when I was on stage: my voice was not loud, brash or bold enough to make myself heard when I shouted my wares.

I found the going so hard I was selling articles for fivepence which had cost me sixpence to buy wholesale. Even at knock-down prices I would sometimes stand for hours on my pitch without selling anything at all.

By now I was really worried about my future. The impossible had actually happened to me and like many of my friends, I was a casualty of the Depression.

On 3 May 1926, matters came to a head, not just for me but for the whole country. It was the start of the General Strike, called by the Trades Union Congress in support of the miners, who were already on strike.

A friend and I put our heads together. To replace the strike-hit newspapers the government was issuing a daily news sheet, which always seemed to be in short supply. My friend and I hired an old-fashioned copying machine on which we reproduced copies of this newsheet, for sale to delivery boys at one penny each. The price at which they retailed them to the news-hungry public was their own affair. My pal and I were inundated with delivery boys: we could not keep up with the demand. Just as our enterprise was becoming too big for us to handle the government stopped not only us, but all the other unauthorized entrepreneurs reproducing their publication.

Trying to keep busy, I then answered the call for volunteer bus-drivers, replacing the striking regular bus-drivers. Like the other volunteers, I sat at the wheel of my General Bus with a policeman beside me in case I needed protection on my run from Shepherd's Bush to Marble Arch, Piccadilly Circus and back again.

A mere two days after I started this job the nine-day strike ended and the regular drivers returned to work.

Once again I was stuck for some way to earn a living.

A friend, Sydney Jay, at that time probably the only film agent in London, made a suggestion. 'How would you like to be in the movies? I can put you in as an "extra" for crowd scenes. You won't have to speak lines and no one will even notice you.'

In that long-forgotten film I was one of the crowd of soldiers attacking a castle. I got killed in the first scene. After eight takes I was a bit fed up with having to fall down and roll on the wet grass, acting 'dead', but for my magnificent pay of £3 a day I endured it.

While I had no ambitions to be an actor, during my few days on location I became intrigued with the business side of movie-making. I had new notions of becoming a film agent, or a producer.

Who knows? I might indeed have ended up as a movie mogul. But at this point my mother stepped in. She was now Mrs Jack French. During the First World War my new stepfather had run a tin-roof theatre on the Sussex coast at Shoreham-by-Sea, frequented by local fishermen and the convalescing Canadian soldiers. When the war ended, so did his audience, and he had now set up in London as a theatrical agent.

With her husband working in town, and her family grown up, my mother wanted some interest outside her home and I was to be included in her plans. She applied for the licence for the St James's Tavern in the City, not far from Petticoat Lane, and put me behind the bar. It was all a novel experience for me, not just a new trade, but for the first time I was spending my working life in the East End environment of my grandparents.

Our little public house was a lively place. On Sundays we became a kind of overflow annexe to Petticoat Lane market, leasing space in our saloon bar to two men who ran a jewellery business. We were the only pub in London with a permit to sell jewellery during licensing hours. I would watch, fascinated, as the jewellers put out their brooches and bangles on the green baize-covered tables. They sold some quite expensive stuff.

On weekdays our lunchtime customers were gentlemen from the nearby shipping offices. Knowing these City types liked a little snack with their pink gins and gin-and-its, I would spend a good part of my morning cutting cheese into cubes to be served with biscuits. I left the job of setting up the 'pins' – fitting pouring taps into the barrels of Toby ale – to our cellarman, Jack.

One day, when Jack was off work, sick, I volunteered to deputize and do the 'pins' myself.

'You won't manage,' warned my mother. 'It's not as easy as it looks.'

'Rubbish! I know what to do. Jack fits the tap with just a flick of his hammer.'

I wielded the hammer. The whole barrel shattered, and I was drenched in pungent beer.

'Serves you right!' laughed my mother. 'You think you know everything, don't you? One day, perhaps, you'll listen to people who know better.'

The tale of my mishap caused much merriment that evening when our regular Jewish clientele came in for their drinks. The mainstay of our evening trade consisted of my mother's relatives, the Assenheims. Her 17 surviving brothers and sisters and all their in-laws provided a healthy nucleus of customers.

Some of my uncles had taken up cab-driving. Uncle Jack was a long-distance lorry driver. One aunt had married a Petticoat Lane grocer and another a Petticoat Lane fruiterer.

My grandfather Joe Assenheim's hokey-pokey business was flourishing. Handcarts selling the famous Assenheim ices were now touring the streets of London, and my Uncle Solly and Uncle Ike, helped by various aunts, still ran the original Sunday stall in Petticoat Lane market.

I'd go round to Stoney Lane, where the ice cream was made under the supervision of Uncle Mark, and willingly give a hand in turning the freezers. Electric mixers had not yet been invented – nor, as far as I knew, were there any hygiene regulations. Still, we kept our operation as clean as possible, and we used only the best-quality eggs and milk.

Our neat squares of vanilla with a streak of raspberry through the middle were placed on the stall, each with its own sheet of white paper to protect the customers' hands.

'They're luvverly! Try 'em! They're luvverly! Penny a lump! That's the stuff to make you jump!' cried Uncle Solly and Uncle Ike in their raucous Cockney voices. People of all nations and colours would stand in a line, throw their pennies on the stall and pick up their portion of hokey. When the day's business was over the whole Assenheim family would gather round to count up the sticky pennies.

Like the Assenheims, I loved the warmth and energy of the East End. For me, those were good days down the Lane, though it was just a brief period in my life. Our pub in Creechurch Lane did so well that my mother and I decided to move on. We took a bigger pub, with a restaurant upstairs, next to the Holborn Empire, nearer the West End.

For me this was another mistake. As I now admit, I allowed myself to be led astray.

I was never a man who could carry a load of liquor. I get affected very quickly. When customers asked me, the barman, the inevitable question 'What are *you* going to have?' I should have stuck to lemonade. But for the sake of conviviality and good business I would serve myself spirits.

One night, when I was drunk, I reeled out into the street for air . . . and the next thing I remember is a policeman picking me out of the gutter and carting me off to the lock-up.

This experience taught me yet another sharp lesson. From then on I have always been careful not to drink too much: one glass of wine is my limit.

My one hour of imprisonment sobered me up forever. I was overcome with shame. As I waited for my mother to arrange my release I realized how far I had digressed from my original goal to be a showman, a credit to my parents' good name.

I felt a re-born determination to get back to the profession where I, and all my family, fitted best: entertainment, vaudeville, music hall.

Fortunately, the solution to my dilemma was right at hand. I went to work with my theatrical agent stepfather, Jack French, who had an office above the fire station in Shaftesbury Avenue, London's theatre district.

At last I was back on course.

4

Settling Down

When I started work in my stepfather's theatrical agency I was in my late twenties and I knew this might well be my final chance to get established in show business. I had put behind me the follies of my youth.

I brought with me useful experience, running theatres, budgeting for shows, managing touring companies, but I had never been a theatrical agent, getting work for performers. None the less, I soon realized that Jack French, whose one-room office I shared, couldn't help me much as his own business was very small.

Instead, I devised a job all of my own. In the late 'twenties and early 'thirties there were dozens of touring companies and plenty of audiences for them. Apart from the 60 music halls in and around London, there were at least four in each major city and two in the smaller towns. Any town with only one music hall had to be a real one-eyed dump!

I studied the show-business newspapers listing the names of the various touring revues, and then wrote to the revue proprietors. Once again using my late father Will Collins' name to introduce myself, I promised that if they would let me have a list of their bookings I would try to get them work in the vacant weeks. Writing to theatre-owners, offering these revues on commission, I would go into raptures about the beautiful girls and wonderful scenery and costumes. I never went to see any of these productions I commended so warmly. Yet by pure luck I never sold any 'duds', and the customers always seemed satisfied.

My service to the theatres, which made my job viable, was helping them comply with a complicated professional code about 'barring areas'. It was a West End rule that a revue must not appear on stage within a mile of any music hall where it had been seen in the past 16 weeks. For provincial theatres the distance was six miles and the time limit 40 weeks. There were other legal conditions about when and where a show could be staged. My task was rather like putting together some intricate jigsaw puzzle. For the sake of the artistes' goodwill I also had to avoid the many run-down theatres around the country, built in the music-hall boom of the early 1900s, never renovated or even fumigated and falling into disrepair. No artiste of status wanted to set foot in these smelly places, derided – with accuracy, I'm afraid – as 'fleapits'.

While I was doing this desk work I began to meet a few performers, the small-time dancing acts who called at the Jack French office hoping for bookings. Though none of us could have guessed, many of these hoofers were men I would encounter in business throughout my career, for when their dancing days were over they too became theatrical agents. There was Keith Devon, Don Ross, and a 24-year-old East End chap who had just returned to Britain after dancing his way across Europe: his name was Lew Grade.

Back in the 1920s Lew (later Lord Grade of Elstree) and his brother Bernie, now entertainment chief Lord Delfont of Stepney, were mere show-business hopefuls trying to get established, and with less know-how than I had.

Sons of a Russian immigrant, Isaac Winogradsky, a trouser-presser and buttonhole-maker, and his forceful wife Olga, they had got their start through winning charleston competitions. In the 'twenties and 'thirties the Grade brothers had various dancing acts with various partners, but when I first met Lew he had gone solo as a so-called 'eccentric dancer'. His billing was 'Lew Grade, the Dancer with the Humorous Feet'.

I don't know to this day why, of all the agents in London, Lew Grade latched himself on to me. Perhaps it was just that I too was young and keen, and had more time for him than some of the more established agents. For Lew was not handsome and he did not have outstanding talent. He just had a shrewd head on his shoulders and plenty of push.

Lew was most persistent. When I arrived at my office in the mornings he'd be standing at the locked door, waiting for me to open up. We'd go for coffee at a place in Old Compton Street where we sat on stools at the U-shaped bar and talked of nothing else but where we could find work for Lew Grade.

Actually, Lew sold himself to me very quickly. I found him some engagements. And he came up with a proposition which I knew had possibilities.

'I've managed to fix up a booking myself,' he told me one morning. 'Cine-variety. I've got a spot on stage just before the main feature film. It's at the Grange Cinema in Dagenham' [Essex]. 'If you like, I can get you an introduction to one of the cinema's owners – Johnny Kaye – and maybe he'll book some of his other stage acts through your agency.'

This was the kind of opening I wanted. I had not ignored the simple truth that cinemas were winning the audience battle against music halls. Yet this was still a transition period in entertainment tastes. Though the public were now flocking to 'the pictures', they still liked to see a few 'live turns' on stage.

In the perspective of most of the twentieth century, this mixture of movies and music hall was probably the best entertainment value for money ever offered.

Just for the price of a seat you got two major films, a 'short', a newsreel, some variety acts and an organ recital: the public had special affection for the man rising out of the floor in his glistening white satin tail-coat, playing away at his mighty Wurlitzer.

Oh yes, cine-variety, I knew, was a good slot for many of my clients, and an ideal one for Lew Grade. As 'the Dancer with the Humorous Feet' he did a novelty version of the charleston, squashing his hat down over his ears and pulling funny faces. This act, lasting twelve minutes, was performed on a small table.

I calculated if I could book Lew three cine-variety spots in one evening he could tot up £30. There was just one snag. How could Lew transport his 'prop', his table, from one cinema to another in the allotted time? He did not own a car.

I offered him a deal. 'Tell you what: you can put your table in the back of my motor car and I'll take you to your engagements personally. *You* can pay for the petrol.'

Apart from the petrol money, I took 10 per cent of Lew's

earnings for the agency, to be shared equally with my step-father.

Providing turns for cine-variety was my real introduction to the agency business. After Johnny Kaye of the Grange I became friendly with the booking managers of the big Gaumont and Paramount cinema circuits, who would engage acts through me to perform in two picture palaces a night – two shows in one cinema, three in the other.

I tried to interest my stepfather in this developing side of our business, but he couldn't be persuaded. I soon realized this nice old chap was a bit of a fuddy-duddy. He did not want challenges and change. In any case, apart from his theatrical agency he was doing very well in a less demanding line.

When I first went to work with Jack French I wondered why our little office was crammed with sacks, all full of rags. Through some of our visitors I discovered that my stepfather had contracts among clothing-manufacturers and was buying their leftover fabric clippings. What he did with these clippings, where he sold them, I never did learn for myself, and he never told me.

Realizing my father's mind was on his rags rather than finding work for performers I knew our business association must end, and that I must set up my own company.

I had a particular incentive to get ahead, in the form of a very special girl I had met through a pal of mine, Hal Monty.

Hal Monty, real name Albert Sutan, was teamed in a dancing duo with Lew Grade's brother Bernie. At first they called themselves Grade and Sutan, but due to confusion with Lew they changed their title to the Delfont Boys. Bernie (his real name is Barnet) became Bernard Delfont, officially. Albert changed his name to Hal Monty when he went solo as a comedian.

He was a handsome, genial sort of chap, full of get-up-and-go and a great lady chaser.

'Come with me and relax a bit,' Hal suggested one evening after a show. 'I know a very good nightclub in Regent Street . . . first-class band, charming dance hostesses.'

'I can't be bothered,' I said. 'It'll be expensive, and you know I can't dance.'

'Well, it's time you learned. At this club they have a dance teacher, a ballroom dancing champion. She's a gold medallist.'

Hal offered further incentive. 'You might as well come along. It could be worth your while. You could meet the club-owner and get bookings for your artistes in their cabaret.'

I went to the club with Hal purely for business reasons . . . but it did not work out that way. For he insisted I should take a lesson from a dance instructress, Miss Elsa Bessant.

She was a smiling, slender girl with blue eyes and blonde hair arranged in neat waves around her face, the type of looks which have always attracted me. In her dress of flame-coloured chiffon, with flowers at the shoulderline, she looked a picture.

Miss Bessant led me to the dance floor. As the band played the jumpy 'Tiger Rag' I was so intent on listening to her instructions, trying to get my feet in the right place, I did not attempt conversation. I stumbled on Miss Bessant's toes and tried in vain to follow her instruction.

'You're wasting your time, trying to teach me to dance,' I gasped finally. 'Let's just shuffle around for a bit and talk.'

I can't remember what we talked about. It was the kind of chat you might expect between a single girl and a single fellow in a nightclub.

Then I came to the point. 'I'm an agent. I only came here to get bookings for my acts.'

'Then you'd better meet the booking manager. I'll introduce you.'

It was a fruitful meeting. I did provide that club with acts. And though I never attempted more dancing lessons, through my visits to the club I got to know Elsa better.

She had beauty, she had charm, she was easy to talk to; I started taking her out every Sunday, on trips to the Sussex coast, to my beloved Brighton, or Shoreham-by-Sea. We started making up a foursome with a friend of Elsa and her young man, and after the girls had finished work we'd drive off to our favourite bungalow-style hotel.

Then Elsa invited me to her home for Sunday tea with her family. In those days that meant a girl was 'serious'. And, at the age of 29, no dallying youngster any more, I was 'serious' too.

The Bessants, who lived in a fine Georgian house in Kennington Road, South London, were the kind of people who are the backbone of Britain, industrious, stable, good-hearted and unpretentious.

Elsa's father Bill, a railway porter when she was born, now drove a tram. He and his wife Ada had eleven children, all grown up, working and bringing money home. It was a prosperous household.

In a room upstairs lived Elsa's Grandma Sarah. She never joined us when I came to tea, but I often saw her nipping out of the house, dressed all in black, with a little black bonnet, carrying a jug to fetch her ale from the off-licence.

I became very fond of Elsa's mother, Ada Bessant, who reminded me of my dear, stalwart grandmother, Leah Assenheim. Ada was stout, jolly and forever rushing around keeping her home clean and tidy. Every day she polished the furniture in her immaculate parlour, though that room, the family showplace, was hardly ever used.

When I came to tea I sat with the rest of the family round the kitchen table, which was laden with plates of bread and butter and dishes of cockles, mussels, shrimps and winkles. I had never eaten food like this. My own family would have considered it beneath them to serve these squiggly, maggot-shaped bits of things from the sea. But I was fascinated, especially when we were each given a hairpin to spear the tit-bit of our choice. Cockles and winkles became one of my favourite dishes.

I enjoyed going to tea with the Bessant family. They were all so cheerful and even-tempered, so different from the volatile show-business crowd. In Elsa's home there was never any shouting, no raw nerves or uncontrolled outbursts.

Soon, as I had anticipated, Elsa's dad wanted to know my 'intentions' concerning his daughter. I told him, with clear conscience, that they were honourable.

By now I was sure Elsa was the girl I wanted to marry. She was just right: three years younger than me, home-loving, very feminine and she certainly would not develop into the aggressive type of woman who might try to interfere in my show-business life.

Future events proved me right. Throughout our marriage Elsa was good to me; she fed me well, she looked after me and was a perfect mother to our three children, Joan, Jackie and Bill. With her bright personality she complemented me ideally in our social life with my show-business friends and their womenfolk, but she never tried to influence me in decisions about my work. She never complained when some emergency kept me out till the early hours of the morning, nor when my job took me away from London.

Our girls, Joan and Jackie, have said there were times when Elsa should have asserted herself more. But their mother was too gentle, too peace-loving ever to shout back at me. It wasn't in her make-up. She never waivered in her role of the supportive wife, and we loved each other.

When I proposed to her she accepted me – despite my unromantic approach! 'They say two can live as cheaply as one. We might as well get married. But for goodness' sake, don't let's make a fuss!'

1932: Franklin D. Roosevelt was elected president of the United States. The president of France, Paul Doumer, was assassinated. George Lansbury – grandfather of actress Angela Lansbury – became chairman of the British Parliamentary Labour Party.

For me, Joseph William Collins, that year was a turning-point in my life. On 9 February Elsa and I were married at Paddington Register Office in West London and set up home in a four-room flat in Castellain Mansions, behind Maida Vale.

At the time Elsa was earning more money than I was, so it was she who bought all the furniture and paid the first month's rent. I had no cash to spare. Apart from running my car – always my top priority – I was putting aside all the money I could for my next venture.

That spring I leased a one-room office from the film agent Sydney Jay, in the same building as my stepfather's variety agency, above the fire station in Shaftesbury Avenue. (I had become so used to conducting business to the tune of clanging fire-engine bells I could not work without them.) I opened my first bank account, and made a down-payment of a guinea (£1.05) on my first typewriter, an Underwood, price 12 guineas (£12.60).

As my telegraphic address I chose the word 'Limelight', to me so evocative of the old-time music halls of my childhood. In the days before electric spotlights, a gas flame playing on a lump of lime threw a magical beam of light across the stage. This was 'limelight'. Though people today talk glibly of 'being in the limelight' most of them have no idea of the literal meaning of the phrase.

Printed in bold letters on my glass-panelled door was 'WILL COLLINS THEATRICAL AND VAUDEVILLE EXCHANGE'. I felt I owed it to my father to perpetuate his name. The 'Theatrical and Vaudeville Exchange' part, though it sounds old-fashioned today, was a totally accurate description of my business. I was running an employment exchange, a job centre, for jugglers, acrobats, ventriloquists, conjurers, comics, singers and dancers . . . the very stuff of music hall.

I dealt in all types of audience-pulling attractions, some of which would be frowned upon today, for I arranged tour dates for what was then called a 'freak show', entitled *Would You Believe It?*, which had been offered to me by a Scottish agent, Horace Collins (no relation). Today the expression 'freak' is considered belittling to people facing physical disability, but in 1932 such sensitivity was rare. The artistes in those shows did not feel loss of self-respect; they were grateful for being able to earn a good living and were always well looked after by the impresarios.

I still have a prized souvenir of those early days of my agency from a comedy duo, brothers whom I had booked into the Empire Theatre, Newcastle-upon-Tyne, a very prestigious venue.

When I told them the good news of their engagement the brothers were stunned.

'A week up in the north east!' they exclaimed. 'We can't do it.

We haven't got the fare . . . haven't got a penny piece between us.'

'Don't be stupid! You *must* be there for rehearsal on Monday morning, otherwise you're out forever,' I warned.

'Joe, it's impossible. We're skint!'

I knew why these boys had no money. They were always short: they wasted everything they earned on gambling. I wanted to help them out, but knowing about the ways of gamblers from past personal experience, I was not going to offer a loan they'd never repay.

I struck a deal. 'Give me something as security, and I'll let you have thirty pounds.'

'All right. We'll go home and find you something.'

When the brothers returned to my office carrying three brown-paper parcels, I was astounded to find that they contained, not the junk I had expected, but three valuable Meissen figurines.

I handed over the £30 in cash, and the boys handed me the priceless porcelain. I still have the figurines. And the brothers still have my £30.

Apart from the hundreds of barely-remembered acts, I was beginning to find engagements for famous names too.

I brought Bruce Bairnsfather, the First World War cartoonist who was known for his character Old Bill, the hardened soldier, into music hall for an illustrated lecture tour.

Max Miller, the Cheekie Chappie, and master of innuendo, who ranked in popularity with Gracie Fields, asked me to book a tour for him. We sold all the seats everywhere, except the Theatre Royal, King's Lynn, for the staid and starchy Norfolk folk did not appreciated Max's vulgarity. They thought the way he dressed – loud check suit, violet kipper tie, diamond-studded cane – was in appalling taste. When he minced across the stage, raised an eyebrow and pouted 'Well, what if I *am*?' there was not even a titter from the audience.

Max ended his week at King's Lynn very depressed. 'How were the box-office receipts? How did we end up?'

'Not too good,' I admitted. 'I lost a hundred pounds.'

1954

MAY 3RD

SOUTHEND, Odeon

✓	1	WALLACE, DENISE & JEANETTE	(E. Taylor)	5%	45 — .
	2				
✓	3	3 IMPS	(S. Royle)	5%	55 — -
✓	4	MICHAEL BENTINE	(frade)	5%	175 — -
✓	5	EVE BOSWELL	(Foster)	5%	300 — -
×	6	Wallace Denise & Jeanette		—	— — —
✓	7	PETER SELLERS	(frade)	5%	175 — -
✓	8	ROSITANDA & GERDA	(M.CA)	5%	55 — -
✓	9	JANET BROWN	(F Barnard)	5%	105 — -
✓	10	HARRY SECOMBE	(F Barnard)	5%	300 — -
		Al Read & Bauch		nett	150

✓   KENTISH TOWN, Forum   66% ....

"MUSICAL EXPRESS"

CAMBRIDGE, NEW   55%

✓	1	MARSHALL & BRETT		10%	18 — -
✓	2	EARL & VAUGHAN	(fraden)	5%	30
✓	3	WILBUR WHEELER & PARTNER	(J Head)	5%	25 — —
	4	DENNY BERRARD			
✓	5	RIKI LINTANA & DIANE		12%	25 — .

"STAIRWAY TO STARDOM"

KING'S LYNN, I.R.   66%

✓	1	NORMAN & NIKI GRANT	(Joe Hayes)	5%	25 — .
	2	IDRIS	(Foster)	5%	22 10 -
	3	REXANOS			
	4	DAVE KING		10%	27 10 —
	5	DIANA COUPLAND & PIANIST		5%	50 — —
	6	— INTERVAL —			
	7	NORMAN & NIKI GRANT		+	— — —
	8	DOLORES VENTURA	(Heath)	5%	40 — -
	9	MAX MILLER	(Dorewski)	neft	400 — - gu
	10	DON LEE		10%	15 — -

A few reminders of some past clients, including Peter Sellers, Michael Bentine, Janet Brown, Harry Secombe, Dave King, Diana Coupland and 'cheekie chappie' Max Miller, from one of Joe's old ledgers.

'Mmm,' Max digested the information. 'Well *you* don't have to worry, Joe. I'll see you right.'

In my post next morning was a cheque from Max for £100, covering my loss. In a tough business like mine, this was a most heart-warming gesture, especially coming from a comic who had a reputation for being so tight with his cash he would never even pay for a round of drinks.

A lively agent will always get excited when he spots new talent – even when he has no chance of acquiring this talent for his own books. During the early years of my agency I was finding engagements for a trick cyclist working with his wife in an act called Red Fred and Rosa. I went to see their bottom-of-the-bill spot at Stratford Empire, in East London. Second-from-the-bottom were a pair of comics, Flanagan and Allen.

I was hoping to approach these two about future business . . . then in the bar in the interval, I met Val Parnell, then Moss Empires' booking manager.

'What did you think of those comics?' I asked.

'What did I think of them? Just you wait and see.'

A few weeks later those two unknowns, Flanagan and Allen – fellow soldiers of the First World War who had met up again by chance on a London bus – were right at the top of their profession. Val Parnell had put them into the star spot at the London Palladium. Bud Flanagan, the down-and-out in the shaggy fur coat, and the 'gentleman' Chesney Allen, with their wild humour, their songs like 'Underneath the Arches' and 'Run, Rabbit, Run' became all-time greats of British entertainment. Teamed with other lunatic slapstick comics to form the Crazy Gang, their shows at the Victoria Palace in London were the favourite theatre treats of the entire royal family. Flanagan and Allen were a national rage.

While I was booking 'live' acts for cinemas a Mrs Welsh from Dagenham, Essex came to see me about finding work for her 13-year-old daughter. Mrs Welsh felt her little Vera was worth a spot at their local picture palace, the Grange.

'She's been in the children's troupe and she's a very good singer,' Mrs Welsh assured me.

As Mrs Welsh had not brought her daughter to my office I

had no chance of hearing for myself how well the girl sang, but I was prepared to give her a break.

'Well, as you live locally, I dare say we can put her on at the Grange for three days,' I agreed. Vera became a professional vocalist. Years later I got bookings for her when she sang with the Ambrose orchestra, but I never met her. Still, I would recognize her voice anywhere. . . For Vera Welsh became Vera Lynn, Sweetheart of the Forces, and is now Dame Vera. With her 1952 record 'Auf Wiedersehn, Sweetheart' she broke new ground as the first British girl singer to top the hit parade in Britain and the USA.

Though I found work for anyone I could, the mainstay of my business was still the dancers, with Lew Grade no.1 on my list.

The other dancers came and went, getting bookings through any agent willing to place them. Lew was the first person I actually signed to a sole agency agreement. By now we were good pals.

One evening in 1933, over a fish-and-chip supper, we got talking about an agent who had just left the country, probably for good. His departure left a gap, for he had brought in all the best continental acts.

'I wonder who'll fix them up in Britain now?' I mused.

'You will, of course!' said Lew, quick off the mark as ever.

'It's a great chance, Joe. You can do it! I'll advise you. I've worked in Europe myself and I know 'em all . . . know all the circus folk, the Chinese acrobats, all the best speciality acts from Germany, France, Italy. Where I don't speak their language I can communicate in Yiddish!'

Lew was away. 'Now for a start, I can get you the Quintette du Hot Club de France. You've got to book 'em, Joe. They're the best.'

I knew the Quintette were indeed 'the best'. Their leader, Django Reinhardt, the guitarist, and Stephan Grapelli, the violinist, were — still are — famous.

I put a proposal to Lew. I had long felt this smart young man was wasting his time as a performer.

'Look, Lew, why don't you forget about your dancing? Come and work with me as an agent.'

I suspect the idea was in Lew's mind already, and he had prepared his terms.

'Only if I'm a partner,' he replied instantly.

We shook hands on the deal. I changed the title on my door to just four words: 'COLLINS AND GRADE AGENCY.'

Lew and I were now close both in business and socially. It was only natural that when Elsa and I had our first child, a daughter, Lew should accompany me to see her as soon as she was born, on 23 May 1933.

We arrived at the nursing home in Bayswater, near Hyde Park at 7 am. Elsa, I was delighted to note, looked very well. The baby was just a dark little nothing . . . a scruffy little child with a few tufts of hair. Very ordinary.

I watched in silence as the nurse put her into Elsa's arms.

'Well, what do you think?' Elsa smiled.

Not a man to show emotion, I made a joke. 'What's that bit of scrag you've got there?'

'Well, if it's scrag, it's your fault. You did it!'

'Do you forgive me?'

'Ask me in few years' time.'

We decided to call our baby Joan, a feminine version of my own name, Joseph. For her second name we chose Henrietta, after my mother.

During those first hours in the life of Joan Henrietta Collins it never so much as crossed my mind that one day my little girl would become a superstar. I am not given to such flights of fancy! I did not even think of her carrying on the Collins line of show-business folk. Had someone suggested it, I would have dismissed the idea as a hard life for a girl, too competitive, too many men around ready to take advantage of her.

What I wanted for my new baby daughter was simply that she would be healthy. Being a traditional kind of man, I also hoped that when she grew up she would find a good, traditional sort of husband who would protect and care for her.

I could never have guessed that 50 years on I'd still be voicing the same wish.

5

The Agency

My daughter Joan has led a charmed life. Like me, she has resilience. Like me, she has been foolish, self-indulgent, made wrong decisions – and still come out on top in the end. She has also had miraculous escapes from disasters outside her control.

In June 1985, when she was in Germany doing publicity for a new BMW car, she was due at Frankfurt Airport to catch her plane when a bomb ripped through the terminal killing three people. Joan missed this horror. She was still standing in the lobby of the nearby Sheraton Hotel, waiting for transport to the airport.

In 1964, in Paris, when Joan was married to Anthony Newley and their daughter Tara was a baby, the three of them were rescued just in time from a terrible fire which had broken out in the lift at their hotel.

And in 1933, when Joan herself was a baby, she escaped what could have been a fatal fire at our flat in Maida Vale, London.

In those days it was my Sunday routine to drive down to Brighton to visit my mother. Sometimes Elsa and I took the baby with us; sometimes we left her with our young live-in help.

That particular Sunday afternoon Joan was fractious, cutting her first teeth, and Elsa suggested she might feel more comfortable if we took her with us.

Luckily I agreed. For as we drove up Maida Vale on our return from Brighton we saw fire engines outside our apartment block and our little 'help' in the road.

The poor girl sobbed, 'I'm sorry, it was my fault. I was smoking a cigarette and I don't know what I did with it. The firemen say I must have dropped it on Joan's cot.'

The whole flat was burnt out. . . absolutely gutted. As we no longer had a home to go to, we were given temporary shelter by a neighbour, Jock Jacobson, an agent whose clients later included comedian-singer Max Bygraves.

Our other trips to Brighton in those first six years of Joan's life were less eventful . . . or seemed so at the time. They were just a day with the family. My grandmother, Leah Assenheim, who lived with my mother in the King's Road house, would be there, and so were many of my Assenheim aunts, all vying to hold our pretty little Joan. She would be passed round to Auntie Sadie, Auntie Minnie, Auntie Bessie, Auntie Hannah, Auntie Annie.

Joan was my mother's first grandchild – neither of my sisters had children – and I think now it was Mother who, from Joan's earliest years, fostered her determination to be a big star. Joan has certainly inherited many of my mother's qualities: her talent, her charisma, her springy, hip-swaying walk, the provocative twinkle in her eye when facing an audience.

My sisters, Lalla and Pauline, had started out with promise, winning the top prizes at their dancing schools and going straight into top West End shows. But Lalla had given up the stage on marrying, and Pauline, by the mid-'thirties, had moved to the agency side of show business.

In Joan, Mother saw a new generation carrying on the theatrical tradition of our family: before anyone else, she saw in Joan that special spark – star quality. I never had the heart to tell Mother I did not approve of the way she was encouraging the child.

My mother taught Joan the music-hall numbers she had once performed herself, complete with accompanying gestures. She taught Joan dance steps and acrobatic movements. Even at the age of 70 my Mother could still do the splits!

When regaling Joan with tales of her youth I noted that Mother did not dwell on the rigours of music-hall life – the cramped, cell-like dressing-rooms, the lack of washing facilities, the endless travelling, the rivalry over billing and the clashes of ego.

She did not tell her that if an audience didn't like you they would hoot you off the stage or pelt you with tomatoes. Mother emphasized only the glamorous side of her calling, including those legendary admirers, the backstage Johnnies.

'Lovely bouquets were handed up to us every night, and

always with a little trinket hidden among the flowers, like a pearl ring, or a locket studded with jewels. . .'

Joan drank it all in. If I'd guessed the deep impression such talk was making on her I'd have warned my mother to stop romanticizing.

One day I caught Joan standing in front of a mirror apparently poking at her eyes with matchsticks.

'What are you doing? Mummy and I have told you not to play with matches!'

Joan turned to me innocently. 'Granny taught me this. She says if you balance matchsticks on your lashes it makes them longer and stronger.'

At six, Joan was already a right little actress striking poses and very keen to look nice. Elsa and all the many women of our families pandered to Joan's love of pretty dresses, worn with matching bows in her hair. My sister Lalla gave her a little coat made of white rabbit fur and a tiny beaded vanity bag to go with it.

Joan would preen herself and sashay round the room, hand on hip. 'I'm a lady going to a ball.'

Joan was our solo star for about five years. Then our second child entered the world, to share the spotlight with her.

By now we had moved to a new block of flats, Hillcrest Court, in Shoot Up Hill, on the border of Hampstead, between Kilburn and Cricklewood. Our new daughter was born in a nursing home in Fordwych Road, just round the corner from where we lived.

Elsa and I decided that with a Joe and a Joan in the family we'd stick with the letter 'J', so we named our daughter Jacqueline Jill.

At first we addressed her as 'Jackie Jill', rather like the nursery rhyme, then it became just 'Jackie'.

But for the outbreak of war in 1939, Jackie, like Joan, might have been influenced towards show business by her Grandma Hettie. However, the children were being evacuated from London, and Jackie saw little of my mother during her early years. She remembers her grandmother only as a 'sweet old lady'.

A top name in British show business: Will Collins (formerly Isaac Hart), Joe Collins' father.

The young Isaac Hart, before he changed his name to Will Collins.

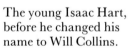

Joe's mother Hettie Collins in her dancing days. At the age of 70 she could still do the splits.

Joe Collins, aged five, with his baby sister Pauline on their nanny's lap.

Joe at Rottingdean School.

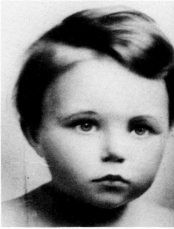

Joan Collins at three years old.

1907. The Collins residence in Pennard Road, behind Shepherd's Bush Empire in West London. Joe's sister Lalla, aged two, stands in the doorway.

Hettie Collins (centre) with her first grandchild, Joan. On her left, Hettie's sister Sarah; on her right, her sister Minnie.

Now Lord Grade of Elstree, in the early 'thirties Lew Grade was 'the dancer with the humorous feet', the first artiste Joe Collins signed to a management contract.

LEW GRADE

THE DANCER WITH THE HUMOROUS FEET

Variety Season—
MOSS, STOLL, SYNDICATE and Principal
Independent Halls

Booked by WALTER BENTLEY'S AGENCY
Cabaret Arrangements—Joe Collins, Esq.

Joe Collins' sister Pauline, dancer in West End shows of the 'twenties.

Mother and daughter: Elsa Collins and little Joan.

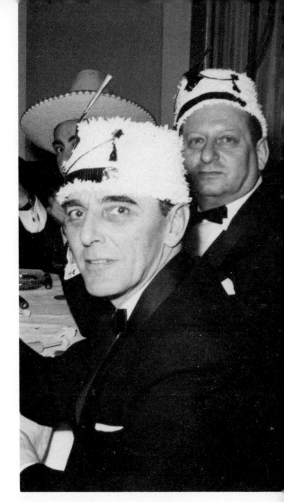

Party time: Joe Collins with Lew Grade, his first London business partner.

Dave King, an entertainer whom Joe Collins built into a star. In 1956 he turned down Hollywood opportunities for his first chance to head the bill at the London Palladium.

THE LONDON PALLADIUM

APRIL 2ND TWO WEEKS 6.15 MATINEE AT 2.40 EACH SATURDAY 8.45

DAVE KING

FIRST TIME HERE

TELEVISION'S STAR COMEDIAN

HASSANI TROUPE WHIRLWIND ACROBATS | GEORGE CARDEN DANCERS | PIERRE Continental Jugglers BEL

GEORGE AND BERT HELD OVER FOR TWO MORE WEEKS | RADIO, T.V AND RECORDING STAR JOAN | WALTON &

Joe with Joan, aged three, on the beach
at Brighton.

Two little girls in party frocks – Joan
and younger sister Jackie.

Proud of the new addition to the family:
Joan – aged 13 – and Jackie with their
baby brother Bill.

Joan at 17, already heading for a film career. She wrote on the bottom: 'I knew it would happen one day! Fame at last!!'

Joan Collins, Hollywood star.

Joan – pin-up by the sea.

Joan and Jackie Collins, bikini-clad teenagers staying with their Aunt Lalla in Cannes.

The Agency

When we took Jackie to visit my kin she was a mere baby, who tended to be restless on the journey to Brighton. I learned later she hated the smell of the car's leather upholstery, which explains why she was always quieter than usual when we arrived.

Our little daughters were very different in personality. Joan was an outgoing child; Jackie was very sensitive. From babyhood she was always very protective towards animals, and was overjoyed when we gave her a little poodle as a pet. When this animal messed on our much-prized Chinese carpet and I started shouting in anger, little Jackie burst into tears and became so upset she has never forgotten the incident. Nor have I! To this day the stain is still visible on the carpet.

I do admit, I did shout at my children, quite a lot. Except on stage or in markets I always was a good shouter! Shouting was my way of getting my children to behave themselves, and it worked. Yet for all the noise I made, they never appeared scared of me . . . not as I was scared of my own father's temper. He too had disciplined me by shouting, though he once gave me a good hiding – for flicking a pea across the dinner table at my sister Lalla when he was entertaining important company.

I never smacked my own children. Elsa would have been very angry if I'd done anything like that. Even in my most furious outbursts I never slipped into foul language either: blasphemous or rude words were never spoken in our household.

Today, when I hear Joan use bad language I'm shocked. Jackie nowadays writes four-letter words in her books, but I've never heard her actually *say* anything distasteful. My son Bill does not swear either. I've never heard him make suggestive remarks or tell a dirty joke. And neither does my youngest child, Natasha . . . not in *my* hearing.

By the end of the 'thirties I had accepted that it was my lot to be the only male in the household with three females. In my teens I'd been an only son with a widowed mother and two sisters. Now I had a wife and two daughters.

My business life too was becoming dominated by women, for in the early days of my partnership with Lew Grade the goodwill of two particular influential ladies was vital to our business.

To obtain Home Office permits for continental artistes to work in Britain, Lew and I needed proof that they had a fixed run of engagements. This meant getting them bookings on the two major theatre circuits, both of which employed women as their bookers.

Cissie Williams, Artistes' Booking Manageress of the Moss Empires circuit under Val Parnell, was a martinet, very formal and correct. It was impossible for an outsider even to make an appointment to see her.

Flo Leddington, who booked the Syndicate Theatres, was less forbidding. Married to a comedian, she was reputed to be a gentler type of woman.

When Lew and I started bringing in our European acts, I was the one who took the initiative and telephoned Flo Leddington's office.

'Miss Leddington will be late this morning,' said her secretary. 'Her husband is away on tour and there's no one else to walk that wretched dog of hers. She has to do it herself.'

I saw my opening. Always the diplomat, when I spoke to Flo Leddington later that day, instead of sales talk about my acts I asked about her dog – a greyhound – and encouraged her to tell me about her 'walkies' problem.

'I'll help you out,' I volunteered. 'I'll come over to your house tomorrow morning and take him for a run.'

Flo Leddington lived in Barnes, in south-west London, miles from my own home. Her greyhound was a massive, lively creature of seemingly boundless energy. But I'd made my promise. For quite some time I'd start my day by driving to Barnes and doing my strenuous chore as a dog-walker.

Once the animal was exercised, I'd give Miss Leddington a lift to her office in my car, and gradually we became friendly. Flo Leddington duly booked our acts for the Syndicate Theatres and also gave me an introduction to the formidable Miss Cissie Williams. Collins and Grade owed their future success to Flo Leddington's greyhound.

One thing I had not anticipated was the amount of paperwork and patience involved in importing the continental acts. Copies of a permit application had to go to the Home Office, the Variety Agents' Association and to Equity, the actors' union, any of whom were likely to challenge you.

'Why all this fuss over a down-bill Rumanian juggler?' I asked a Home Office official who had cross-examined me concerning this particular artiste.

'We have to be careful,' he answered drily. 'He might be a spy.'

As the Collins and Grade workload increased, Lew Grade brought his two younger brothers into the firm. First, in 1937, came Bernie Delfont. He was a good-looking 28-year-old, still getting well-paid work as a dancer. His duo with a girl partner, Delfont and Toko, and his duo with Hal Monty, the Delfont Boys, could easily command £20–£30 a week. But with an eye to a future when his feet were less nimble, Bernie now wanted to learn the agency side of the business.

Written in my ledger for the year 1937 is the record of the first booking he ever arranged, for a comedian singer: 'Harry Jerome, Argyll Theatre, Birkenhead, £10 for the week.'

Bernie's share of the commission was 7s 6d (37½p). The future Lord Delfont had taken his first step towards his present status as an international show-business figure.

Bernie remained in the office with Lew and me for several months before quitting to start his own agency, booking acts for a group of dance halls.

Bernie was a nice lad. I liked him and I was sorry to see him go.

The youngest of the Grade brothers, Leslie Grade, was a commercial traveller (what is today termed a sales rep) with no experience at all of show business. When Lew suggested we should start him in our office I was dubious, not knowing how he'd fit in.

I need not have worried. Leslie, whom we paid £1 a week, got the hang of the business very quickly. He started making contacts of his own and became friendly with Billy Cotton, the genially smiling band-leader whose cry of 'Wakey! Wakey!'

followed by a few bars of 'Somebody Stole My Gal' rang out on radio each Sunday. With Cotton putting business his way, Leslie Grade too left our agency to start up on his own. The Leslie Grade-Billy Cotton friendship has endured to the next generation. Today Billy's son Bill Cotton and Leslie Grade's son Michael are both big wheels of BBC Television.

With or without the younger Grades, by 1937 Collins and Grade was a well-established business. Anyone with the slightest interest in the entertainment industry knew our names. Apart from our agency we had branched out as show-business managers and we presented variety bills of our own around the country. We offered talent for every type of vaudeville patron, from the grand folk in the fauteuils (as we called the orchestra stalls in those days) to the less affluent people up in the gods (or gallery). Pleasing the people in the gods was most important. They sat on hard benches three tiers up – above the stalls, the dress circle and the upper circle – and if they couldn't hear what was happening on stage or didn't like the show they let the performers know about it by stamping their feet and disruptively catcalling.

There was still a big following for those 'speciality' acts of a kind rarely seen today except in a circus; among the ones we booked I remember Dudley's Midgets, Locarno's Pigeons and the Royal China Acrobatic Troupe.

The younger people wanted to see in person the big bands and star musicians they knew from the radio: Henry Hall and his Band, Jack Hylton and his Band, the Silver Sax Six, the Kit-Kat Saxophone Band, trumpeter Nat Gonella and organist Robin Richmond. None of these people, big names in their time, earned the millionaire income of today's recording stars, but they did all right.

Just as in the 'eighties an impresario can make good money from the stage spin-off of a high-rated television series, in the 'thirties you could fill a theatre with a stage version of a popular radio variety show. My tours of the radio shows *BBC Bandstand*, *Music Hall*, and *Old Town Hall*, obtained on licence from the BBC, did very well indeed.

One of our top attractions, a big hit on radio, was a comedy duo, the sisters Elsie and Doris Waters, who played sketches in the guise of charladies – Gert and Daisy.

Dressed in second-hand clothes and carrying shopping bags they would meet, centre stage, and gossip about their lot in life and their fictitious menfolk, Daisy's husband Bert and Gert's sweetheart Willy, who sent her love-letters which she would read aloud. (One of them, I recall, began: 'I am writing this very slow because I know you don't read very fast . . . .')

In real life Elsie and Doris, daughters of a funeral furnisher, were women of the utmost refinement who had studied at the Guildhall School of Music – a most unusual training for playing querulous Cockney cleaning ladies. The sisters were inseparable and neither ever married.

They had a brother, Jack, a graduate of London University, who had raced cars at Broadlands and was now a motor salesman. Jack was impressed with the career I was building for his sisters and decided to go into show business himself. He changed his name from Waters to Warner and later became a British television favourite in the guise of a typical kindly English bobby, 'Dixon of Dock Green'.

Having conquered show business, Lew and I, like all ambitious entrepreneurs, felt the time had come to diversify. In 1937 we opened an exclusive West End nightclub, El Morocco, which we modelled on the New York night spot of the same name.

It was situated in premises below street level, for we knew that descending into a basement gives people a greater sense of anticipation, of doing something daring, than when they climb a flight of stairs.

To suit the ambience we wished to create, the ceiling was designed like a romantic night sky – deep, velvety navy, with electric 'stars' – very sensual, very chic. This Eastern promise was somewhat dissipated by the two fashionable, very Western dance bands we engaged, led by Jack Harris and Lew Stone.

We wanted the smartest people in town to be our patrons, and we got them. Lady Charles Cavendish, the former dancer Adele Astaire, who had partnered her brother Fred on the West End stage in the 'twenties, was at the opening party.

Our enterprise had the intriguing label 'bottle party', which in itself attracted customers. For owing to the quirky British licensing regulations in those pre-war years, it was not permitted to dispense drinks at night clubs. To circumvent the law the liquor shops in nearby Soho stayed open late to accommodate us and similar club-owners. Our clientele would fill in order slips given them by the waiters, who handed them to the cycling boys, who collected the bottles from the shops.

If a customer's bottle was not empty by the end of his night out, it was labelled and put aside for his next visit – all very stupid, but it made our customers feel happily conspiratorial and was advantageous to us because we charged 'corkage'. That was where we made our profit.

When my brother-in-law Mark Godfrey, my sister Lalla's husband, saw how well we were doing he became anxious to have a share in our club; in fact we sold the whole business to him.

As a less exotic venture, Lew and I also opened a cigarette kiosk at Marble Arch, staffed by the Grade brothers' only sister, Rita. The kiosk got bombed in the Second World War and Rita married a doctor, Joe Freeman, so that was the end of that!

I had been in partnership with Lew long enough to know he was what is now called a 'workaholic'. I felt he would have welcomed an extra day in the week, so he could work eight days instead of seven.

'I've got my wife, my family, my work. That's all I want!' Lew has reiterated through the years.

I did not intend copying his style. I never did consider Lew's great appetite for toil a virtue; in any case, I couldn't function that way. I need some time to re-charge my batteries. I need leisure to look around quietly and observe the world.

In the 'thirties I had my routine for a long weekend. Fridays I went fishing, Saturdays were for football and on Sundays I took my wife and children for an outing in the car. Although, in principle, I worked a four-day week, I put in far more hours at business than most people. In London, after my day at the office, I'd study the time-sheets of the stage acts I wanted to see and visit at least three theatres a night, checking on my clients and looking for promising new faces. I travelled to theatres round the country, seeing our shows and looking for fresh ones, keeping an eye on possible competition.

When I visited the theatres my wife Elsa rarely came with me, or if she did she would usually wait at the stage door while I went up to the dressing-rooms. Elsa was a lively companion in my social life with my associates and their families. Her particular friends were Lew Grade's wife Kathy and Kathy's sisters, Norah, who married agent Solly Black, and Phyllis, who married Vaslov, the photographer.

Most of Elsa's activities, however, centred on our little daughters. She was a diligent and doting mother.

I was startled when, soon after Joan was born, she produced a printed notice which she fixed to the baby's pram: 'PLEASE DO NOT KISS ME.'

'It's bad for children if strangers kiss them. They might catch germs,' Elsa assured me. When Jackie came along, and later, when our son Bill was born, out came that same notice again.

I did not interfere. In rearing children, Elsa knew what was best. Having enough to do outside the home, I was content to leave Elsa to bring up our family. She looked after everything, even their schooling.

I don't know if Elsa ever told Joan and Jackie about what we used to term the 'facts of life'. Elsa and I never uttered a word about sex in front of the children, and would never have discussed human reproduction the way some parents do today.

As I was at home so little, when I did spend time with the girls I was a strict father. I insisted they had good manners and treated their elders respectfully. I don't remember either of them as tots ever throwing a tantrum. They were good kids, in a secure environment. Though not wealthy, we were comfortably off, with a pleasant home, good food, and a car.

Actually, though my children never knew it, there *were* times when things were not as good as they seemed, for in show business, as in other businesses, the cash flow can sometimes be a problem.

One particular financial emergency occurred early in 1939. The Nazis were in power, the German army was advancing across Europe and Britain had opened her doors to refugees. I had an urgent call from Syd Hyams, one of three brothers who owned a chain of cinemas.

'Can you do something for me, Joe? I want you to help me get a Hungarian Jewish theatrical company out of Europe. They're stranded in Prague. Their impresario Robert Koralek, a friend of mine, is desperate. He says the German army is expected any day.

'Can you get the permits to bring them to Britain? Fly out to Prague and see what has to be done? We *have* to save their lives!'

Of course I had to help. My only worry was financing what might prove a costly operation. I feared there might be a few officials to bribe.

When I told Elsa my problem she did not answer. She simply walked out of the room and came back with her jewel case.

'Take this diamond ring to a pawnbroker. We can always redeem the pledge later.'

Arriving by plane in Prague I went straight to the theatre where the Koralek company were putting on a folk entertainment called 'Ma Vlast' (My Country), based on a cycle of symphonic poems by the Bohemian composer Smetana. It was all very cultural. The cast, in national costume, presented a song-and-dance performance depicting the life and legends of Czechoslovakia.

Watching them was a most moving experience, particularly as it now seemed certain that Czechoslovakia was about to be crushed by the Nazi regime.

Without delay I made arrangements for the 'Ma Vlast' company to leave the country and come to Britian, where the Hyams brothers had engagements waiting for them. To my relief, it was a straightforward procedure, no bribery involved. Then I caught the next plane back to London.

When I first set off on my mission I had tried to close my mind to the political implications. It seemed everyone else around me was playing the same game, for in Prague everything seemed normal. However, under the surface, the tension was there . . . just as it was with me.

When the plane bringing me back to Britain made an

emergency landing, actually because of bad weather, I thought in my panic that the German Luftwaffe had intercepted our flight and we had landed in Germany. I expected to be greeted on the tarmac by an SS man toting a machine-gun. I had no idea we were in Rotterdam, Holland.

After this, I could not get out of Europe fast enough. Instead of waiting for the next day's flight to London I rushed down to the docks and caught the first ferry-boat. I think it sprang a leak. As the sea lashed against by bunk I was scared out of my wits. When I finally landed and telephoned Elsa she cried with relief.

On 14 March the 'Ma Vlast' company arrived in Britain. I had succeeded in my mission just in time: two days later it was announced that Hitler had annexed Bohemia and Moravia and proclaimed them a German protectorate.

The 'Ma Vlast' company put on its show at the Trocadero Cinema, Elephant and Castle, then transferred to the Troxy Cinema, Mile End Road and eventually disbanded and dispersed. The only member of the troupe I kept up with was its director, Robert Koralek, whose family owned the Ronacher theatre in Vienna. He settled in London, joined my agency and worked with me for many years, bringing continental circus and 'speciality' acts into Britain. After he left me he did similar business with the United States.

During my short stay in Europe it had become clear to me that Prime Minister Neville Chamberlain's hopes for 'peace in our time' were unrealistic. Knowing, first-hand, that war was inevitable, I started making plans to get Elsa, 6-year-old Joan and baby Jackie away from London and the bombing raids to come.

I rented a house with a garden for them on a newly-built estate in Bognor on the Sussex coast where Elsa's mother, Ada Bessant, was now living. Elsa's sister Renee was in Bognor too: her husband, George Hillman, who worked for me, had joined the forces. Lew Grade's mother, Olga Winogradsky, took a house two doors away from ours.

In August 1939 my wife and daughters moved to what we thought would be their wartime home. Little Joan was alarmed by these changes and knew something drastic was happening, but she couldn't work out what.

'Are you sending us away, Daddy? Why are you doing it?'

How can you explain what war is to a 6-year-old child?

Without Elsa and the girls our latest London flat, at Alexandra Court, Maida Vale, was a very lonely place. I invited my agent friends Bernie Delfont and Keith Devon to move in with me. They were delighted with the arrangement; I felt almost like a bachelor again.

On 3 September 1939, the day Britain declared war on Germany, I stood on my balcony with Keith and Bernie, looking down into the street. Everything was so quiet. Then the air-raid sirens sounded and we heard the buzz of aeroplane engines. It was a false alarm (the planes were British), but all the same I was thankful that Elsa, Joan and Jackie were somewhere safe.

6

The War Years

As soon as there was a lull in the bombing attacks I brought Elsa and the girls back home to Maida Vale. But then the raids started again and I had to find another new home for my family. Returning to Bognor was out of the question. Elsa's sister Renee Hillman warned us of the dangers. 'As the Germans fly in over our coast they're even shooting at innocent people walking on the promenade,' she reported.

Bognor being too risky, I took a flat in an area west of London, on a quiet part of the river Thames at Maidenhead, Berkshire. I was able to move there too as I could commute quite easily to London – and could spend my weekends fishing!

We did not stay long in Maidenhead. During another lull in the Blitz, Elsa and I took a chance on going back to London again. We had been foolish, for the very night we settled in the Maida Vale flat there was another raid, a really bad one.

During the Blitz, all the families would check with each other next day on how they had fared in the previous night's air raid. When I told my sister Pauline that we had bundled our sleeping children down the road to take cover in the crowded Underground, she suggested we stay with her. Pauline, now married to the theatrical agent David Marks, was living at Portsea Hall, a block of flats near Marble Arch – not far from our own place – which had an air-raid shelter in the basement.

That night, after we had moved to Portsea Hall, the air-raid warning sounded again. David Marks did not come with us to the shelter. He always preferred to sit at his open window and watch the raid.

I considered this habit strange and foolhardy, but that night I saw his point, I would myself have preferred to see what was happening outside, for in the basement I felt trapped. We heard the roar of planes, the shriek of bombs, the explosion, the crashing masonry and we knew it was all happening only a few yards from where we were huddled.

In the morning, feeling lucky to be alive, Elsa and I set off up the road with the children heading for our own flat. It wasn't there. Alexandra Court had been sliced clean in half. I opened the door of our bedroom and found. . . nothing. The girls' bedroom was gone completely, not so much as a wall or a door left.

Elsa was by now under great strain, with baby Jackie to care for and Joan so frightened that she had to sleep with the light on. I felt that if this state of affairs went on much longer my daughters would grow up nervous wrecks.

This time Elsa and I decided the girls must be taken right away from London, the prime enemy target, to settle down in some quieter place. We made up our minds that for the duration of the war Elsa and the girls would live in Ilfracombe, a hilly, picturesque seaside resort in North Devon, on the estuary of the Bristol Channel. My sister Lalla and our friend Hilda Burns, wife of the agent Sidney Burns, had already settled there and liked the place.

On that journey to Ilfracombe I had some inkling what it must be like to be a refugee. I drove my family there in my little Ford car, with Elsa in front beside me and Joan, Jackie and their nanny in the back. We were a pathetic sight. Jackie's pushchair, our bed-linen and our blankets were all tied to the roof and as it was raining heavily everything was soaked.

We did not reach Ilfracombe till well after nightfall, and because of the wartime blackout I had no idea where I was driving. Not knowing the roads, I was worried that in the pitch darkness we might have an accident.

Then, to my relief, I saw a sudden flash of light, picking out the shape of a man at the roadside. It was Lalla's husband, Mark Godfrey, with a flash lamp. He guided us through the blackout to our new home, a flat above a sweetshop on the seafront promenade.

That night, for the first time since war broke out, the air-raid sirens sounded in Ilfracombe. We heard the familiar buzz of approaching aircraft, then the blast of bombs as they were dropped on Swansea, South Wales, the opposite side of the Bristol Channel. Ilfracombe itself was never bombed.

There was another problem I had to tackle. Ilfracombe is 200 miles from London, wartime train connections were appalling and with petrol on ration it seemed I would be visiting my family very rarely.

I had a plan. I knew that farmers were allowed extra petrol because they were growing vital foodstuffs. I hoped to find a farmer willing to let me have petrol on a 'barter' system, if I could provide *him* with some other commodity in short supply.

Finally, after knocking on many farmhouse doors, I found someone willing to co-operate. This farmer agreed to let me have petrol in exchange for cheese, which for me was no trouble for in the London street markets you could buy any rationed food you liked if you were willing to pay over the odds.

If all this sounds odd or dishonest now I would like to point out that very few of us who lived through the war could say, hand on heart, that they did not try to get 'a little extra' on the black market when they had the chance.

Some folk were more enterprising – if that is the right word – than others. My Devon farmer friend, for example, and my brother-in-law, Mark Godfrey, were partners in a scheme. 'Goddy' had heard of a ship which had sunk in the mouth of the Thames with a cargo of currants, almonds and raisins. When this cargo was salvaged the fruit had solidified and, condemned as unfit for human consumption, was due to be sold as animal feed.

The farmer bought the ruined fruit officially for his cattle, and he and Goddy rented a high-street shop in Barnstaple, the nearest big town to Ilfracombe. Here they unloaded their sacks of booty on to the floor and got busy scrubbing the coagulated contents with scrubbing brushes.

When the fruit looked respectable they parcelled the currants, almonds and raisins into half-pound and one-pound packages, took them round the bakeries of Devon and sold the lot. No one questioned the source and no one ever complained of food poisoning from the bakers' fruitcakes.

Having cleared his stock of dried fruit, Goddy used the same shop premises to sell ladies' silk stockings, also in short supply, which he bought from London market traders.

Where they had obtained them no one knew, not even Goddy, and he certainly did not try to find out. The women of Devon, weary of clothes rationing, never asked questions either; they were delighted with Goddy's service.

My thoughts at this time were on keeping my theatrical business ticking over, if I could, and waiting to be called up. My partner Lew Grade joined the army, I failed the medical examination because of chronic stomach ulcers.

So I joined the Home Guard, now laughingly called 'Dad's Army' instead. We were trained as soldiers, but were only to be sent into battle as a last resort, if the worst happened and the Germans invaded Britian.

Though I rose no higher than the rank of private in the Home Guard, I was in a ritzy platoon. We had headquarters at one of London's smartest hotels, Grosvenor House in Park Lane, conveniently near my new West End offices in Triumph House, Regent Street.

In my schooldays I had trained with the Officers' Training Corps under canvas in Wiltshire, but now I had forgotten all I ever learned about combat. My only memory of that time is the discomfort and embarrassment of using the communal latrine, a pole across a ditch.

I would, I fear, have made a terrible soldier. When a sergeant of the Guards from Buckingham Palace put us through our paces with full pack and rifle, I fainted half-way through the exercise. As you can imagine from this, I am not what you would call a strapping fellow.

One of my later Home Guard jobs was to help with casualties during air raids. I was stationed opposite the London Palladium in a two-room basement beneath the goods entrance of the department store Dickins and Jones, where we Home Guard personnel, plus our ammunition, occupied one of two cellars. By a dangerous mistake of wartime planning, despite the presence of explosives, the other cellar room was an air-raid shelter for the public and there was just one staircase for both rooms.

When the sirens sounded it was chaotic: we six Home Guard fellows would be rushing upstairs to do our duty while the public rushed down to take cover. We had to fight our way out.

At the start of the war I had expected changes for the Collins and Grade Agency. All the London theatres went 'dark' (except for the Windmill, home of 'girlie' entertainment) because it was thought people would not be in the mood for shows, or want to venture out in the blackout. The government, however, soon insisted that the theatres open up again. This meant that audiences coming into the West End risked becoming air-raid casualties – and so did the artistes.

I did what I could to ensure their safety. The building where our agency was situated had a 'safe' basement two floors below street level, which I leased and equipped as an air-raid shelter. We filled the place with mattresses and invited all our agent friends – Solly Black, Dennis Selinger and the rest – to pass on the news that all artistes appearing in the West End were welcome to use our shelter, with our obliging caretaker providing an all-night running buffet. Though bombs dropped all round us in the course of the war, and one morning we surfaced to see Oxford Circus ablaze, we in our basement were safe.

By 1944 I had become used to operating under wartime conditions, business was booming again and I felt ready for my first venture as a West End producer: it would be the biggest thing I'd ever done, the type of production which would make people forget the drabness of the war.

I decided to present a lavish operetta, but I wasn't sure which one to choose. There was someone on hand to advise me: the musicals and plays side of my business was handled by Leslie Bloom, chairman of that dedicated bunch of theatre enthusiasts, the Gallery First Nighters. Leslie recommended Emmerich Kalman's *The Gipsy Princess*, a romantic show I remembered having seen when it first was staged in the 'twenties. Set in mythical European country called Voyvodinan, it was about a prince, Ronald, betrothed to a countess but in love with a gipsy girl. Feeling a little updating would be in order, we amended the script, put in a few topical references to such things as the wartime meat 'spam', while the Voyvodinians greeted each other with the 'V' sign – the patriotic V for Victory. Our star was Tessa Deane, a big name of the day.

After a pre-London tour, that summer our show opened at the Saville theatre in Shaftesbury Avenue and received good reviews from the critics. We were also praised for 'discovering' a new star, our romantic lead James Etherington, a former schoolteacher we had found at our open auditions. (Sadly, James Etherington died before he became a truly established name.)

My hopes that *The Gipsy Princess* would have a long West End run seemed justified. But within 48 hours of the London opening Hitler chose to launch his latest weapon – the flying bombs, known as 'doodlebugs' because of the buzzing sound they made. For civilians they were the most frightening weapon of war yet devised.

Business at all the West End theatres slumped instantly, for people were too scared to leave their homes, let alone venture into a crowded part of London. I looked at the rows of empty seats and decided to go back to the provinces. It was a wise move, for the tour made quite a lot of money.

During this period of coping alone in London I was able to visit my family in Ilfracombe once every two weeks, thanks to my Devon farmer. Elsa and the girls had settled in quite well. My sister Lalla, our friend Hilda Burns and Elsa opened a business there, a little drinking club called the Odd Spot, frequented mainly by the Canadian servicemen.

It was the smartest place in Ilfracombe. Frankly, there wasn't anywhere else to go! Lalla and Hilda ran the place and Elsa, though occupied with caring for Joan and Jackie, sometimes lent a hand too.

Occasionally something happened which brought the war nearer to Ilfracombe. On one of my trips to visit my family there was a great excitement because a German bomber plane had landed in a field a few miles outside the town. The pilot, so the story went, had mistaken the Bristol Channel for the English Channel and had brought his plane down thinking he was safely back in Germany. He was taken prisoner but his plane had not been moved, so I took my daughters to see what an enemy aircraft looked like at close quarters. Joan recalls also seeing a bayonet I had acquired. She has never forgotten the grisly sight of the blood-stained blade.

One of my greatest regrets, though, is that I spent very little time with Joan and Jackie during their childhood years. Seeing them only once every two weeks I missed out on sharing this period of their lives.

I love my daughters, but I am not the kind of parent who deludes himself that his children are superior to everyone else's. I did not think of them as outstanding in any way. I saw them as quite pretty, quite nice . . . and quite ordinary. I could see that Elsa was controlling them well. But there was nothing about them I would have termed 'special'. Even today, while I would describe Joan and Jackie as very successful I would never say they were 'special'.

In Ilfracombe, the girls' school reports provided assurance that my children were reasonably intelligent, though not exceptionally so. And as neither Elsa nor I were academically inclined ourselves we would never have driven Joan, Jackie or Bill (who was born after the war) to be top of the class.

Though we did not do this consciously, our parental attitude allowed the girls to neglect the subjects they did not like and concentrate on those which appealed to them most. Joan was good at drama, English and art. When I came to visit the family in Ilfracombe she'd do delightful little drawings for me.

As soon as Jackie was able to read and write, even though she couldn't spell very well, she was way ahead of the rest of her class in English composition, already proving herself a born storyteller. When the girls were playing at home she'd compose little tales to go with Joan's drawings. Later she found two characters of her own, Lucky Lucy and Roger Rat, and wrote about their adventures. (The word 'Lucky', now the name of one of her characters and the title of a bestselling Collins book, has always been a favourite in her vocabulary.)

Jackie's way of keeping me up to date was to write things down that had happened to her and turn them into stories. As her dad I of course found these tales very interesting but it never crossed my mind that one day she would be a professional author.

It did not occur to me either that my girls were missing out on a very particular pleasure of my own early childhood: owing to our wartime separation they had no chance to come with me to music halls, and I wouldn't have taken them even if they had been with me in London.

When friends asked me if I intended to bring my daughters into show business, carrying on our family tradition, I would shake my head.

'No thank you! I'd never put them on the stage. I know the game too well. Too many pitfalls. Too many failures. I wouldn't expose them to that!'

I did not guess that Joan and Jackie would develop very strong minds of their own, and that what I had to say would not stop them!'

The day the war ended, in 1945, I stood amid the elated crowds outside Buckingham Palace. Everyone was cheering; everyone was your friend; complete strangers were hugging one another.

I brought Elsa and the girls home to London at last, to a flat I had rented in Portland Court, Great Portland Street, in the West End, and we began to settle into life as a family once more.

Elsa began to look for a bigger place, where the girls could each have a room of their own. She found a wonderful flat in Harley House, Marylebone Road, a huge, dignified building on the site where a monastery had once stood, and very close to Harley Street, where top doctors and dentists had their consulting rooms.

Our new residence was a semi-basement, which meant the rooms were never sunny, and we had a paved yard in place of a garden, but we had plenty of living space – two huge reception rooms, four bedrooms and two bathrooms. There were other advantages: porters on duty night and day at each of the five entrances to the block and the use of a large private garden attached to nearby Regent's Park, with swings, a sandpit for the children and a tennis court. The tribunal-controlled rent for all this was £10 a week. Though I remained at Harley House for about 30 years this rent control meant that even at the end of my stay I was still paying only £40 a week; today apartments in that block are rented at £200–£400 a week.

Harley House is the place Joan and Jackie still think of as their 'old home', and both were married from there (first time round). Elsa and I lived in the block until her death in 1962, and I stayed on as a widower and into the first few years with my present wife, Irene.

Gradually other show-business people moved into the block too. The Australian manager Peter Gormley had both his offices and a residential apartment there; occasionally his artistes Cliff Richard and the Shadows stayed the night. In the 'sixties Mick Jagger leased an apartment, where he lived with the delicately pretty blonde singer Marianne Faithfull. I will always have great affection for Harley House.

Soon after the war ended, my business set-up also changed. Lew Grade, newly demobbed from the forces, decided not to come back to the firm; instead, he formed an agency with his brother Leslie.

Though taken by surprise I did not mind too much. I really did not need a partner. I was a recognized name in show business and, in all modesty, one of the top agents.

Once more I changed the sign on my door. This time it read 'WILL COLLINS LTD', which eventually I changed to 'JOE COLLINS LTD', the title I use to this day.

7

Little Women

The big event of 1946 for Elsa and me was the arrival of our only son, William Richard, born at Queen Charlotte's Hospital in west London on 1 May. He was a lovely fair-haired baby, weighing 8 lbs 9½ oz. He brought a new dimension to our family life. He was the apple of Elsa's eye, and I welcomed a male ally at long last.

I bought Bill a train set, which I played with more often than he did. Bill preferred his model cars. As soon as he could crawl he was fascinated by anything with four wheels and an engine. Cars became little Bill's passion, and he was given literally hundreds of them. Almost 40 years on he still has them all, each wrapped in cotton wool, in perfect condition – and worth a fortune.

Today he is an expert on cars and can tell you anything you care to ask, from the value of a vintage motor vehicle to the advantages or disadvantages of the latest model. Cars are an interest Bill and I share. I began by teaching him everything I know about them, and now he teaches me.

When they were children Bill's car collection became Jackie's favourite toys, too, and as he learned more and more about motors, so did she: Jackie can still talk with authority about the engines and bodywork of the various models. She also gets sentimentally attached to her cars, and when she went to live in Los Angeles in the early 'eighties she took her pet '65 Ford Mustang with her.

Jackie, by the time she reached her teens, was a self-sufficient little person, quite happy with her own company. As long as she had her exercise book to scribble in, she was content. At eleven she wrote her first 'grown-up' story, a fantasy about a girl who wanted to be a film star; it was a natural enough choice of subject, for she and Joan were crazy about movies and their stars.

Jackie was also an avid reader – too avid for my peace of mind. Not wishing my innocent children to be corrupted, I put my copy of D.H. Lawrence's *Lady Chatterley's Lover* into a crumpled brown paper bag and hid it away among my shirts. Jackie managed to find it. When I caught her reading it in my bedroom I exploded.

'I'm disgusted with you! That book's pornographic. You must not read books like this!'

Jackie kept her cool. 'You're too late, Daddy. I've nearly finished it.' She looked me straight in the eye and asked: 'Have you read this book?'

'Yes, I have.' I felt my face go red. Realizing that my modern daughter was actually far less embarrassed than I was, I let the matter drop. I reasoned that if Lawrence's writings were indeed liable to 'deprave and corrupt' the damage had now been done as far as Jackie was concerned.

After this incident I found a different hiding-place for my second 'naughty' book, Henry Miller's *Tropic of Cancer*. Jackie tracked it down to the tool-box in my car.

Looking back, I wonder now if Jackie learned a useful tip through me; even a non-reader like me will buy a book if everyone is talking about it, saying it's 'spicy' and 'shocking'. Perhaps that is why she chose to write such books herself. I wonder what kind of novels Jackie would have written had I kept shelves full of classics!

During their formative years, other traits of mine were also shaping Joan and Jackie's future. Sometimes, unconsciously, I was providing guidelines. They came to understand the qualities of a good business agent: drive, foresight, shrewd judgement. Today Jackie, like me, has a good grasp of business; Joan too is a good negotiator.

Though I did not take my girls to variety theatres, they all met the top variety stars and also the top agents.

One special group I belonged to would meet regularly in each other's homes for a Friday-night card game of six-handed gin rummy. There would be Lew Grade, the agent Dennis Selinger, the comedian Davy Kaye, the impresario David Land (who launched the careers of composer Andrew Lloyd Webber and lyricist Tim Rice), all of us sitting in our shirtsleeves, endlessly smoking cigars and cigarettes, playing till dawn, with just an interval for smoked salmon sandwiches and tea. When it came to my own turn to be host, Joan and Jackie would sneak into the room and pinch our food.

Though my children were growing up in a theatrical environment, for them this was not the exciting side of show business. Joan and Jackie would have far preferred to be meeting film stars.

There had been a film connection in our family. In the 'thirties and early 'forties my sister Pauline had worked in film casting for producer and agent Herbert de Leon, finding roles for Greer Garson and Margaret Lockwood, and for a hopeful gap-toothed, uppercrust young man called Terry-Thomas, who was usually cast as a waiter or croupier.

After her marriage to David Marks, Pauline had given up her job. Then, in 1948, after dear David's untimely death, she carried on his variety agency, so by the time Joan and Jackie were old enough to be interested there was no real family contact with this glamorous world.

To my girls, Hollywood was the ultimate dream-fulfilment. I think that apart from their upbringing by Elsa and me the movies and the fan magazines were the biggest influence on their future lives. They were ready to believe all the publicity stories, the glamorized versions of reality. Joan and Jackie's bedrooms were full of film magazines and pin-up pictures. Jackie's favourites were Tony Curtis and Rock Hudson, while Joan's was a British star, Maxwell Reed.

Although, at this stage, Joan's fantasies did not touch on her real life, she had started preparing herself for a time when they would by taking dancing and drama lessons. Elsa thought they would be a nice hobby for her, but Joan, with the backing of Grandma Hettie, was fancying herself as a star.

The year Bill was born Elsa and I let Joan have her way and sent her as a boarder to a top theatrical school in Hertfordshire, hoping it would get this film-star nonsense out of her head.

Sure enough, a couple of weeks later, Joan telephoned us to complain. 'It's impossible here! I have to make my own bed and clean my room myself . . . even scrub the floor. *And* they insist I wash my hair with scouring powder.'

Elsa lost no time in bringing Joan home again. I reasoned that if my daughter would not endure a bit of discomfort for the sake of theatrical training, then she was not cut out for show business – a thought I found reassuring.

I had further proof that acting, to Joan, was just a game. During her flirtation with juvenile dramatics she was chosen to play one of the two children in Ibsen's *A Doll's House*, in a production at the Arts Theatre in London.

Elsa and I, waiting to witness our daughter's West End début, were puzzled and worried when she failed to appear. Later she admitted she had become so engrossed in a schoolgirl adventure yarn in the magazine *Girl's Crystal* that she had missed her entrance cue.

By the time she was a teenager, I had lost count of the number of schools Joan had attended, but now she tells me there were thirteen in all. This was, of course, due to the war. As I moved my family from one safe area to another, then back to London again when the bombing eased up, she was always making a fresh start with new teachers, new curricula.

The last school Joan attended, with Jackie, was the exclusive Francis Holland School. Here both girls showed they had inherited my own type of brain, totally one-track, which stops us ever being distracted from our ultimate goals.

Though the girls had their favourite subjects, neither distinguished themselves academically. (This, I must stress, was not the fault of the school, for my youngest daughter Natasha has done very well there.) Joan was still fond of anything to do with English language and drama. She was absolutely enthralled when she went out with a school party to see Laurence Olivier and Ralph Richardson at the Old Vic in Shakespeare's *Henry IV, Part 1*.

By now I thought she had come to appreciate fine acting without wanting to involve herself. So around the time of her sixteenth birthday when she announced she had definitely decided to be an actress, I was absolutely stunned.

Thinking back, it should have seemed a quite logical idea that

Joan should go into show business, considering her childhood drama studies and the family background. She had played out little acting games all her young life, and my friends were now telling me – and her! – that she was so beautiful she should be in the movies. Yet when she told me, seriously, that the time had now come to make a start, I could not take it in.

I floundered. 'Joan, the last time we talked about your future you said you wanted to be a fashion artist.'

'Daddy, that was ages ago. I've changed my mind.'

'Then you'd better change it back again,' I shouted. 'You don't know what you're letting yourself in for!' More calmly, I began explaining the facts. I told her of the high unemployment rate among actors and actresses. I reminded her that even if she did get parts regularly, acting can be a very short-lived career for a pretty girl unless she progressed to 'character' parts.

'You could be famous at 20 and forgotten at 27. You could get very hurt. If you do become a big name everyone will want to know you, invite you to their parties, butter you up . . . and a year or two later, once you're not doing so well, they'll walk right past you in the street as if you were a stranger.

'It's a profession where you'll meet lecherous men who try to take advantage of you. The very word "actress" attracts all kinds of hangers-on. . .'

I told her all that, and more, but Joan was not heeding my warnings. Like me, when I was a youngster, she didn't listen to what she didn't want to hear. And her mind was made up.

'Daddy, I'm aware of the pitfalls,' she said sweetly. 'And I'd still like to do it. I want to audition for RADA. If I get in, will you let me train there?'

With Joan's words I felt a weight lift from my shoulders. I knew that at the Royal Academy of Dramatic Art, Britain's premier training school for actors and actresses, only 20 applicants in 250 were given places. The high standard of entry, the sheer weight of competition, meant my daughter would not stand a chance, and so I agreed.

It might seem that I had been absolutely blind not to recognize Joan's potential, or simply determined to deceive myself. But the truth is that I never expected her to make any sort of an impression at the RADA audition.

But she passed that entrance exam with flying colours. I must admit I was absolutely thrilled about it, and Elsa even more so. I made a total about-turn and decided to back her every inch of the way.

When Joan had settled in at RADA, I made arrangements to fulfil my promise and spoke to Leslie Bloom, my firm's drama agent.

'I'd like to try something new, Leslie – put on a repertory season. Can you get a company together for me?'

Leslie was instantly eager. 'Of course I can. Good idea!'

'I'm really doing this to help my daughter,' I confessed. 'She can play small parts and help backstage. She's good at art, so she can paint scenery.'

My new repertory company, the Eros Players, duly opened at the Palace theatre, in Maidstone, Kent, in March 1950, and when the RADA summer vacation came round Joan joined them. I paid her £3 10s a week; as she was living at home, this was quite enough. Joan did not actually appear on stage until the last production of the season, in September, when she played the maid in Terence Rattigan's comedy *French Without Tears*.

Our plays at Maidstone included Eugene O'Neill's *Anna Christie*, *Honeymoon Beds* by Cedric Richards, *The Anonymous Lover* by Vernon Sylvaine (described on the billings as 'witty, gay and frankly naughty') and *Damaged Goods* by Eugene Brieux, about the dangers of venereal disease, then as much talked about as AIDS is today. They were good choices for that particular era, but this repertory season was not among my successes. I lost money practically every week. The only production in the Eros Players' repertoire which actually packed the house was *The Respectable Prostitute* by Jean-Paul Sartre, for though the story had nothing to do with prostitution the title pulled them in.

I did not mind being out of pocket, for I had set Joan on her way – as she herself put it, 'bought her a rep'. The real motive was to give Joan a reference and bring her to the notice of prospective employers.

I took a page in *Spotlight*, the casting directory, showing her

JOAN COLLINS

EROS PLAYERS,
MAIDSTONE REPERTORY COMPANY

Management :
WILL COLLINS Ltd.
Triumph House
189, Regent Street, W.1
REGent 7328/7329/7320

Height 5 feet 5 inches   *Jack Emerald, A.I.B.P. 1950*

JASMINE DEE

" BUOYANT BILLIONS "
                    — *Princes Theatre*

" CINDERELLA "
                    —*Emile Littler*

Management :
HERBERT DE LEON, LTD
30, South Audley Street
Grosvenor Square, W.1
GROsvenor 1641/4

Barry Hicks 1947

Available: young Joan's entry in *Spotlight*.

98

photograph, stating that she was appearing at Maidstone and informing interested parties she could be contacted through my agency.

Within days I had a telephone call from Bill Watts, a leading agent who specialized in finding work for eye-catching young ladies. To be taken on by him, to be one of 'Bill Watts' girls', was a feather in any young beauty's cap.

'I saw a picture of that girl you're representing, Joan Collins,' Bill began. 'She's a great-looking kid. Who is she?'

'She's my daughter.'

'Good for you, Joe! Well, I may have something for her. They're looking for a girl to play the lead in a film about beauty queens. They want a new face. Can I put your daughter's name forward?'

'Sure you can.'

'Can she be available to audition in London next Wednesday, late afternoon?'

I did a quick calculation. By late afternoon Joan should have been on her way to Maidstone. I wasn't sure what she was doing in the play that week, but I could not take a chance. So that Joan would not miss her film audition I simply cancelled the Eros Players' show that night, duly paying the cast their usual salary and refunding the ticket money to the patrons who had booked seats.

Joan was not given the lead in that film, *Lady Godiva Rides Again*. A girl named Pauline Stroud got the main role as the winner of a beauty contest, while Joan was cast as one of the runners-up.

Now Joan was launched I made what I am sure was a wise decision, and asked Bill Watts to take over as her agent. I was not the right person to find work for her in plays and films. From that time onwards, though Joan has come to me for professional guidance, I have never been involved officially in her career.

My faith in Bill Watts was justified. Within months he had steered her towards her first important film role – which she won against great competition – in *I Believe in You*. This starred Celia Johnson as a probation officer, with Joan playing a young streetwalker in her care.

99

Watts negotiated a seven-year contract for Joan with the Rank Organization; she was the first player it had put under contract for more than a year.

At that time British movie-makers favoured English rose blondes to play their heroines. They saw Joan, with her dark allure, as the contrast to this virtuous image, just as we're used to seeing the 'goodies' in screen westerns wearing white hats and the 'baddies' wearing black ones. Joan made a run of movies in which she was almost inevitably cast as a wayward girl, bold, flashy and sultry.

She did not finish her course at RADA. Instead, she learned her craft through practical experience. It was not luck which brought Joan to where she is today; it was hard graft.

In career terms, getting starring roles in movies while still in her teens was an advantage. On the personal side, though, she was flung suddenly into the environment she had craved since childhood, without having a chance to recover her balance. Eager to be 'in the swim', she accepted almost every invitation to a smart party which came her way. She never seemed to spend an evening at home.

As her social life was not interfering with her work I could not object. After a night out she'd still be punctual on the set early next morning. She was never too tired to give press interviews, or to pose for that inevitable sideline, pin-up pictures. When she was 18 the British photographers gave her the title 'The Most Beautiful Face in Britain'. Joan has continued to be co-operative with the press, always saying something newsworthy and never keeping photographers hanging about.

In 1982, some 30 years after she first started making news, the American Women's Press Club gave her a Golden Apple Award as 'the star with the most news impact and the best entertainment image'.

In the early 'fifties Joan became a trendy name so quickly that the more carping journalists said that all this publicity was certainly not warranted by her acting ability. Yet none of them ever denied that she had personality, individuality and – most important to her employers – box-office appeal.

'Joan is alive, she has a bodily arrogance and vitality,' wrote doyen Beverly Baxter in the *Sunday Express*. I consider this a good assessment. Other writers expressed themselves in more lurid terms: one description was 'Coffee-bar Jezebel'. Coffee bars were the regular teens-and-twenties hangouts of the time. Visiting them, you could see a host of Joan Collins look-alikes, dressed in bright-coloured shirt blouses with tight-waisted skirts, a style which suited Joan, accentuating her very slim waist.

Joan's great admirer, my mother Hettie, was dismayed by the public image of her beloved granddaughter. She was shocked when patrons at her local Brighton cinema greeted Joan's entrance on screen with wolf-whistles.

I reassured her that although she was a bit of a gadabout, she was really very innocent. I knew on the best authority, namely her sister Jackie, that Joan *was* innocent. Jackie was always kidding Joan about her prudish attitude to her dates. Jackie's nickname for the budding star was 'Goody Two-Shoes'.

Jackie herself went through a wayward phase long before Joan did, though I did not learn until years later about Jackie's early fling.

As a girl, despite her pigtails, Jackie looked older than her years, and people did not realize there was a five-year age gap between her and Joan. For a start, Jackie, at 5 foot 9 inches, is 5 inches taller than Joan. All the same, to me my younger daughter seemed a prim and proper young girl, much quieter than her elder sister. While Joan was so occupied with her outside interests, Jackie would help in the home, would always find time to play with Bill, and could even cook a meal.

When our poodle bitch went into labour, Jackie was the only member of the family to stay up with her all night and help deliver her litter of five puppies. One of them, Candy, became Jackie's own pet and lived to the age of 17, an amazing lifespan for a canine.

One day when she was 12 years old Jackie arrived home from school really scared. 'A man came up to me on Baker Street station and asked me to come to the movies with him. He frightened me. I ran away.'

Elsa turned pale. 'You must never speak to that kind of man!

Don't even go near him! He could stick a needle in your arm and drug you and you'd end up in China!'

Elsa's warning could have scared Jackie away from men forever. Actually, it only scared her away from Baker Street station for the time being.

When Jackie was not yet 14 we let her go with Joan for their first holiday without Elsa and me, to stay with my sister Lalla at her villa in Cannes. Although I warned her not to let them out of her sight, she let the girls go out unchaperoned to enjoy themselves.

The news came back to me that my two attractive daughters, in their bikinis, were the belles of the Cannes beach, and a particular hit with the personnel of USS *Coral Sea*, an American ship anchored in the harbour. Jackie lost her heart to one of the sailors.

When the girls returned to London, Jackie wrote to him. Elsa insisted that Jackie tell her beau her correct age – and the jolly Jack Tar never even sent her a reply.

Jackie says now that her romance with the young sailor was the start of her being attracted to American men. I think myself she was already influenced by her American heroes.

Unknown to Elsa and me, in her mid-teens Jackie used to sneak through her bedroom window and across the back yard at night to jazz clubs, and for rendezvous with boys from the American school just up the road from where we lived.

While she kept these late-night escapades secret, I did find out that Jackie had been playing truant from school in order to go to the cinema.

Elsa and I became alarmed. I warned Jackie that she'd end up in a juvenile court, but she took no heed. At the age of 15 she left school. I was very displeased with her, and had I known the real reason I'd have been even more displeased. She had been expelled for smoking a cigarette while wearing her school uniform. Perhaps Jackie told Elsa the full story but, guessing how I would react, neither of them told me.

However, even the thought that Jackie was not completing her education as I would have wished made me very angry. As we discussed her future, Jackie told me seriously that she would like to go into journalism, but she did not know how to make a start. Neither did I, for although I had a large circle of friends and contacts it did not include any editors, and I was aware that it was hard for an 'outsider' to get a junior's job on a newspaper or magazine, especially a girl who had not completed her schooling.

Instead, knowing I had been wrong concerning Joan, I suggested Jackie should follow the rest of our family into show business and become an actress. 'I'll do what I can for you,' I promised, 'and as Joan's doing very nicely, maybe she can help too.'

Looking back, I see I was mistaken. I should have encouraged Jackie to write round to the various publications, asking for a opening. She would have made an excellent reporter and feature writer. I also wish Jackie had held out for what she really wanted to do. Actually, when I suggested coming into show business she seemed quite amenable to the idea, and as she loved the movies I was convinced she had aspirations in that line.

It never crossed my mind, nor Elsa's, that Jackie might spend frustrating years in a profession where she was always in Joan's shadow. Jackie had the right attributes: good looks, a superb figure and acting talent too. But throughout her acting career she was always tagged 'Joan Collins' younger sister'.

Of course, everything turned out well in the end. Jackie started her working life in a world where she found authentic backgrounds for her novels. She saw the glamour and the tawdriness, the successes of the few and the humiliations of the rest. Though she was an actress, this time was really her traineeship as an author. Her mind was always on her writing, committing her observations to paper.

Jackie was always concerned with the people around her and curious about what made them tick – more so than most performers, whose overriding interest is usually their own persona and own careers. The people Jackie met who *were* successful enjoyed her company. She was a sympathetic listener, and they confided in her.

By 1968 she had acquired plenty of material. In that year she at last completed one of the many novels she had started – *The World Is Full of Married Men.*

Many times in her teens Jackie regretted having followed Joan into acting. By her late twenties, when her acting days were over, she was glad she'd done it.

8

Father of the Bride

When Joan was 19 years old she made the most disastrous move of her life. She married Maxwell Reed.

It was an unhappy and traumatic time for Elsa and me, causing the first and only serious friction between us. Joan herself found the marriage set an unfortunate precedent for all her future relationships.

I was familiar with Maxwell Reed's face in our home long before he materialized in person. Joan had his picture on her bedroom wall and her eyes went dreamy every time she looked at it. He was the male image of her youthful fantasies. I only wish he had never become more than a glossy photograph.

I have to concede – much as I came to dislike the man – that Reed was the ideal beefcake film star: tall, dark and handsome, what they call a heart-throb.

Fourteen years older than Joan, he came from Larne in Ireland, and before being 'discovered' for movies he had been around the world, serving with both the RAF and the Merchant Navy. After a spell of acting in repertory at Scarborough he was recruited to the Rank Organization's Company of Youth – the so-called 'Rank Charm School' – and was soon getting his picture into the fan magazines bought by young girls like Joan and Jackie.

Reed's best-known film was *The Brothers*, set in a small Scottish community, with Reed and his screen brother both in love with a girl from Glasgow, played by Patricia Roc. In other films he was cast as an underworld character or a boxer. Rank's publicity people saw fit to dub him 'The Beautiful Beast'.

Joan met Reed when she was 18, through the future star Laurence Harvey, then a young man of about her own age, with whom she had appeared in *I Believe in You*. She went out with Harvey a few times. I considered him a 'safe' companion for my well-brought-up daughter, for at the time Harvey was more interested in an older woman, the actress Hermione Baddeley.

One night Joan came home very excited. 'Larry introduced me to Maxie Reed. He *is* gorgeous.'

I gave her a stern look.

'Now don't go silly over him,' I warned her. 'He's a lot older than you and a big star and he makes the most of it. I've heard he makes scenes in nightclubs. He has a bad reputation around town. The man's a roué and he's not for you!'

Joan didn't answer, but I had the feeling that in cautioning her I was wasting my breath. I was right: within weeks Joan brought Reed home to Harley House and dropped her bombshell.

'Mummy, Daddy . . . Maxie and I want to get married.'

Joan looked eagerly from her mother's face to mine. She genuinely wanted our approval and was hoping against hope that I would be pleased that at least Reed's intentions were honourable.

Reed stood beside my daughter, a smirk on his face. For him, this visit to his 'intended's' parents was simply a necessary formality. As Joan was under 21 he was legally compelled to seek my written consent to their marriage.

At first I tried to be civil. I invited the loving couple to come into the lounge and sit down and talk it over. But as they faced me, side by side on the green velvet settee, my feeling of anger and outrage was choking me. I could see my beautiful, impressionable young daughter was mesmerized by this flashy, worldly man, so much more experienced than she was. I was aghast at his complacency at having captured his prize.

I cleared my throat and began to speak, choosing my words carefully.

'Mr Reed, I have to tell you that you are not the type of husband I envisage for my daughter.'

Reed's smile did not waver. Seeing the mockery in his eyes, my voice rose. 'For heaven's sake, man, you know how old Joan is, don't you? She is too young to know what she's doing. You've got an absolute cheek in coming to my home and confronting me with what you have in mind. I'm telling you here and now that I will not agree to this marriage. Is that clear?'

I stood up, expecting Reed to follow suit and leave my home. Instead, he remained seated, smiling, sure of himself.

Joan's eyes were filled with tears. She was noting my words, even if Reed was ignoring them. 'Daddy, please, I do want to marry Maxie.'

'Joan, be quiet!' I brushed aside her plea and continued to berate her suitor, hoping that at least I'd have the satisfaction of seeing him lose his temper.

'If you want to know the truth, Reed, you're nothing but a dirty. . .' My flow of language got less polite. If Reed felt insulted as I ranted on at him, he didn't show it. He knew he had the upper hand.

'Mr Collins, Joan and I love one another. I am well able to provide for your daughter. I have a very nice flat in the West End –'

'Reed, will you please get out of here – '

'Stop it, Joe, please stop. . .' This was Elsa's voice, soft, conciliatory. 'Don't go on like this. Think about what he's saying. Be reasonable. Lots of young girls get married and it all works out. Why are you so sure this marriage is wrong for Joan?'

I couldn't believe what I was hearing. I just stared at my wife in total shock. She had never before disagreed with me on any important matter.

For the first time in our marriage I felt Elsa was betraying me, just at the moment when I needed her backing more than ever before.

Seeing that he had won an ally in Elsa, Reed played his trump card.

'Well, Mr Collins, it's like this. If you don't agree to us getting married we'll just go off and live together.'

Never in my life have I committed an act of violence. But at that moment I wanted to knock Reed's block off. As he was a muscular 6 foot 3 to my slim 5 foot 10, even in my rage I realized this was not a practical solution, but I could not take any more of his impertinence.

'I've had enough of this!' I shouted to my wife and daughter. 'You can go on talking it over as much as you like. I am not going to be browbeaten.'

I turned to Reed. 'You're a lunatic, and you can go to hell!'

Then I turned to face Elsa and Joan: 'If you won't take any notice of what I say now, you'll have plenty of time to think it over. I'm leaving home and I'm not coming back!'

With that I marched out of the flat, slamming the heavy oak front door behind me. As I stomped off into the night I was still shouting insults at my prospective son-in-law.

For six hours I walked the streets of London in a fury of misery. It was not that I wanted the earth for Joan. I was not hoping she would marry an international star, a millionaire, a man at the top of his profession. What I wanted for her was simply a marriage with some man who would respect her and understand her . . . someone who, if I were truthful, would fit in with our family. If he were successful and rich, that would be a bonus, but it was not essential. Joan, I felt, was not yet mature enough for marriage anyway, but even if she had been, Reed was exactly the type of husband I did *not* want for her!

Eventually, as my temper cooled, I began to worry about Elsa. Though she was wrong in even beginning to consider this marriage, she meant it for the best. She always did. I knew she would be very upset if I stayed away from home overnight in my present frame of mind. Besides, I did not even have a toothbrush or overcoat with me!

When I returned to the flat at dawn Elsa and Joan were waiting up. Elsa followed me into our bedroom and started reasoning. She was quite firm.

'You heard what Maxwell Reed said, and he meant it. If you refuse them permission to marry she'll go and live with him. You can give children as much advice as you like, but interfering is another matter. It doesn't work. In the end they go their own way.'

I nodded. I had reached the same conclusion. While I saw the sense of Elsa's argument, I was still angry and very hurt.

'All right,' I said. 'If you think it's the only way, *you* can tell them they can get married. I'm not going to get involved in this. *You* can handle it.'

In the end, I too gave in to the inevitable. I put a good face on it and agreed that Joan should have a dignified wedding. It was a register office ceremony at Caxton Hall, Westminster on 24 May 1952, the day after Joan's 19th birthday.

As we stood in the forecourt of Harley House before leaving for the ceremony, I put aside my misgivings about my future son-in-law and appraised my daughter in her bridal outfit.

Trying to match her groom's sophisticated image she had chosen not the traditional white I would have preferred but a short dress in oyster and gold brocade, with a nipped-in waist. She looked very nice, though I was a bit worried about her choice of shoes, with their 4-inch heels. I was afraid that, in her excitement, she would slip on the register-office steps.

After we left Caxton Hall Elsa and I entertained family and friends at a reception at Ciro's Club. I was pleased that Joan's old headmistress from Francis Holland School, Miss I.C. Joslin, was among our guests. The presence of this respected lady assured me that Joan's marriage to Maxwell Reed was not so shocking to other people as it seemed to me.

Next day there were wedding pictures in all the newspapers. I comforted myself that at least Reed was doing well in his career and so, thankfully, was Joan.

One photograph, with Maxwell Reed feeding Joan from his own plate, sticks in my mind. They looked such a glamorous couple, providing glossy imagination fodder for the kind of girl who looks at a film star's photograph and imagines she's in love with him. Perfect reading for silly girls like my Joan!

Even a glamorous star must sometimes transform herself into a housewife. Joan had never done 'women's work' in our home, being too busy with her own work and her social life. Elsa had a maid to help run our home smoothly, and with Jackie always willing to lend a hand too Joan's lack of contribution had never been missed. I wondered how she would make out now with the usual domestic duties Reed had a right to expect from her, like cooking his meals.

I know Joan did cook for Reed – and for her subsequent husbands and three children – but I don't know how well she cooked. I cannot remember Joan at any time cooking a meal for me. Whenever Elsa and I visited Joan and Reed we just picked them up and went out to a restaurant to eat.

The 'nice flat in the West End' Reed had mentioned on our first meeting had a good address – St George's Street, off Hanover Square – but it was in a ramshackle building and you had to climb several flights of stairs to reach their small apartment.

The furniture looked to me like second-hand junk from film sets. He kept an unusual pet, too – a monkey. The creature, who was not house-trained, had a huge cage in the living room, and the stink in that flat was appalling. It hit you as soon as you opened the door. Even Joan's fashion sketches on the walls were impregnated with the stench. It was altogether a most unsavoury set-up, and did nothing to help my antagonism towards my son-in-law.

I never missed an opportunity to tell Reed what I thought of him and his lifestyle. The man knew I couldn't stand the sight of him. I wished secretly that he would carry out one of the wilder schemes he sometimes talked about and go off to hunt for treasure in the South China seas.

Joan and Reed had been married for less than two years when I knew for certain I had been right in my judgement. One day I overheard Elsa speaking to Joan on the telephone. Elsa was obviously distressed.

I demanded to know what Joan was saying. Elsa put her hand over the mouthpiece. 'He's been hitting her,' she said simply.

I took the telephone. Joan was crying. 'Daddy, I can't stand it any longer,' she burst out. 'Maxie's leading me a hell of a life and I want to run away from him.'

'Where are you speaking from?'

'I'm at home. Maxie's gone to the studio.'

'Now do as I tell you: just get in a taxi and come home to your mother and me. Don't bother to pack. Just get out of that place!'

Joan needed no persuading. She came home at once. Elsa and I calmed her down, and settled her into her old room again. Then I drove over to their flat with a friend to collect her clothes.

I don't know if Joan confided in her mother about the details of Reed's violence. She never told me, and I didn't ask. If she had any marks on her body I never saw them.

But this was not the end of Reed as far as Joan was concerned. His career went on the slide and even after their divorce settlement, in 1956, from which he gained financially, he kept chasing after her for her money. Knowing he was broke, she gave it to him.

Eventually, though, Joan did lose touch with Reed and it was only when I sent her a clipping from the London *Evening Standard* that Joan learned he had died.

In retrospect, I am sure that during their relationship Reed had his justifiable frustrations. His career began, inexplicably, to peter out just as Joan was becoming a real star. Joan, so young, having fallen in love with his film-star image and not the man himself, lacked the understanding and compassion vital to pull a marriage through a bad patch. She had no trust in her husband. When Reed became violent Joan had only one instinct: self-preservation. She was frightened of him.

I believe this bad marriage has influenced Joan's emotional life ever since. And it took many years – 34, to be exact – before Joan herself at last turned to me and said, 'Daddy, you were right!'

I am glad that the Maxwell Reed episode did not inhibit Joan from introducing me to the subsequent men in her life. She has always been eager for my approval – though whether I give it or not is another matter! Joan knows I have an instinctive gift for making a quick and accurate assessment of the people I meet. In private life as well as in business I am a good judge of character and can spot insincerity or dubious intentions at just one meeting. The more sensible side of Joan appreciates this gift of mine. But of course she does not always act in accordance with my judgements. When she is in love she goes her own way.

The trouble Joan was having during her marriage fortunately did not interfere with her work. The fact that, through no fault of hers, the films she was making were mediocre did not stop her progress either.

In 1952 she went to Rome, where Elsa stayed with her, to shoot a biblical epic with Jack Hawkins. *Land of the Pharaohs* was her first American picture. My daughter played a princess and wore a jewel in her navel. That film, though again mediocre, helped her land a big Hollywood contract with 20th Century-Fox, who bought her contract from Rank. The movie-makers had assessed her potential to earn money for them. As an actress she was a good all-rounder. They knew that whatever role they gave her she would play it well, and Joan had the basic qualities for exposure to the camera: good features, good bone structure, expressive eyes. As it does all ladies, a bit of artifice helps Joan too, but other qualities account for her lasting physical appeal.

Joan, by the time she was 21, was very confident of her own commercial worth. She researched the kind of money she ought to be getting. Disregarding what she had been offered by 20th Century-Fox, she asked for – and got – a $65,000-a-year film contract.

While filming *Land of the Pharaohs* Joan fell in love with one of her co-stars, Sydney Chaplin, second son of the great Charles Chaplin by one of his former wives, the actress Lita Grey. I had a tenuous connection with Charles Chaplin: in his youth he had been in a troupe run by Fred Karno, a friend of my father's.

When Joan brought Sydney to Harley House to meet the family, I was disappointed. He seemed to me to be a dissatisfied young man with a chip on his shoulder. His father – claimed Sydney – was not doing enough to help him in the film world.

I was not impressed with Sydney Chaplin. I do not care for young men who blame their parents for their shortcomings. As Joan was not yet divorced from Reed I hoped this new romance would fizzle out before she was free to make another matrimonial mistake.

Joan went off to America to take up her new film contract at the end of 1954. As we waved her off at the airport (she was looking very pleased with herself in her first full-length mink coat) I had no doubt she would hold her own against the other pretty and talented young actresses in Hollywood. But I could not quell my misgivings about how she would conduct her personal life. At 21, to my mind, Joan was still very childlike.

'Daddy, I'm not going to play around in Hollywood the way I sometimes did over here,' she promised me. 'I'm going to get down to some hard work. I hope they'll give me good parts, not those awful 'bad girl' roles. I've had enough of that Baby Temptress label.'

None of us realized then that even as Joan matured the 'temptress' stamp would prove indelible.

I remember the London premiere of one of Joan's Rank films, a comedy called *Our Girl Friday* (in America *The Adventures of Sadie*) in which she was shipwrecked on an island with three men (George Cole, Kenneth More and Robertson Hare).

While Elsa and I were standing in the foyer, waiting for the stars to arrive, I heard a woman behind me talking to a companion.

'I'll tell you why that Joan Collins has done so well! She's Joe Collins' daughter. He's a big theatrical agent. My daughter was at drama school with her, but *she* didn't get the breaks!'

Joan entered the foyer, on the arm of Maxwell Reed – then her husband – all in white and looking very lovely. The resentful woman behind me fell silent. I think, after just one look at her, she saw for herself that Joan's success was not attributable just to being 'Joe Collins' daughter'.

This was the last time I heard anyone label Joan this way. After she went to Hollywood, *I* became labelled 'Joan Collins' father'. It was a tag I could not escape. When I took over theatres for pantomimes and variety seasons the local newspaper reporters were more interested in writing about me – and my daughter – than in the artistes I was presenting in their town.

For example, at the start of a season at the Theatre Royal in Norwich I was photographed holding a programme while the caption described me as 'well known in the variety field and perhaps equally famous as the father of Joan Collins who has been making a name for herself in Hollywood'. The bill headliners I was bringing to Norwich, who included American star Billy Daniels and Billy Cotton and his band, were accorded fewer column inches and no photograph.

Soon after Joan went to America I was invited to make my television début on a chat show. Naturally, I was flattered. 'What's the subject? Vaudeville in the old days? The future of music hall?'

'No, no,' said the producer. 'We want you to talk about your daughter Joan.'

None of this new attention actually changed my standing in my profession. I was too well established for it to make the slightest difference. I had a high reputation as an agent and entrepreneur even before I became tagged 'Joan Collins' father'.

In the 'fifties my business was thriving. I had a new outlet for the performers on my books – in television. I was careful about the names I put forward for this developing medium. They had to be top-class artistes. For in those days practically every television show went out 'live' – no pre-recording, no retakes. If an artiste's standard was not consistently good his career could be permanently marred by just one 'off-form' television appearance.

Years later, former television producer Richard Afton wrote in the London *Evening News*: 'Joe Collins was the one agent from whom I would book an act 'blind'. If Joe said an act was o.k., that was good enough. And in the cut-throat agency business you can't give a higher compliment than that.'

In the early 'fifties I was approached by a girl, Della Sweetman, who partnered her brother, Vic Templar, in a trick-cycling act. They wanted my backing for an ice-show enterprise. The British public, I knew, has always loved watching skilled skating so I became the first agent in Britain to introduce ice pantomimes in music halls. Thanks to me, troupes of comedians, dancers and singers started taking skating lessons! My first show, *Cinderella on Ice*, and all the subsequent pantomimes we put on did marvellous business around Britain.

Then we had an invitation to take one of our ice shows to Turkey. This was where I made a slip, for when Della and I arrived in Istanbul we realized our impresario host had somehow got the wrong idea. There *were* touring companies, including British ones, in which the term 'dancer' was a euphemism for a member of another old profession . . . but our company was not one of them. So I was rather put out when the impresario asked, 'Can you show me pictures of your girls? I would like to pick out the ones I think suitable to sit with the customers after the show, and be nice to them. We'll see they get well paid.'

'No, certainly not!' I choked. 'Our girls are professional skaters, not . . . '

I flew back to London with Della feeling sore about our futile journey; and to make matters worse, on landing in London I was the one passenger on the plane taken away from the rest, put in a little room and subjected to a bodysearch. The customs officer had me starkers!

My emotions went from bewilderment to anger, and finally sarcasm. 'Do I *look* like a crook . . . or have you stripped me because you fancy me?' I leered. The customs man remained impassive. He just went on with his search of my person and my luggage, even poking his fingers into the hook-toed Turkish slippers I was bringing home for my daughter Jackie.

To top it all, when I joined the airport coach bound for central London all the other passengers from Turkey, who had been held up half an hour because of me, were giving me odd looks, as if I were a villain.

When I arrived home and told my family about my mishaps, Jackie's face was quite anguished. 'Daddy, how could they do such a thing to *you* of all people?' Her reaction restored my self-esteem.

In seeking new markets for British talent I decided to forget about Turkey. Doing business with Russia, another country showing interest in British talent, sounded a better bet. And for a satisfactory Russian deal I did not even have to leave my own land. Along with other leading agents and promoters I was invited to the Russian embassy in London to discuss an exchange of artistes.

Everything was conducted in a most civilized way. Our hosts received us in a grand room and plied us with the most famous of their foodstuffs. Tables were positively groaning under a load of caviare . . . black, grey, blonde, red, the lot.

It was the first time I had ever tasted this luxury, and I liked it. Since that evening Russian caviare has been my prime extravagance in food, and I have passed this expensive taste on to every member of my family. Rest assured that when Joan spoons up the caviare with gusto in *Dynasty* she is not acting.

In the 'fifties the main form of live entertainment that was threatening to replace vaudeville was the touring revue. I was soon putting together almost as many of these as straight-forward variety bills.

One of these new shows, called *Hot from Harlem*, featured music of black American origin – shades of the famous Cotton Club – but the cast were all British black people. In the 'fifties there were far fewer black performers in Britain than there are today, and when I came to casting the soubrette I was stuck. I just could not find the right girl.

An agent friend of mine, Sidney Burns, stepped in. 'I've got someone you could try. Heard her singing in some dump in Tiger Bay' (the dockland area of Cardiff). 'That's where she lives. She's only singing part-time . . . works as a waitress too. She's still very raw, but I think with the right presentation she would be fine. Her name is Shirley Bassey.'

I interviewed Shirley Bassey in my office. She was just a skinny little thing in her mid-teens, yet I sensed she had stage presence and could be made to look stylish. I did not bother to hear her sing. I reckoned that even if she wasn't much as a vocalist, she would fit my show if she were dressed the way I had in mind.

I telephoned the fashion designer Eric Darnell. 'I want this girl, Shirley Bassey, to look feline and seductive. She's only a scrap of a kid. You haven't got much to work on. But do what you can. I'm willing to spend forty-two pounds on her clothes.'

That sum of money was no fortune, even in 1954, but it was not too bad either, considering I was spending it on an unknown artiste in a touring revue.

I paid Shirley Bassey a weekly salary of £18, which worked out at £1 10*s* (£1.50) per performance.

You could say I got a bargain. Shirley Bassey put the heat into *Hot from Harlem* . . . fingers snapping, hips working over-time, she was a right little tease, with a seductive, growling voice. Sometimes the wolf-whistles from the audience drowned her singing. Both the audience *and* the rest of the cast went wild over her.

Contracts

Hot from Harlem

Name		£	Role
Ashley Harney	M	£12	C.C. Coy
Amos Gordon	M	£12	" "
Dusty Daniels	F	£11	" "
Roy Bent	M	£10	" "
Val Richmond	F	£11	" "
Woods & Jarrett		£60	Comedians
Harold Holmes	M	£20	C.C. Coy
Eddie Williams		£30	Comedian
Shirley Bassey		£18	Soubrette
~~The Two Tokas Duncan~~		~~£36~~	~~Juv.~~
Charlie Woods		£16	Manager
Harriet Scott	M	£10	C.C. Coy
Nadia Lane	F	£12	C.C. Coy
Rupert Brown	M	£12	C.C. Coy
Angela Freeman	F	£12	C.C. Coy
Teresa Davis	F	£8	C.C. Coy
Cyril Lagey		£30	Comedian
Eddie Atkins		£12	Mus. Dir.
Mrs " (Madam Rita)		£6	Wardrobe
~~Robert Mitchell~~		~~£11~~	~~Stage Director~~
~~Joyce Taylor~~		~~£8~~	~~Chorus~~
Shirley Caesar		£8	"
Iris Freeman		£4	"
Birgé Parker		£8	
Terry Link	F	£14/10/-	C.C. Coy
Jimmy Russ		£44	Musician
2 Horns	1	£11	
Jack Raymond		£9	S.M.

Another page from an old ledger: it must be some years since Shirley Bassey has worked for so little money, but this all-black showcase certainly helped to get her launched.

The Tigress from Tiger Bay never went back to waiting on tables in Cardiff. She got a spot in London at the Astor Club, then in 1956 went on to a bill at the Adelphi theatre in the West End. Her version of 'Burning My Candle at Both Ends' stopped the show. That was the start of her international career.

I like to think that my interest in her clothes also played a part in pushing Shirley upwards. Though in private life I am not particularly observant about women's outfits, I have always had a very keen eye for their stage clothes. I know the right dress, something which emphasizes an artiste's personality, can make a very positive impact on the audience. A performer's clothes are a talking point, part of the show. Though artistes often fail to see this for themselves, they play an important part in promoting a career.

I have great regard for Darnell, the designer who dressed Shirley Bassey for me. His creations are theatrical, dramatic and glamorous. I first met Eric and his business partner Eric Plant when they were performers themselves. Plant was a pantomime dame, Darnell a drag artiste – one of the people I had urged to learn to skate for my ice pantomimes. When Plant and Darnell set up in the fashion business my daughter Joan, then married to Maxwell Reed, was among the first clients I sent them. Joan, in those days, did not always dress expensively. She was a sweaters-and-skirts girl. But I insisted that for premieres at least she should look like a star. Joan, who has excellent taste in clothes, was delighted with Darnell's work.

Another star I pointed in his direction was Diana Dors. Diana was a railwayman's daughter from Swindon, Wiltshire and two years older than my daughter Joan. She was the youngest student in the so-called 'Rank Charm School' mentioned earlier, which was started in 1946 because there were not enough young stars for the number of films then being made in Britain. Diana was with Joan in the film *Lady Godiva Rides Again*, also playing a beauty-contest runner-up, and the only one to show off her assets in a daring (for the time) bikini.

A voluptuous, eye-catching blonde, Diana exuded a bold, inviting sex appeal, which attracted publicity. At the same time, she had far more talent as an actress, even in her early years, than she was given credit for. Like Joan, Diana had married for the first time at the age of 19, but although their paths often crossed, the two girls were never close friends.

Though Diana did not get her Hollywood break until two years after my daughter went there, she was a hit with British film audiences. She also had a sideline career as a singer – which was how, in 1954, I came to meet her.

My good old pal Hal Monty – Bernie Delfont's former dancing partner, who married my cousin Leah Levy – saw Diana performing in variety at the Wood Green Empire, Essex, and reported back to me.

'You could be on to a good thing with Diana Dors, Joe. The girl needs an agent. Why don't you go to Wood Green and catch the show?'

I did go to Wood Green. When I saw Diana's stage act I could not believe my own eyes: all her efforts to seem naughty and seductive were being thwarted by the way she was dressed. She wore a black crinoline gown, cut too low on her bust (which was not all that well rounded!) and concealing her stunning hipline and beautiful legs. Even with her brassy hair and full lips she looked no more tantalizing than the young Julie Andrews.

When I was introduced to Diana in her dressing-room, she was obviously flattered by my interest. She agreed almost instantly that I should be her agent for stage and the light entertainment side of television. Then I broached the subject of dress and suggested sending her to Eric Darnell. As I expected, Diana bridled.

'So you're criticizing my clothes sense, are you?'

'Yes, I am!'

'Do you tell your daughter Joan what to wear?'

'When necessary, of course I do.'

'Does Darnell design clothes for *her*?'

'Yes, sometimes.'

That dispelled any doubts Diana may have had about my taking her in hand. What was good enough for my daughter, the Hollywood star, was good enough for Diana.

I did not tell Diana that neither Joan nor my younger

daughter Jackie needed me to teach them dress sense. Like their mother, Elsa, they had an instinct for choosing the right wardrobe.

Darnell's dress for Diana was an absolute masterpiece: a figure-hugging sheath embroidered with 257,000 cerise sequins (yes, Diana actually counted them, she claimed). All the newspapers asked for photographs of her in that dress.

Shortly afterwards Diana Dors went to America for her Hollywood début in *I Married a Woman*. She won outstanding reviews for her performance as a girl condemned for murder in *Yield to the Night*. Between movies she continued to work in variety theatres too and I looked after that side of her business, negotiating fees for her in the £300–£1000-a-week range.

By the late 'fifties Diana's confidence was at its peak. She decided she was popular enough with theatre audiences to form her own variety company, enabling her – and possibly me too – to earn more money on a percentage basis. She was the top-of-the-bill attraction, of course, and the other acts were engaged to complement her.

As compère of the show, and to be a foil for Diana, I engaged a £100-a-week entertainer called Dickie Dawson, a former bus conductor from Gosport, Hampshire. I little realized this small-time comic had very big-time ideas. In fact, he took over Diana even to the extent of marrying her.

Certainly, at the time the Diana Dors tour set off around Britain this turn of events would never have seemed possible. Diana had an estranged husband, Dennis Hamilton, and a close friend, Tommy Yeardye, termed her 'business manager'. I would have thought she had enough to cope with without a third man in the picture, but by the summer of 1958 Diana was openly introducing Dawson as 'my new friend'.

Eventually she confronted me. 'Joe, I am in love with Dickie. We work well together. In the future Dickie will look after me *in every way*. And that,' she added, 'includes my business affairs. I no longer need you, or anyone else, to advise me.'

I did not argue. I knew that Dawson was now the only person to whom Diana would listen. Tommy Yeardye was out of the scene. In January 1959 Diana's husband Dennis died; three months later Diana and Dawson were married in New York.

For the ceremony, which got massive television coverage, Diana wore a sensational gown in slinky gold lamé . . . designed by Darnell. The marriage ended in divorce. When she married her third husband, actor Alan Lake, with whom she lived happily until her death in 1984, Darnell again designed her wedding dress.

Diana had rejected my business expertise. But she had continued to endorse my ideas about how she should present herself.

9

The Entertainers

Not long ago I read a newspaper article about Peter Sellers' will. He left £4 million and there is money still coming in from his 'Pink Panther' films. Out of curiosity I got out my old ledgers and checked the salary I had arranged for him in the 'fifties.

I found that 30-odd years ago, for his performance as a supporting act on a variety bill at the Odeon, Southend-on-Sea, I had paid him £175 for the week, working out as £12 10s (£12.50) per performance. The show's bill-topper was Harry Secombe, with a fee of £350.

The two men had been partners in Prince Charles' favourite radio programme, *The Goon Show*, surrealist, anti-establishment, anti-bureaucracy humour written by their third partner, Spike Milligan, who devised such exploits as conquering Everest from the inside and transferring the Albert Memorial from London to the moon.

For all their joint popularity on radio and in theatres, Harry (now Sir Harry) was a bigger draw than Sellers. Audiences loved his singing and his sense of fun. His sincerity projected well across the footlights.

Sellers, as a comedian and impersonator, could draw a character most skilfully on radio or film. He was excellent when hiding behind someone else's personality, be it Sir Winston Churchill or his Goon characters – half-wit Henry Crum or pompous Major Bloodnok. But when facing a live audience with his act 'Speaking for the Stars' Sellers lacked personal warmth and communication.

He was withdrawn and morose in private life, too, reminding me of another artiste I booked, Anthony Newley. I was quite surprised to find the two men were good friends. I often wondered what they found to talk about, apart from shop. In general conversation neither of them had much to say to a mere businessman like me.

On stage, Newley was the more entertaining of the two performers. He had started in show business as a child, and when I booked him to top a touring bill – at a fee of £250 a week – in 1959 (long before he married my daughter Joan), he was a consistently good all-round entertainer. Apart from working on the variety stage and in films he had become a charting pop singer, with the big hits 'Idle on Parade', 'I've Waited So Long' and 'Personality'.

Today, though our paths no longer cross, I have continued to respect Newley as a brilliant artiste and composer, although socially I never found him interesting.

Looking through my ledgers of the 'fifties it gives me pleasure to note how well some of the artistes in my books have done in later years.

In 1954 I billed Bruce Forsyth as 'The New Style Funster' and paid him £30 a week, £20 a week more than his previous earnings. Bruce, with his jaw jutting like a peninsula, his flair for off-the-cuff cracks and catchphrase 'I'm in charge', did not become a real star till four years later, when he compèred the weekly television show *Sunday Night at the London Palladium*. Bruce, who came into show business at the age of 14, had been slogging away for 16 years at his dancing, his singing and his comedy patter before he found recognition.

Janet Brown, when I booked her in 1954, commanded £100 a week. In her mid-twenties she was already an experienced, proven talent: she had starred in variety, in the television series *Friends and Neighbours* with her husband Peter Butterworth, and acted in the West End and in the film *Folly to be Wise* with Alastair Sim. All this happened long before Janet put on her present hat as an impressionist famed for her perfect take-off of Margaret Thatcher. (Actually Janet is of much more slender build than the Prime Minister.)

Apart from my variety shows, I was always scouting talent for my Christmas pantomimes. I had heard about a holiday-camp entertainer so genial he didn't even mind the children throwing him, fully clothed, into the swimming-pool. He always came up smiling. This man, Des O'Connor, I considered ideal to play

123

Buttons in my 1957 production of *Cinderella* at Croydon, Surrey, and I paid him £60 a week.

Des expected to crawl rather than shoot to star status. When I drove him back to central London from Croydon one night he sat beside me working out his sums. He reckoned at the rate he was progressing it would take him about 50 years to afford the Rolls-Royce he so craved. In fact diligent Des reached the Rolls-Royce bracket in the early 'sixties, and has stayed on top. In 1985 he featured my daughter Joan in the Christmas party edition of his weekly television show.

Another contribution I have made to entertainment as an impresario was giving Danny La Rue, then an all-round entertainer, a chance to wear gorgeous female clothes. I cast him and his partner, Allen Hayes, as Cinderella's Ugly Sisters at Gloucester and York, at a fee of £90 a week between them. Today that sum would not pay for the jewelled hem of one of the fabulous gowns Danny wears on stage, now he has become a most glamorous 'lady'.

It makes me smile when I think back to my early memories of burly Don Arden, known for his 'tough-guy' tactics as a record industry boss. Don started out in show business as a pantomime villain, growling threateningly at the children in the audience, who were not scared at all. They loved to hiss back at him. I paid Arden £40 a week to play the wizard Ebanazer in *Aladdin* at Gloucester and York. He was so good I upped his salary to £45 to play the same role the following year at the Hulme Hippodrome, Manchester. Arden had a fine singing voice and might have continued to do quite nicely had he not changed course, started promoting rock tours and eventually become the millionaire manager of the Electric Light Orchestra.

The astute Arden was one of the first people to appreciate the vast money-making potential of rock 'n' roll tours. But by the second half of the 'fifties all of us in the variety field had got the noisy message too. We knew that if we wanted to fill theatres, rock 'n' roll took precedence over every other brand of entertainment. In comparison with other artistes' earnings, the rock stars' fees were astronomical.

In 1957, when Lonnie Donegan, the Glasgow-born skiffle

king, was clocking up millions of record sales for 'Rock Island Line' and 'Cumberland Gap', I paid him £750 for just one concert, at the Regal cinema, Great Yarmouth. The vocal trio, the Mudlarks, after just two big hits in Britain, merited £200 a night.

Compared with some of the skilled entertainers who had spent years perfecting their craft, polishing every gesture, achieving the perfect timing for a joke, some of these new pop performers gave poor value for money. Except when they sang their own hit songs they were boring. But the audiences had bought their records, and were now prepared to pay to see them in person.

While all the rising and established talent vied to be in Joe Collins presentations, or be signed to my agency, the one person in the family indifferent to my business was my growing son Bill. Always even-tempered (except when very roused!), quiet and level-headed, as a child Bill seemed immune even to the reflected glory of having a film star sister. To Bill, show business was just a job like any other.

Given Bill's fanatical interest in motor cars, the only time he felt proud of any of my achievements was during my one-time connection with the motor business. The only celebrity Bill ever asked for an autograph was the racing driver Stirling Moss, who wrote his name for my son on the back of a cigarette packet. (Bill would have scorned to carry an autograph book.)

After my nightclub and cigarette kiosk with Lew Grade in the 'thirties, my 'forties sideline business was a betting office. I simply financed the venture, run by a friend, Percy Silk (a theatrical agent whose heart was really in horse-racing), and my brother-in-law David Marks, my sister Pauline's husband.

Then, in the 'fifties, I set up my former brother-in-law Reg Levy (my sister Lalla's ex-husband) in a used-car business. He had fallen on hard times, and my aim was to get him back on his feet.

Bill took great delight in exploring the 'showroom', an outdoor site in Kensington Church Steet. Sometimes I put my own car on display in the front line of vehicles there. That car, my pride and Bill's too, was a Bristol 405 convertible model, one of the first on the road, which I had ordered at the Earl's Court Motor Show at a price of £2,000 – enormous money for those days. My super model, royal blue with Mexican tan leather upholstery, did for the motor site what Joan's posters did for her films. It attracted the passers-by, but was definitely not for sale!

If Bill was impressed by anything else about me it was my being on friendly terms with professional footballers. One day, when Joe Mercer, captain of Arsenal in 1956, came to Harley House, I went too far in trying to cut a dash.

We were kicking a football around in the hall. Stupidly, instead of putting on strong shoes I was still in my carpet slippers. 'I used to be good at this game myself. Captained the soccer team at Rottingdean School,' I boasted.

Joe kicked the ball towards me from the other end of the hall. I put my foot on top of it, but my footwear was not firm enough for me to get a good grip and I slipped.

I lay on the floor, yelling in pain. I had broken an ankle.

I tried in vain to get Bill interested in show business. As soon as he was old enough to understand I would show him the show-business newspaper *The Stage*, pointing out the list of productions I was putting on around the country.

'Is there anything you would like to see with me? We've got *The Jane Show* at Aldershot' (a revue based on the *Daily Mirror*'s saucy strip-cartoon character), 'a musical at the Windsor theatre, Salford, *Zip Goes a Million* . . . or how about a trip north, to Scarborough to see Joan Rhodes, the Strong Woman? She can tear telephone directories in half.'

My sales talk was wasted on Bill. 'No, I don't want to see shows with *people*. Please, Daddy, take me to the Arcadia in Skegness, where you've got the *animal* acts . . Gloria's Educated dogs, Dash's Chimpanzees, Scott's Sea Lions and Vogelbein and his Bears.'

One star singer I represented did impress Bill: Dorothy Squires, an ebullient lady with an amazing flow of language. Bill enjoyed visiting Dorothy and her husband, handsome actor Roger Moore. They had a fabulous home in Kent, with a swimming-pool (an unusual luxury for Britain in the 'fifties) and a billiards room. Roger would frequently escape the chit-chat of the assembled celebrities at Dorothy's parties to play snooker with young Bill.

A policeman's son, Roger had similar gifts to those of my daughter Joan. He could act, and was good at art too. Like Joan, he rejected a career as an artist in favour of RADA.

When Dorothy Squires first met Roger she was a big star with a huge and devoted fan following. As a performer she could 'sell' a song better than anyone else, putting enormous emotion into a performance. Even the young Elvis Presley, though their styles were so different, listed Dorothy as his favourite female vocalist. She was clever too, writing many of her own numbers.

At this time Roger, eight years Dorothy's junior, was just another struggling young actor.

After the couple married – in New Jersey, USA in 1953 – Dorothy confided in me, as her agent, about her ambitions for Roger. She was sure that square jaw, the keen blue eyes, the classic male beauty, would go down well in Hollywood. She encouraged Roger to try his luck there.

After unmemorable roles in the Elizabeth Taylor-Van Johnson film *The Last Time I Saw Paris* and *Diane* with Lana Turner, and a few similar movies, Roger returned to Britain disgruntled.

His sense of humour, though, was unimpaired. 'In one film they asked if I'd mind working with a vocal coach as my accent was a little too English,' Roger told me. 'This was odd – considering I was playing the Duke of Wellington's nephew.'

Roger always sees the funny side of things. He has no inhibitions about sending himself up and will relish an anecote in which he comes out the fall guy.

In the mid-'fifties Roger was given the title role in *Ivanhoe*, a British television series based on the Walter Scott classic. During the shooting we went to a party at the Moores' place in Kent. Roger was limping. 'Got kicked by a horse on location yesterday,' he explained. 'The horse obviously shares my opinion of the series.'

Though Roger was obviously not satisfied with the parts he

A little Roger Moore artistry on a restaurant menu, caricaturing (left to right) Joe, Irene Collins, Luisa Moore, Roger, Jackie Collins and husband Oscar, Joan and husband Tony Newley.

was getting, he never gave the impression that he considered them unworthy of his talents.

He was never big-headed or self-obsessed. He felt that his wife Dorothy was more gifted than he was, and he appreciated her support. He was very concerned that I did my best to promote her career and he made sure she got good terms.

When we were not discussing Dorothy's business affairs Roger and I still found plenty to talk about. He was what used to be called a 'man's man' – a sportsman, like me, and a good card-player, particularly adept at gin rummy.

And another thing we had in common: we had both suffered from bad stomachs. I told him how my ulcers had prevented me joining up in the Second World War. Roger was also careful about what he ate, claiming that his first wife Dorn, an ice-skater, cooked so badly she had ruined his digestion.

The era of lavish parties with Dorothy and Roger ended when

Roger went off to Hollywood again for more films and the *Alaskans* and *Maverick* television series.

Lew Grade, by this time boss of ATV Television, contacted me with another suggestion for my Adonis friend. 'We're going to make a series based on the Leslie Charteris character, the Saint. We want a big name, a handsome, active chap for the title part. You know Roger Moore. Why don't you get him to come over and do it?'

Obligingly – and hoping to be a party to pleasant business arrangement – I wrote a personal letter to Roger in Hollywood, but to my disappointment the reply came not from Roger himself but from a show-business agent who told me politely that Roger was 'too busy' to consider the project.

Later, when Roger *was* fixed up to play the Saint, the deal was done by someone else. I never had an opportunity to do business with Roger. However, we stayed good friends, even after he parted from Dorothy in 1961. Dorothy went out of *my* life too. After I had represented her for many years we had an argument and agreed to disagree.

When Roger married his present wife, Luisa, I was one of the few wedding guests. At the time I was a widower. As soon as he knew I had married Irene, he insisted we all go out to dinner.

My daughters, Joan and Jackie, who first met Roger at those parties in Kent, have remained good friends with him, are very fond of his wife, Luisa, and Joan is godmother to their son Christian.

Years ago, when he was starting to get famous, Roger told me, 'I wish they would stop giving me parts where I have to fire a gun. Every time I fired one in my last series I blinked, and they had to edit the film, taking the blink out.'

This, I hasten to add, was before Roger became the screen's 007. I assume that with all the target practice he has had as James Bond, Roger has now overcome his blinking problem.

Not so long ago I was walking down Marylebone High Street one morning when a chauffeur-driven limousine drew up beside me. 'Hi Joe! How's it going?'

Roger, whom I had not seen for a while, stopped his car and sent away his driver. We sat in a little coffee bar – the Stage

"ROGER & LUISA"

or

"Two's coy. 4's a Family"

CALL SHEET. NO. 1.

Production "THEIR WEDDING" Date 11th April, 1969.

Set AS BELOW Stage HAPPY

Director THE REGISTRAR Unit Call AS BELOW

ARTISTE	CHARACTER	D/R No	MAKE-UP CALL	SET CALL	

1. INTERIOR CAXTON HALL. AT 11 A.M.

ROGER MOORE — GROOM

LUISA MATTIOLI — BRIDE

KENNETH MORE — BEST MAN

LUCIA MATTIOLI — MAID OF HONOUR

CROWD

10 MEN

GENERAL OBSERVERS

10 WOMEN

PROPS — Wedding Rings - Buttonholes - Flowers For Bride - Confetti - Rice - Hankies for crying.

NOTE — Immediately after completion of Caxton Hall ceremony main unit move to next location by own transport.

2. INTERIOR, SUITE ADJACENT TO ROYAL ROOF, ROYAL GARDEN HOTEL - KENSINGTON. AT 12.30.

ROGER MOORE — OLD MARRIED MAN

LUISA MOORE — OLD MARRIED LADY

KENNETH MORE — OLD BEST MAN

THE COLLINS' — VERY RICH AGENT & BRIDE

LUCIA MATTIOLI — SISTER OF BRIDE

GEORGE MOORE — FATHER IN LAW

LILY MOORE — MOTHER IN LAW

Don't be late.

CROWD NOTE — (ALL SMART FOREGROUND ARTISTES ONLY)

FROM ABOVE

PLUS SIXTY MORE — WEDDING GUESTS

PROPS — Champagne - Glasses - Hors D'Oeuvres - Cigarettes (practical) - Tea Trolley not required.

3. INTERIOR - ROYAL ROOF - FOR LUNCHEON SCENE -

ALL PRINCIPALS & CROWD

FROM ABOVE "

PROPS — Practical Food - Champagne - Wine - Cigars - Cigarettes.

SIGNED:

PRODUCER

Roger and Luisa Moore's wedding invitation.

Door, run by my friend Lew Lee – talking over old times, then he walked back home with me and telephoned for his car to pick him up.

After he left I had to face a furious showdown with the family 'treasure', Doris 'Dodo' Hugill, and another woman who was our housekeeper at the time.

'Why didn't you ask us to make a coffee or something for you and Mr Moore? All the time you were with him we were sitting in the kitchen waiting.'

'But we didn't want anything. We'd just had a coffee before we came home,' I answered innocently.

'Oh, you *are* silly,' chided Dodo. 'You should have asked us for something just to give us a chance to come into the room and have a good look at him.'

Roger Moore's modesty contrasted with the attitude of someone I still claim was the biggest talent of the 'fifties to come my way. I refer to Dave King.

In the last decade King has been in plays on television and at the National Theatre. But in the 'fifties he was all the rage as an all-round entertainer . . . impressionist, comedian, singer.

King had been a baker's boy and a bookie before joining the Morton Fraser Harmonica Gang and becoming its leader.

In 1953, when a solo comedian on the same bill at the Hippodrome, Manchester fell sick, King had deputized for him and brought the house down. Encouraged by this success, King had asked Fraser for a salary rise of £1 a week, which would have brought his wage up to £11. Fraser refused.

At this point another artiste, Len Young, billed as 'The Singing Fool', brought King, then 23 years old, to see me.

'If you can get work for me at £11 a week I'll sign with you,' King said eagerly.

'I'll do better than that,' I promised, 'I'll get you £12 a week.'

I duly booked King into the Wood Green Empire, Essex for one week and put him into the opening half at the New Theatre, Cambridge the following week. Then, having seen his potential for myself, I signed him to a five-year contract.

Through my association with King I fulfilled the ambition of all good show-business agents. I found an unknown artiste of outstanding talent and helped him to make the most of it. In short, I kept him in work, built his career, made him a star, made his fortune. But, as is the way with many fulfilled ambitions, there were snags. Sad to say, on a personal level, my association with King brought little satisfaction.

For a start, as his popularity grew, so did his ego, making him very unpopular with fellow entertainers. The comedian Tommy Trinder, a good friend of mine who shared a bill with him, quipped, 'Hats come in three sizes .. big, very big and Dave King!' Tommy had it right.

I would plead with my protégé, 'Can't you try to be a bit more pleasant and friendly and not so full of yourself?'

'No, I'm too honest,' he insisted. 'I can't put on the phoney humility. Anybody who has the nerve to get up on stage, hold an audience enthralled and then says afterwards he isn't vain is a liar.'

At best I considered King eccentric. Married to a glamorous dancer, Jean Hart, he was so influenced by the westerns he read incessantly that he named his two daughters after Red Indian tribes, Cheyenne and Kiowa.

He had a big train set, which he fitted up in my lounge at Harley House because his own place was less spacious, but such was his nature that none of my family, nor anyone else for that matter, was allowed to touch it, let alone operate the signals. So Bill and I would play with Bill's model railway in one room and let King play alone with *his* in the next room. I'm not surprised Elsa thought us ridiculous.

King could be altogether unco-operative. When he began to make hit records and was inundated with fans' requests for autographed photographs, I ordered postcard-size pictures, but King refused to sign them. I had to sign them myself.

After his early hits, in 1956 ('Memories Are Made of This' and 'You Can't Be True to Two'), his recording manager, Dick Rowe, telephoned me. 'I've got a great new song for Dave. Can you get him to the studio next week to hear it?'

'What are you trying to do, turn me into a pop star?' King demanded. 'I'm not interested. Leave me alone!'

He was lucky his recording deal was not terminated there and then.

King was not an ungenerous man. I remember he once gave me a set of toby jugs, a reminder of the days when I sold Toby ales in the pub I ran with my mother. What King lacked was team spirit. He would never join in fund-raising activities, for instance. This I could not comprehend, for I have always done voluntary work myself. For many years I was Vice President and Hon. Treasurer of the Entertainment Agents Association Ltd, a body which helps to see that our profession is run smoothly and fairly. As a barker of the Variety Club of Great Britain I supported fund-raising campaigns such as Sunshine Coaches for the Disabled, and both Joan and Jackie can look back on some Variety Club function as their first 'grown-up' evening-dress outing. My girls and their brother Bill have always respected the show-business tradition of helping people in need.

Dave King never let me involve him in charity events. Yet, I have to repeat, I always respected King's talent. He broke house records at the Winter Gardens, Blackpool, where I booked him at £450 a week. From here he went on to star at the London Hippodrome where the two bosses, George and Alfred Black, not only paid King's salary but made me a personal present of an additional £1000. With King in such demand, they felt I had done them a favour by letting him appear at their theatre.

Even when things were going so well, there was a barrier between King and me. One day I felt compelled to spell it out. 'I can't say, honestly, that I like you very much.'

King's reply was revealing. 'I don't like myself much either,' he answered miserably.

In 1956 I flew with King to the USA – my first long plane journey. The turbulence over New York was so bad that everyone on board was sick, excepting me. I was too excited to be sick. I had got King a booking on the Ed Sullivan show, and fixed for him to make a screen test with Mitzi Gaynor in Hollywood. My daughter Joan's studio, 20th Century-Fox, wanted to groom him in the Jack Lemmon mould.

King and I had no sooner checked into our Los Angeles hotel

when I had a phone call from London. It was Leslie Grade, the brother of my old partner Lew Grade and Bernie Delfont, about to disrupt all my plans.

'Can Dave King be free to top the bill at the London Palladium? They want him in two weeks' time!'

I did not know what to say. Topping the Palladium bill was the highest honour for any variety artiste.

I turned to King. 'Do you want to play the Palladium, or stay on here in Hollywood?'

King didn't hesitate. 'I want the Palladium,' he answered promptly, 'but only on condition they pay me £1000 a week.' In those days that was top whack. Grade didn't quibble.

Shortly after our return to Britain King and I parted. If I had any regrets, they were only professional ones.

King, in fact, did work regularly for a while in the US. He was the first British comic to be given his own television series there. But that was later on.

On that first trip to the US, before he returned to appear at the Palladium, I took King with me to visit Joan at her studio, where she was working on the film *The Opposite Sex*, with June Allyson and Ann Sheridan, based on the Claire Booth Luce novel *The Women*. Joan played a chorus-girl minx out to steal the husband of an older woman (played by June Allyson).

The director, David Miller, gave me a report on my daughter's progress. To the public it might have appeared the kind of 'reference' more suitable for a diligent secretary than a so-called star, but to directors stars are like any other workers.

'Mr Collins, I'm pleased to say your daughter is very satisfactory. She's a strict timekeeper, very co-operative, very reliable.' Then he added, 'When you're keeping an eye on your budget, this is important. Temperamental actresses can be ruinous.' I knew exactly what David Miller meant!

I did not learn till much later, though, exactly how co-operative Joan had been on his film. For her bathtub scene they had used a strong washing powder to create bubbles, and her body below the waterline was covered in painful blisters. Yet Joan never took time off for them to heal: she is a trouper.

At this time, in an American poll, Joan had just been voted Most Promising Star. She was pleasing both directors and the public. In her career she was doing fine.

I hoped her private life too would soon be in better shape. She was, at last, about to be divorced from Maxwell Reed and had a new man friend, Arthur Loew Jr, a film producer who had recently made the Paul Newman film *The Rack*. Arthur came from a prominent American show-business family. His grandfather Marcus Loew had founded MGM, his maternal grandfather was Adolph Zukor, while Arthur Loew Sr ran the theatre and cinema chain of the family empire. Being of show-business lineage myself, I considered this an excellent pedigree. I was delighted to be meeting young Arthur.

My first evening in Los Angeles I called for Joan at her little apartment and she took me straight to Arthur's home, a ranch-style house up in the Hollywood Hills, where the rich folk lived. What impressed me, though, was not the man's opulent home, but the chap himself. Arthur was the first man in Joan's life I positively liked. Unlike her previous boyfriends he was not particularly good-looking, but he was suave and smart. He received me with the courtesy a man has a right to expect from his daughter's boyfriends but does not always get.

As I had anticipated from what Joan had told me, Arthur and I could communicate. Both being businessmen, we talked the same language.

After this meeting with Arthur, I offered Joan a few hesitant words of caution: 'I hope you're being sensible this time. Don't treat sex as an aperitif.' For me, to utter a sentence to my daughter that included the word 'sex' was very outspoken. Joan was too embarrassed to reply.

I treated her to another piece of wisdom. 'Now you've met someone nice, instead of wanting to run around all the time, it would do you good to stay in occasionally and watch television.'

Joan stared. 'Daddy, what are you talking about? Watch television! I hate the horrid thing.'

My daughter's outraged response reminded me of old-time vaudeville stars getting huffy if someone suggested they go and see a movie. They preferred to ignore the expanding form of entertainment which, they felt, threatened their own livelihood.

Neither Joan nor I could have guessed that television would one day turn her into a superstar. (Today Joan has changed her ideas about television viewing: the set in her bedroom is the size of a cinema screen.)

After I returned from America I visited my mother in Brighton, who was all a-gog for first-hand news, especially anything I could tell her about Joan's life in Hollywood.

Mother had just been to see Joan's film *The Girl in the Red Velvet Swing*. Of all the movies her granddaughter had made, this was her favourite – and mine, too.

The story was based on a real-life turn-of-the-century scandal, much discussed in my parents' show-business circle. The 'Girl in the Red Velvet Swing' was Evelyn Nesbit, a Gibson Girl from the *Floradora* chorus, who married a playboy, Harry K. Thaw. She also had a lover, an architect called Stanford White – shot dead by the jealous Thaw. This character was played by Farley Granger, Ray Milland was White and Joan had the leading role of Evelyn Nesbit.

I'm glad that my mother – who died at 76, in 1957, two years after the film was made – had the sentimental experience of seeing her granddaughter playing one of her own, and my father's, Edwardian stage contemporaries, and playing it so well, for Joan was very, very good in the part. It was her opportunity to draw on the inherited experience of our show-business family, and to draw on her Grandma Hettie's early schooling in stagecraft.

Mother was altogether thrilled about what was happening for Joan. She had nothing but praise, praise, praise. She approved of everything Joan said and did.

Well, almost everything.

While I had been in America, Mother had kept a particular press clipping which she now read to me. 'What do you think of this? Joan says, "Men like to be kissed and I like kissing them. If people don't like me, that's just too bad!" '

Mother put aside the clipping. 'You see! She's learning to stand up for herself. Speaking her mind. People will talk about her, take notice of her.'

Then she frowned. 'I wonder just how much kissing she's doing?'

'Well, she's got this nice new boyfriend now . . .' I started to explain. Yet even as I told my Mother about Arthur Loew Jr I was worried. I felt that for all her bold words in print, Joan was still very vulnerable.

10

A Writer Wrong-footed

In December 1983, when a photograph of my daughter Joan in the nude appeared in *Playboy* magazine, my phone never stopped ringing. People expected me to be shocked. Far from it – I was proud. Joan has a great body, and in show business, posing is part of your living. Joan has proved that a woman of 50 can still be in perfect shape.

I really don't understand anyone making this fuss about a nude picture, particularly nowadays, with all the topless sunbathing. Attitudes have changed so much since the 'forties and 'fifties, when nudity was considered 'naughty' and people would actually buy theatre tickets just to see some girl, not necessarily a pretty one, posing on stage in the buff, or near-buff. As a showman I knew that by putting a nude into the cast of a revue I could get the production a full year's bookings around the country in just an hour of telephone calls.

At one time I was in the pantomime and review business (which included revues that featured nudity) with entertainer Davy Kaye, a man who compensates in personality for what he lacks in height. An indefatigable fund-raiser for show-business charities, Davy is much liked by the royal family, and when he was King Rat of 1984 Prince Philip joined him in an impromptu comedy double-act, screened on television.

For the many shows Davy and I put on he was the comedian producer and I was the impresario.

We would have a laugh, thinking up titles for our shows with naked ladies, each of us trying to outdo the other with bills like 'Nudes of the World', 'Evening Nudes', 'Fanny Get Your Fun' and 'Piccadilly Peepshow'.

Our posers were not engaged in advance. The first day of rehearsals we would line up the chorus dancers and make our offer of an extra ten shillings (50p) a week for any girl prepared to do it. We were never short of volunteers.

The law in those days demanded that a nude poser must remain quite motionless on stage: she was usually presented on a pedestal, like a statue. We had our own way of getting round the 'no-movement' rule. When the curtain went up to reveal the nude, the stage manager in the wings would get busy with the wind machine, creating a gale which made the girl shiver, causing involuntary movement. As she was cold, her nipples would stand out.

These shows were really harmless fun, and I was irritated that some people within our profession objected, complaining that stage nudity was spoiling the reputation of the music hall as family entertainment. I did not accept this argument, for there were still plenty of variety theatres around the country offering a different type of presentation.

If anything did kill stage variety, in my opinion it was the wealth of new pastimes being offered: evening football matches, dog-racing, ice-skating, and the new passion for television.

The biggest direct threat to the variety theatre was the trend towards good cabaret staged in clubs, which meant the patrons could watch a show without being held to the rigid seating arrangements and timetable of the music hall. In a club you could have a meal, have a drink, see a few acts and come and go as you please.

Despite all the various other ways of spending free time, it was still possible to get a full house in a top-class music hall with an attractive bill.

This I proved myself. One of the outstanding attractions for which I was agent was Carroll Levis and his Discoveries, a talent show which could always fill a provincial theatre for a two-week run instead of the usual one week.

After Levis had a mental breakdown his name faded, but in his prime he was a great showman, a strong personality popular both live and on radio. When the buzz went round a provincial town that Carroll Levis would be appearing there, all the local would-be stars would turn up for the Monday-morning auditions, hoping for their break. We were never short of a full bill of hopeful amateurs.

The Carroll Levis show did indeed launch many bright

careers. Humorist Barry Took, comedian-impressionist Eddie Arnold, singer Ronnie Carroll, comedian Ken Dodd, entertainer-actor Jim Dale, who became the toast of Broadway when he played the title role in the musical *Barnum*, are just a few who owe their start to Levis.

In the main theatres Levis compèred his show himself, and for the no. 2 dates he would put in a deputy, most frequently Eddie Lee, formerly of the vocal group the Three Admirals.

Whenever Eddie Lee did a 'warm-up' for the Discoveries show, whatever the season he always sang the same song, Irving Berlin's 'White Christmas'. Hearing him warbling on about sleighbells and snow at the Aston Hippodrome during a heat-wave I ventured to ask: 'Can't you sing something else? Haven't you noticed it's midsummer, and the whole audience is swelter-ing?'

'I'm an amateur psychologist,' Lee answered, deadpan. 'I'm singing "White Christmas" to make 'em feel cool.'

Another Levis presenter at no. 2 theatres was a lovely brunette, Violet Pretty, who, like my daughter Joan and Diana Dors, played one of the finalists for the beauty-queen title in the film *Lady Godiva Rides Again*.

For Violet that film was partly autobiographical. She actually did get her start through winning a beauty contest. Later she changed her name to Anne Heywood, became a film star and married the film producer Raymond Stross.

A third Carroll Levis-show presenter was none other than my daughter Jackie. True to my promise to help her in show business, it was I who suggested Levis should give her the job. Jackie did me credit; she was a very good commère. Not until years later did she tell me she found the whole experience 'abysmal'.

Indeed, today Jackie appears to have few pleasant memories of her comparatively short career as a stage and screen perfor-mer. I don't know why, because although she never became a star she did not do too badly. Certainly she notched up quite a list of credits.

She did a season in repertory at Ilfracombe. At 18 she made her screen début, playing a juvenile delinquent (a similar start to Joan's!) in a film called *The Pay Off*. She was later in a pop film, *Rock You Sinners*, and made another film, *Barnacle Bill*, which starred Alec Guinness. Jackie also appeared on television quite frequently and was in the final episode of the BBC's first successful soap opera, *Compact*, about life on a women's magazine. Ironically, she played a star actress, not one of the magazine writers.

Jackie interrupted her career in Britain to stay with Joan in America. I thought Jackie might get parts in Hollywood films, but though she won a place in the 20th Century-Fox star-grooming school she was unable to obtain a permit to work in the US.

During Jackie's eleven-month visit Joan took her to parties, where she met top stars: she dated Marlon Brando, who in those days was young and slim. Jackie also found her own, younger, crowd, some of them ambitious actors and actresses, others what Jackie termed 'just plain bums'.

In one way or another Jackie was getting to know a whole cross-section of the Los Angeles population, mixing with the people who would form the basis for the characters in her books and earn her a fortune. Jackie never needed to get work as a chambermaid or office receptionist to eavesdrop on what was going on. Though she held herself aloof, she was right there on the scene with those pretty girls willing to degrade themselves for a bit part in a movie, the young studs on the make, ready to turn bi-sexual if necessary, the loose-living producers, the 'chancers' and pretenders, the honest hard workers, the publicity people, the photographers.

At the time Jackie returned from America, though, I had no idea she had been quietly stockpiling material. What Elsa and I did know was that Jackie wanted to free herself from the 'Joan Collins' little sister' tag. We did not like it ourselves when some journalist, unable to reach Joan, would 'make do' by speaking to Jackie. Twice Jackie declared she was going to change her name, first to Jackie Douglas, then to Lee Curtis, but there was little point as people would still have known who she was.

At this stage, when she was not working or posing for decorative pictures, Jackie would spend hours in her room, absorbed in her compulsive writing, with her records or the radio blaring in the background.

I never asked what she was writing, and she never offered to show me. I just did not think about it at all. To be honest, I was too occupied with my own business life to be interested.

Elsa was not curious either. Though she had a very close relationship with Jackie, Elsa, like me, was no reader and did not appreciate our daughter's 'hobby' any more than I did. Because the noise of her records disturbed our peace, Elsa and I were more aware of Jackie's other interest – rhythm 'n' blues, modern jazz and Latin American. She even played the bongo drums.

As a young enthusiast of the new pop music boom Jackie was asked to appear as a guest celebrity in Britain's first television rock series.

'I'm going to be on the *6.5 Special*,' she announced.

I looked up from my newspaper. 'Where to?' I asked absently. For all I knew, the '6.5 Special' could have been a train. However, when Jackie celebrated her 21st birthday, Elsa and I gave a party for 80 guests and invited all the *6.5 Special* folk, including the resident musical director, Tony Osborne, and his wife Joan, and Britain's first big rock 'n 'roll star, young Tommy Steele.

Tommy, who has since played the lead in many Disney movies, soon expanded beyond the rock field. Apart from being an entertainer, his activities include writing novels, painting, sculpture, even conducting an orchestra. At the time of Jackie's party his latest hobby was hypnotism, and to prove his newly discovered powers he put several of the guests into a hypnotic trance and brought them out of it again – in what I must say seemed a most professional and responsible manner. At any rate Tommy's hypnotism made a novel change from the usual party games.

During this 'pop' phase Jackie was friendly with the disc jockey Tony Hall, a very nice fellow. I half expected she might marry into the pop music world.

Then one day, when Jackie was on tour with the play *French Without Tears*, billed above the title (much to our regret) as

'Lovely Younger Sister of Joan Collins', a journalist telephoned with some news.

'Did you know your daughter Jackie got married this morning to the pop star Marty Wilde?'

I was astounded; Jackie had never even mentioned Marty Wilde's name to us.

After a few anxious phone calls Elsa and I learned the marriage story was a hoax by students of Hull University, one of their Rag Week pranks. We were furious. We learned that Jackie and the gangling pop idol Marty, also appearing in Hull, had only ever met once, at a party. They could not even have been described as friends.

Marty himself thought the phoney marriage story quite funny, but his fiancée, Joyce Baker, a singer with the Vernons Girls, was not amused. Fortunately, the incident did not harm their relationship. They've been happily married since November 1959, and have four children, one of whom is pop star Kim Wilde.

In 1960 Jackie did get married, with the wholehearted blessing of Elsa and me, to Wallace Austin, whom she met at a party. Wallace came from a well-known family in the London clothing industry, was educated in the US and at the age of 26 had founded his own firm. Eleven years Jackie's senior, he was now very successful as a dress manufacturer.

The courtship was formal and correct; Wallace gave my daughter an engagement ring with a huge diamond and we all looked forward to a traditional wedding which, according to custom, I would pay for as father of the bride. But when Wallace's mother came round to our home to discuss the wedding arrangements I began to feel uneasy.

'We must hire a ballroom at one of the best hotels,' Wallace's mother insisted. 'I think Grosvenor House would be the right place.'

'Grosvenor House!' I gulped. 'That's a very big ballroom.' Mentally I began to tot up how much this wedding was likely to cost me. 'Well, all right. I want to do things properly for my daughter. How many people shall we invite?'

'About six hundred,' Wallace's mother answered coolly.

I exploded. 'Do you think I'm a millionaire? Who *are* all these people? I can't afford to entertain them!'

To her credit, Wallace's mother took my outburst in good part, whatever her private thoughts.

'That's perfectly all right,' she said calmly. 'Don't worry. As is happens, we *do* have a lot of friends and we don't want to offend any of them by leaving them off the guest list. We will invite them all, and you needn't be concerned about the cost.'

We reached a civilized compromise. I agreed to foot one-third of the bill, and I engaged a top band, Sidney Lipton's, for the dancing. The bridegroom's mother paid the rest.

Jackie's wedding to Wallace Austin in December 1960 was indeed a very grand affair, with Jackie looking beautiful in her gorgeous white satin bridal gown. At least I had seen one of my daughters as a traditional bride.

My Hollywood star Joan flew to London for the occasion, accompanied by her fiancé, American actor Warren Beatty, to whom she had become engaged a few months previously.

Beatty, by coincidence, was now making a film in England – his second big picture, *The Roman Spring of Mrs Stone* with Vivien Leigh. Though his career looked promising, he was not yet very well known, and was still being introduced to people as 'Joan Collins' fiancé, Shirley MacLaine's brother'.

Beatty was obviously a well brought-up young man, with good looks and good manners. But despite his courteous behaviour towards our family, I treated him with a certain coolness. I had a strong feeling that his engagement to Joan was not going to end in marriage: there was a restlessness about Beatty which told me he was not yet ready to settle down.

After a honeymoon in Mexico, Jackie and Wallace moved into a home on a smart new estate near Hampstead Heath in North London, with all the trappings you could expect for a wealthy young couple.

I had a great fondness for Wallace, the only one of my sons-in-law with whom I shared a background in common. Neither he nor I had actually lived in the East End of London but part of our roots were there and we understood each other, were on the same wavelength – and we even went to football together. I looked on Wallace as a close friend.

My married daughter and her husband lost no time in producing a grandchild, Tracy, a lovely little girl, born ten months after her parents were married.

I only wish life could have been continued on this level of contentment. But even as my wife Elsa held her baby granddaughter in her arms we knew she would never live to see this little girl grow up. Elsa had been operated on for a malignant tumour. Ever since then, she had been losing weight. She was not recovering.

It was the worst experience of my life to see Elsa, who had always been so healthy, waste away and gradually lose hope.

My beloved Elsa died on 8 May 1962, at the age of 56. In her last hours my children and I were with her at Harley House. Bill was barely 16 years old. We had tried to conceal from him the gravity of his mother's illness, but there was no way of protecting him from the final truth.

My greatest sorrow about my little family is that Elsa, who doted on her children, never had the pleasure of sharing their adult future. She would have been so thrilled to know that Jackie found a fulfilling career and became a household name as an author. She would have been so proud when Joan – at 51 – was voted the 'Most Beautiful Woman on Television'.

Apart from Tracy, Elsa never had the joy of knowing her grandchildren. They would have adored her.

It is sad, too, that she never saw our son Bill grow up, become successful in business and get married.

Both Joan and Jackie have dedicated books to their late mother. Her name is on the flyleaf of Jackie's first published novel, *The World Is Full of Married Men*. In the *Joan Collins Beauty Book* is the dedication: 'In memory of my mother, Elsa, who guided me in the right direction.'

Those words of Joan's referred to beauty care, but they remind me of something Elsa said, many times: 'You can guide your children to the straight and narrow path, but you can't keep them there. When they grow up they go their own way.'

Elsa and I had 30 good years together. She was a good wife, a good mother. Though I am now happily married again, she is always in my thoughts. My wife Irene understands. Three or four times a year she comes with me to Hampstead Cemetery to plant fresh flowers on her grave.

The early 'sixties brought a further tragedy to our family. Jackie's husband, Wallace, with whom I had been sure she would have an ordered, secure future, had become ill. He suffered very badly from depresssions. Jackie did her utmost to keep him contented, to give him incentive to be happy. But Wallace's state of mind was not receptive to persuasion. One day he drove to the New Forest, in Hampshire, and never returned.

In those fraught days in the early 'sixties, despite her own troubles, Jackie was a tower of strength to everyone around her, especially to my young son Bill, who spent as much time at his sister's home as he spent with me at Harley House.

For my own part, I tried to comfort little Tracy and devoted more time to her than to any of my subsequent five grandchildren. I used to sit with her night and day, reading her stories. I had hardly opened a children's book since I was a child myself, but the stories of Hans Christian Andersen were one of the few books I had enjoyed, other than football, fishing or detective yarns.

Later, in 1972, recalling Tracy's delight at my readings, I started a company, Fable Recordings, and made an album featuring two of the most marvellous voices of our time, that great lady of theatre Dame Edith Evans and the Poet Laureate, Sir John Betjeman. I felt that with Andersen's simple wisdom and those narrators, with their perfect diction, any child would benefit. The record, which also has music by Norman Kay, is still selling – in the US and Canada as well as Britain. Apart from anything else, for sentimental reasons I'm glad I did it.

My priority after Elsa's death was to get young Bill settled. As usual, I had left it to Elsa to plan his education. As a small child she had put him into the junior department at Francis Holland School, then when he was older he had gone on to Eaton House

School in Belgravia. But Bill himself had the last word, declaring that he wanted to leave as soon as it was legally possible – when he was 15.

Bill got his wish and started work in my offices, but after a few months it was clear to both of us that however much he tried, Bill could not raise any enthusiasm for my side of show business.

Though disappointed, I accepted very quickly that Bill must make his way elsewhere. In the end he began his working life in earnest with my brother-in-law Mark Godfrey, my sister Lalla's husband, who dealt mainly in property. He trained Bill well, and today my son is a very able businessman. Bill is level-headed in all matters affecting the family, and concerning his celebrated sisters he has taken a very definite stand. While close to them in the personal sense, he will not be drawn into their working lives in any way, and never gives press interviews. I admire his strength of will.

11

Rocking Around the Clock

Thanks to Jackie and Bill's records blaring throughout the flat, in the second half of the 'fifties I was well briefed that a new fashion in music had arrived. The smooth, sentimental melodies of those bands I had been booking for about 30 years were now being drowned out by a more primitive music. Bill Haley and his Comets, whose frantic record 'Rock Around the Clock' sold like wildfire, caused riots when they appeared in Britain. Elvis Presley was becoming more popular than any film actor, and the British teenagers, taking their cue from what was happening in America, found their own Prince Charming in Tommy Steele, the ex-sailor from Bermondsey, South London, one of my daughter Jackie's crowd.

Some of the sharper-witted, old-style British band-leaders, realizing their own run was over, became impresarios and agents, signing up rough-looking, untrained young lads who fancied themselves as pop performers.

One of the top band-leaders, Bert Ambrose, approached me about our doing some business together. I knew Ambrose well, for in the 'forties I had booked his Ambrose Quartet, all stars in their own right: Vera Lynn, Anne Shelton, Sam Browne and Max Bacon. I respected his judgement but I resisted his suggestion to put on a rock 'n' roll tour.

'I didn't come into this business to find work for scruffy young kids,' I told him. 'They don't rehearse, they're unprofessional and won't even be told how to walk on to a stage properly. Furthermore, I can't stand the noise they make!'

However, I was not immune to new trends, and admitted an interest in that other craze, skiffle.

Ambrose agreed that we should put together a variety bill, to be topped by the Charles McDevitt Skiffle Group, featuring singer Nancy Whiskey. At the time, 1957, their record 'Freight Train' was no. 5 in the charts and selling better than any disc by

Tommy Steele, proving to me that their music had a wider audience than rock 'n' roll. Skiffle appealed to all age ranges, while rock was for teenagers only.

Actually, during the week's run at the Metropolitan theatre near Marble Arch, the bill headed by McDevitt did reasonable business, but the box-office returns did not excite us enough to risk a tour, and Ambrose and I did nothing further in that line.

Still, I stuck to my guns regarding the viability of skiffle music, and my Sunday concerts starring the performer Lonnie Donegan did very well. Apart from Donegan, for my other Sunday concerts I preferred to book what are now termed 'middle-of-the-road' performers: Frankie Vaughan, who had big hits with 'Green Door' and 'Garden of Eden' and later became a film star; Dickie Valentine, last heart-throb singer of the pre-pop era; Jimmy Young, destined to be a leading radio presenter; and a young comic, Benny Hill, whom I paid £175 for two shows at Great Yarmouth, Norfolk. During this era I also promoted Sunday jazz concerts, featuring Ronnie Scott, Stan Kenton and Johnny Dankworth.

Frankly, I was willing to put on anything *except* rock 'n' roll. Eventually, though, I realized I must stop being 'square', for the rock 'n' roll boys were filling theatres with a new, teenage audience. Seats were being sold again even in the top-tier galleries which, with the gradual decline of traditional music hall, had long since been closed. Rock 'n' roll gave many of these theatres a final burst of life before they closed down forever.

I realized it was time to conquer my personal feelings and, keeping up my reputation for being involved in any new trend, I joined forces with another impresario, Harold Davidson, to present pop shows.

By the early 'sixties rock 'n' roll was a regular part of my business. The hit parades were as familiar to me as the multiplication tables, and I always kept an eye on the bottom end of the charts to see who was coming up and could be booked at a reasonable fee before he or she broke really big.

In February 1963 a promotions executive at *The People* telephoned me.

'Can you find us an attraction for our summer ball? Something for young people?'

I recommended a new pop group from Liverpool called the Beatles, and said I'd try to book them.

When I tracked down the Beatles' manager, Brian Epstein, at his family's furniture store in Liverpool, he was happy for his boys to perform at the newspaper ball. We agreed on a fee of £500.

Three months later, when the Beatles had their second no.1 hit, 'From Me to You', the man from *The People* phoned again. 'This Beatles group you're getting for us, I'm afraid they won't be suitable after all for our ball. There'll be such a rush for tickets we won't be able to cope, and there could be trouble outside with their fans. Can you possibly manage to cancel our arrangement?'

When I told Brian Epstein of the cancellation, he did not disguise his relief. Since our earlier agreement the £500 fee I had negotiated had become ludicrously low payment for a Beatles cabaret.

However, this was not the end of my association with Brian Epstein and his Beatles.

Later that same year Stan Fishman, who booked live attractions for the Rank cinema circuit, came on to me. 'Brian Epstein wants to do a Beatles Christmas show, but he has no idea how to go about a full stage production. Can you help him?'

I could, with pleasure! I booked the *Beatles Christmas Show* into the Astoria, Finsbury Park in North London for two weeks, commencing on Christmas Eve 1963.

I organized the scenery, hired some tabs (backdrop curtains), engaged a producer, Peter Yolland, and a compère, the Australian entertainer Rolf Harris. I reckoned that Harris, as a former schoolteacher, would be able to handle a rowdy teenage audience.

The other acts were provided by Brian Epstein. Apart from the bill-topping Beatles, there was a group from Bedfordshire, the Barron Knights, while the rest came from Brian's stable of Liverpool talent, names he had launched that very year: Billy J. Kramer and the Dakotas (who had already had three top hits), the Four Most, Tommy Quickly and Cilla Black, Brian's latest discovery.

Cilla, a toothy, 20-year-old redhead, had recently given up her regular job as a typist. In the 'sixties the rock audiences did not care much for girl singers, but it was customary to include just one female vocalist on a bill, if only to get some variety into the programme. For her act at Finsbury Park, I remember Cilla coming on stage in a pink mini-skirted dress to sing a lesser-known Lennon-McCartney song she had recorded, 'Love of the Loved'.

When I looked at the printed programme for that Christmas show, I noted the credit I had been given: 'Brian Epstein wishes to acknowledge with gratitude the invaluable assistance of Joe Collins in the presentation.' I was actually co-producer.

As the show was intended to be 'special', not just a plain pop bill, Peter Yolland decided that the Beatles should perform a few sketches.

The night the show opened I wandered into the auditorium to witness George Harrison, dressed as a Victorian maiden, being tied to a railway line by John Lennon, in the role of Sir Jasper, the wicked landlord. Then Paul McCartney entered as the heroic signalman who rescues 'her'.

The experience, appropriate to the plot, was like watching a silent film. The boy's dialogue, if they were speaking lines at all, was drowned by the screeching audience. That was the first and only performance of the Beatles as stage actors.

That night at Finsbury Park, I met the Fab Four in person. I went backstage to introduce myself. 'How's the dressing-room?' I asked, sticking my head round the door of the shabby cell they were sharing.

'All right,' said drummer Ringo Starr, who always looked glum even when he was happy.

'Is there anything you need?' I asked politely.

'Yes, there is!' said Ringo promptly. 'Can you find us some flex for our electric kettle? We want to brew up some tea.'

'If you get us a lead for our kettle, we'll give you some earplugs,' George Harrison cajoled. 'You'll need 'em if you go out front!' That I knew already.

Only one thing blighted our run at Finsbury Park. After the Beatles and other Liverpool groups had monopolized the top chart positions for nearly a year, a London group, the Dave Clark Five, suddenly became a threat. Their shattering, thumping 'Glad All Over' ousted the Beatles from no. 1. The newspapers treated this item as a major sensation. 'DAVE CLARK FIVE CRUSHES THE BEATLES!' shrieked one of the headlines.

'Well, we can't be top 52 weeks of the year, can we?' retorted Paul McCartney.

Still, despite those frantic, yelling girls in their Finsbury Park audience assuring the Beatles how much they were loved, Lennon, McCartney, Harrison and Starr were green enough in show business to be upset about that gimmicky newspaper story.

On 14 January 1964, a few days after our show closed, the Beatles's new record 'I Wanna Hold Your Hand' became their first disc to reach no. 1 in America, and by the end of the year they were as popular in the US as they were in Britain.

Young Cilla Black, too, the sole girl on the Finsbury Park bill, was proving too that she had a future.

During our Christmas-show partnership, Brian Epstein had invited me to dinner at his new London penthouse in Williams Mews, behind Harrods in Knightsbridge.

I noted, with some surprise, that Brian's taste in furnishings was very arty. His choice of decor, with thick white carpeting and black leather settees, was not quite what I had expected from him after meeting his family from Liverpool, who were very down-to-earth despite their affluence.

Over our meal Brian talked about nothing else but his plans for Cilla Black.

'She's great . . . absolutely great,' he kept assuring me.

While agreeing that Cilla had a warm personality, I could not agree with Brian that she was 'great'.

He offered me evidence of her potential by playing a new recording of hers. I had already listened to enough music that day, but Brian was my host, so I put on an attentive expression as he switched on the record-player. The disc he played me was 'Anyone Who Had a Heart', a moving ballad by Burt Bacharach and Hal David. I realized Brian's enthusiasm might possibly be justified. He was right: it reached no. 1.

At the end of 1964, to round off the second amazing year of Beatlemania, Brian suggested we should jointly produce another Beatles Christmas show, to run from 24 December to 16 January 1965 at a very big cinema, the Odeon, Hammersmith, in West London.

We engaged two compères, Jimmy Savile and Ray Fell, and the support bill, again all musical acts, included the Manchester group Freddie and the Dreamers, Sounds Incorporated, the Mike Cotton Sound, and a blues-oriented band, the Yardbirds, who had a particularly talented lead guitarist, a 20-year-old lad from Ripley, Surrey called Eric Clapton. The obligatory girl on the bill was a bluesy singer, Elkie Brooks, a baker's daughter from Manchester. Elkie, like Cilla the previous year, was someone whose star potential Brian spotted early in her career.

The printed programme of what we actually called *Another Beatles Christmas Show* is now a souvenir I treasure, for it was illustrated with drawings by John Lennon, taken from the Christmas edition of his book *John Lennon in His Own Write.*

The Beatles, after almost two years of adulation, were now getting worn down by the fervour surrounding them. They wanted a bit of peace, and vistors to their dressing-room at Hammersmith rarely found a warm welcome.

One evening, when I was with them backstage, a Scandinavian representative from their record company EMI came in to be introduced to his bestselling product. He sat for a while in awe-stricken silence, watching them tune their guitars. Then he tried to start a conversation.

'Tell me,' he asked brightly, 'what is the best thing about being a Beatle?'

John Lennon looked up at the man, his face registering no expression at all.

'Best thing about being a Beatle?' he repeated slowly. 'Well, I guess it has to be that we meet EMI sales reps from all over the world.'

I cannot claim that I was one of the people to whom the Beatles wanted to chat, though as the show's co-producer I would always make my routine call at their Odeon dressing-room.

'How's it going, boys?'

'Fine, thank you,' they would answer politely. That was the end of the dialogue. They'd simply stare at me for a moment or two, then continue talking to each other, usually about their music.

'How do *you* get on with the boys?' Brian Epstein asked me eagerly after one of my brief visits to the Beatles' sanctum.

I laughed. 'So far as I'm concerned they're dumb . . . so dumb they're making millions!'

Actually, from my point of view, the Beatles were a headache. I liked their records and even I, then a man of 62, was humming 'She Loves You'. But I found it impossible to enjoy their stage performance. I couldn't stand the way the audience screamed, making such an hysterical noise all the way through the show it was impossible to hear any of the music. The burly security guys worked as hard as any of the performers: they had to fight back at a rush of shrieking girls, apparently intent on storming the stage and tearing their idols to pieces.

Outside in the street before and after the show youngsters would be surging round the building hoping to waylay the Beatles as they left the theatre. The police trying to control these crowds were kicked, bitten and had their helmets knocked off in the frenzy.

Apart from the fact my head was literally aching through the noise, I had a figurative headache, trying to spirit the Fab Four in and out of the theatre without anyone getting injured in the crush.

Like army officers planning a war operation, each day the theatre manager and I would meet with police representatives to devise some new Beatles escape campaign for the evening. We could never use the same method twice for the fans caught on too quickly.

However, at the end of that short Hammersmith Odeon season my head soon got right again, for I had been well rewarded. My personal fee for the two weeks' work was £4,000, made up of my 20 per cent share of the profits and the sale of brochure programmes. In the 'sixties such earnings were a sizeable sum, especially as the Odeon profits were offset against a loss on another show I co-presented with Brian that season, *Gerry's Christmas Cracker,* which played Scottish and provincial dates. I was surprised this show did not make a profit, for it starred the Liverpool group Gerry and the Pacemakers, Epstein discoveries who in 1963 had no. 1 hits with each of their first three records. (Gerry Marsden, happily, made a charts come-back in 1985 with a new recording of 'You'll Never Walk Alone'.)

The Rank Organization was very pleased with my contribution to its coffers, and at the Rank circuit's annual lunch following the 1964–5 Beatles season I was thanked officially by the company's boss, John Davis, for having brought it the Finsbury Park and Hammersmith shows, the most sucessful stage attractions ever in the firm's long history.

My association with the Beatles is a warm memory, not just because they provided a profitable venture, nor because they made a big personal impression on me: as I have said, I had no real communication with them. I was happy to have been involved because Brian Epstein was one of the most pleasant men with whom I ever did business. I found him charming, modest and completely straightforward in his dealings. I considered him a top-class businessman, and a gentleman.

Unlike some other managers and agents, he never regarded any of his artistes as a mere commodity, to be signed up and hired out just to make money for himself. Brian was concerned personally for the welfare and future of each singer and musician he took on. In all my long career I have never met any manager so enthusiastic about his artistes. When we were together he talked of nothing else. He was thrilled that his boys were putting British pop music on the international map. It should not be forgotten that Brian, as a newcomer to show business, had tramped round the London record companies and music publishers literally pleading for a hearing for his Liverpool artistes. He deserves much credit for turning British pop music into a high-earning export.

*

By the mid-'sixties British cinemas were facing the problem the music halls had faced a decade earlier. Their family audiences were dwindling: most people preferred staying home to watch television. As only the young were still eager to go out for entertainment, pop shows now seemed to be the one hope of filling the huge seating capacity of the major movie houses.

Unfortunately for the cinema-owners, there were not enough pop stars around to bring in large crowds regularly. In early 1965, for instance, the only names guaranteed to draw a full house were the Beatles, the Rolling Stones, Cliff Richard and one another name, P.J. Proby. Proby, then 26 years old, was from Texas; his real name was James Marcus Smith and he had earned his living making demonstration records for other singers. He was brought to Britain by Oxford-educated television producer Jack Good, who had launched many of the early British rockers.

Proby, a first-class showman with a bony, handsome face, oozed so much sex appeal he could send females into hysterics with a flick of his finger, let alone his very mobile hips. Though I had been warned by other agents that Proby was erratic and difficult to deal with, I appreciated his talent and was willing to get bookings for him.

Proby had a disarming way of describing himself in superlatives. 'I am the Cassius Clay of the music business,' he told me, in his rich, resonant voice. 'I talk big, and everything I say happens. I have to tell you, Mr Collins, that I won't work for less than I'm worth, which is five hundred pounds a night.'

I don't think I signed Proby for quite that sum, but it wasn't much less. I appreciated the image he had found for himself, with his velvet knee breeches, buckled shoes and his hair in a pigtail, like the fictional Henry Fielding character Tom Jones. He was also that comparative rarity in the pop field, a good singer, with a full-blooded Presley-type voice. If he could only have disciplined himself, his songs – 'Hold Me', 'Somewhere' and 'Maria' – would have kept him on top of his profession for years. But in trying to impress the girls in the audience with his sexuality, appealing to their most basic instincts, Proby went too far for his own good.

One night at the ABC cinema in Luton, Bedfordshire a tear appeared in Proby's tight trousers, just above the knee. When the audience spotted another tear higher up, pandemonium broke out and the manager rang down the curtain.

Afterwards Proby was most apologetic. 'I'm sorry,' he said evenly. 'There must be something wrong with the velvet cloth my tailor used. I've spoken to him, and he'll reinforce the trouser seams. My pants won't split again.'

Unfortunately they did. The next time Proby's pelvic movements ripped his trousers apart on a cinema stage the ABC management told him in no uncertain terms that they would not accept his excuses. They said his performance was 'obscene' and barred him from their cinema circuit.

I challenged Proby myself about what was happening. He was most upset. 'The same thing happens to Elvis Presley. His pants split too, and everyone knows it's an accident . . .' Proby was so plausible I gave him an avuncular lecture and booked him for another tour. Then came more bad news about Proby: just before he was due to open at the Birmingham Hippodrome he lost his voice and was unable to appear.

Before I had even begun to search for a replacement, the agent Colin Berlin came on the telephone to me. 'I've heard what's happened to Proby. I've got just the right chap to step in. Boy with a great voice from South Wales, name of Tom Jones. Yes, that's his real name . . . well, actually Thomas Jones Woodward. If you listen to his new disc "It's Not Unusual" you'll get the idea that he's just right for the Proby audience. And women go wild over him.'

I accepted Colin Berlin's offer of Tom Jones and agreed to engage him for £600 for the week. As I suspected, this newcomer did not fill the seating capacity of the Birmingham Hippodrome; at this stage he was not pulling in anything like the same size audience as Proby.

Jones' record 'It's Not Unusual' made its mark and he became the first new British solo male singer to top the charts since the start of the groups boom.

Tom Jones, singing magnificently, gyrating his hips and (so the saying went) wearing his pants out from the inside, but never splitting them, became a big star internationally.

Proby could have stayed a big star too, if he had only had the sense to draw a line between sexy showmanship and outright obscenity.

Like my earlier protégé, Dave King, Proby would not take direction from those with wiser heads on their shoulders and could not cope with success. He blew it.

By 1965 I was convinced that only pop performers were viable on the commerical concert stage, and anything else was a risk. When an Italian company, Canteuropa, approached me to promote their rather more 'cultural' show I was dubious. Though they had been touring Europe very successfully with their light classical repertoire, I doubted if they could draw audiences in Britain. I offered them just one evening at the Royal Albert Hall in London.

No sooner was this one date announced than I realized my miscalculation. As the news spread among London's Italian community, nearly every restaurant in Soho arranged to close for that evening so that its staff could come to the show. Outside the Albert Hall it was like Beatlemania: the ticket touts were having a field day. I was astonished to see so many priests, who had reserved seats as an investment and were now reselling them to the highest bidder to raise money for their churches.

I did not watch the concert myself. Sir Charles Forte, the millionaire restaurateur, hotelier and leisure-complex boss, himself of Italian origin, telephoned me with an urgent request for tickets for one of his daughters, so I gave him those reserved for my own family and close friends. I was not sorry to miss the show: it would have only reminded me that I could have booked Canteuropa for a full two weeks and sold every seat.

That same year, 1965, I decided it was time to follow my nose again and put on a nostalgic minstrel show, a style of entertainment which I, and other people of my age, would enjoy seeing revived. I have never analysed why white performers of the Edwardian era had this urge to black their faces, but in my childhood what we termed 'coon shows' were all the rage. My presentation *The New Minstrel Show*, which we described in the programme as 'an action-packed musical melange', was staged for a summer season on the pier at the resort of Southsea, Hampshire, with a cast headed by bumbling slapstick comic Richard 'Mr Pastry' Hearne.

Shortly before our opening I received a phone call from another impresario, Robert Luff, who for years had been running the top stage attraction 'The Black and White Minstrels' and was now very cross with me.

When he said that I was copying his idea and was going to sue me, I could hardly believe my ears, but I kept calm.

'Now, Mr Luff, how can you possibly claim that minstrel shows were originated by you?' I countered calmly. 'Would you like to see some pictures of my mother in her coon costumes? I can also show you newspaper clippings about the minstrel shows my father put on. These shows were part of theatrical tradition before you ever thought of doing them.'

Robert Luff accepted my argument instantly and became so interested in discussing the old turn-of-the-century entertainments we struck up a friendship and are now the best of friends.

In the 'sixties more white artistes than ever were latching on to black American music. Though they did not go so far as colouring their faces, they made discs which were often note-for-note copies of those made by the black performers. The more discerning disc-buyers, however, like my children Jackie and Bill, preferred to hear the original versions. On the staircase at my offices in Chandos House, behind the august London Coliseum, I'd frequently meet the new black American artistes who had come to perform in Britain: the whooping Little Richard, Ike and Tina Turner, the female trio the Ronettes, and the male quintet the Temptations. In the early 'sixties these artistes often performed at three different cabaret venues in one evening.

I was never involved with these acts myself. By now I was not only delegating work outside my scope to members of my own staff but renting part of my office building to independent agents and managers.

My Chandos House headquarters has been quite a launchpad for bright, go-ahead people who have been quick to spot some new brand of entertainment.

One of my earliest associates was Mick Hyams, youngest of three brothers who owned a chain of cinemas. Mick anticipated the family business would decline when the street where he lived started sprouting television aerials.

'Movies made specially for television – that's the coming thing,' he predicted. 'I'm off to America to set up a company with some Hollywood people.'

Before leaving to start a new life in the US he came to me ashen-faced. 'It's to do with my girlfriend, Poppy. My family don't approve. They'd have a fit if they knew I was taking her to the States. As my brothers are insisting on waving me off on the boat at Southampton I'll have to hide her.'

He asked me to take Poppy on board ship and pretend she was with me. Poppy, a flamboyant girl, was not the type to be worried by family disapproval. It was I who felt ashamed, standing with her on her deck, pretending we were a loving twosome.

Mick now has a thriving television film business run from West 57th Street in New York.

One tenant of my office space soon after the Second World War was Manny Jay. Manny had a brainwave. During the war, men in military entertainment units had dressed up as women for shows which had gone down so well with the forces audiences Manny was sure civilians would enjoy this type of thing too. He staged Britain's first successful post-war drag tour, *Soldiers in Skirts*.

Another Chandos House entrepreneur with girls – the genuine article! – on his mind was Paul Raymond, a former drummer from Glossop, Derbyshire, who rented an attic room from me at £5 a week. Paul, who had been sending out touring revues with nudes, asked my help with an ambitious plan.

'I've decided to open a club in Soho with the emphasis on nude shows. It'll cost a thousand pounds to start up the place. Would you like to come in with me, Joe – a half-share for five hundred?'

I told Paul I'd consider his proposal and talk it over with one of my sometime partners, impresario Reg Kemp. While I was not prepared to invest the entire £500 Paul Raymond was asking, I would have considered putting up £250 if Kemp were prepared to put up the same amount.

Reg Kemp's reaction, however, put me off the idea entirely. When I mentioned it he stared at me as if I were mad.

'You need your brains tested! How can you think of getting involved in a club with nude entertainment! The place will be closed down in five minutes.'

Giving heed to Reg Kemp, I turned down Paul Raymond's proposal, but knowing him as a man of integrity I did furnish him with a character reference which helped him secure his premises.

I hardly need say that I had been hopelessly wrong about the viability of Paul Raymond's club venture, for the Raymond Revuebar, opened in 1958, soon became not just a London landmark, but a tourist attraction ranking with the Tower of London and Big Ben.

Experience has taught me that women agents have a more personal relationship with their artistes than male agents do, fighting to get good terms for their performers as if they were their own children. Knowing this, I have always been pleased to employ women assistants.

During my early years at Chandos House when Evelyn Taylor, a blonde soubrette with plenty of bright chat, asked if she could come to work for me to learn the agency business, I welcomed her gladly.

Eve, still remembered by the old pros for a particular stage gimmick of hers (she wore cymbals between her knees, which she crashed together) proved a most energetic apprentice and excellent in the job I gave her, booking attractions for night-clubs and American service bases.

Being ambitious, she left my employ when she found an artiste of her own she wanted to build into a star.

This fair-haired boy, Terry Nelhams, an 18-year-old of charismic presence, had been an assistant editor at Shepperton Film Studios. Taking her cue from the Garden of Eden, Eve

161

named him Adam, and as she had faith in him, he became Adam Faith. Adam, with Eve behind him, topped the British disc charts and branched out into film, television and theatre work, before leaving Eve and going into business for himself: he became manager of singer Leo Sayer.

Eve herself, after leaving me, was at one time Britain's top woman show-business agent, with roster of talent including the Irish entertainer Val Doonican; Sandie Shaw, who won the Eurovision Song Contest and was also the first woman to have three no. 1 hits in the British charts; and Jackie Trent, a woman with a superb voice. Eve had a particular knack with female talent, and one girl she managed, Nicola Martin, of the duo Nick and Nicola, obviously learned something from her, because Nicola, in turn, founded the singing group Bucks Fizz.

Another push-and-go young woman who came to me to learn the agency business was Elma Warren, a Jewish girl, intelligent and hard-working. I guessed from the clues she dropped that she originated from the East End of London. Elma put in so many hours at work I thought she had no time for courting, so it came as a great surprise when she brandished in front of me a copy of *The Times* announcing her engagement to Lord Ulick Browne, brother of the Marquess of Sligo.

The announcement described Elma as 'daughter of Captain Andrew Burmanoff, Russian Hussars', which was something I had not known about her background. I never ceased to wonder how Elma and Lord Ulick ever got together, for they were so different. Down-to-earth Elma and her aristocratic, well-educated husband went into the nightclub business together, running a place in Regent Street called the Nuthouse before setting up in partnership as theatrical agents.

Long after Elma left my office I ran into the Brownes at London Airport when they were en route for the US. Elma, looking a million dollars, slapped me on the arm with a length of sapphire mink she was carrying.

'Do you like this pussy cat?' asked Lady Browne. 'It's supposed to be a scarf, but it's far too hot to wear, so I just wave it around.'

Elma then showed me her jewel case, emblazoned with her husband's coat-of-arms. 'This crest is to impress the Americans,' she said with a wink. 'As soon as we get back to Britain we'll have it removed.'

After Elma's death in 1959, Lord Ulick Browne stayed on in the club business, opening London's first discotheque, Brad's.

My list of former staff and associates who did well for themselves extends to the present day.

One of the later people I trained as an agent was Mervyn Conn; his cousins, the comedians Mike and Bernie Winters, whom I represented for many years, persuaded me to take him into the business. Today Mervyn is an international entrepreneur, known especially for his enterprise in the field of country music, and for his big festivals with stars like Jerry Lee Lewis, Don Williams, Tammy Wynette, Johnny Cash and Kris Kristofferson.

Derek Block, a 21-year-old trainee accountant who, as an amateur, booked artistes for charity concerts, decided that show business was a more exciting life than keeping the books for some big conglomerate. He rented a £5-a-week office from me and got busy. Today Derek is a top promoter, arranging tours and concerts for Bob Hope, Johnny Mathis, Diana Ross and anyone else big enough.

An ex-journalist, Tony Stratton-Smith, once the youngest sports editor in Fleet Street, also decided show business was his true forte and started up under my roof in a £5-a-week room. Today he heads Charisma Records, with a catalogue including the band Genesis and John Lennon's son Julian.

When I reached my mid-sixties I began taking stock of my career, thinking how entertainment had changed since I first became a theatrical agent. Sometimes, during my lunch break, I would take a sentimental stroll up Shaftesbury Avenue, to the fire-station building where, 35 years ago, I had set up my first one-room office. In those days, before television, before pop concerts, entertainment had been so much more exciting.

I would have loved to return to the variety world of a few decades ago: to sit in one of those old theatres, sniffing the aroma of greasepaint, beer, and that perfumed disinfectant sprayed by the usherettes in a vain attempt to drown the other odours. I would have loved to see a bill of trampoline acrobats, performing dogs, trick cyclists, jugglers, stilt-walkers.

How many of the new pop music fans, I wondered, would even known what was meant by the term 'teeter-board team' – those acrobats who jumped on a see-saw springboard, causing the partner at the opposite end to catapult into the air. They'd been my favourite act of all. I still respect the dare-devil, skilled entertainers now practising these arts only in circuses.

I had followed my parents into show business because I, like them, loved 'vor-dor-vil'. When music hall went out of fashion, by using foresight and keeping abreast of trends I had stayed the course, built up a fine business. But, when I faced the truth, I had to admit that with the decline of music hall my own true enthusiasm had declined too.

Finally, after much thought, I made my decision to remove myself from the hassles of the new-style entertainment industry, with its new-style agents and new-style hype.

I handed over the keys of my Chandos House premises to Mervyn Conn and started operating my business from home in Harley House, where there was plenty of office space. I was a widower, my daughters Joan and Jackie were grown up and gone away. Only my son Bill was living at home with me.

Several of the other old-established names had also given up their big offices and were now working from their homes. I was in tune with them. I too had decided I did not want to be a front-runner any more.

12

Falling in Love Again

The mid-'sixties saw not only total change in my business life, but the whole pattern of Collins family life. Within four years, 1963 to 1967, Joan, Jackie and I embarked on our second marriages.

Joan was the first: it was almost ten years since she had parted from her first husband, Maxwell Reed, she was now approaching her thirtieth birthday and I had long been wondering whom she would produce as a new son-in-law for me. I did not want her to rush into anything, but I was still surprised she waited so long before remarrying.

When her mother Elsa was already very ill, and Joan came to stay with us in London, she was friendly with the actor Robert Wagner, her co-star in the film *Stopover Tokyo*. He would call for her at our flat to take her out for the evening, but he did not hang around for conversation with the family. Obviously, I thought, this friendship was not 'serious'.

Then, while I was still mourning Elsa, before I was even aware what was happening, Joan fell in love with Anthony Newley. Tony, whom I had booked for a variety tour a few years previously, had now become a very big name indeed and his musical show *Stop the World – I Want to Get Off*, which he co-wrote with Leslie Bricusse, was a West End stage hit.

When Joan said she and Newley were actually considering marriage I was astounded. Knowing his unsociable ways, the total opposite of my gregarious Joan, I would never have thought him her type of man, and I told her so.

'Daddy, you're wrong about Tony. When he's with me he isn't morose at all. I make him laugh. You *must* see his show. He's a genius.'

I did go to see Newley's show and was impressed, but I still thought him the wrong man for Joan.

Joan and Tony were married very quietly in Connecticut, and

I did not see them again for quite some time after the marriage, but to my delight they started a family.

When their daughter Tara Cynara was born on 12 October 1963 in New York Tony was as proud a father as any grandfather could wish. He wrote me a charming letter, telling me of the happy event. 'It's a beautiful, blue-eyed girl,' he wrote. 'She was born at approximately 2 pm, weighs seven pounds and looks like her mother. Joan is doing well and we are both very happy.'

Two years later Joan and Tony had a son, my only grandson, named Alexander Anthony (but always known as 'Sacha', the Russian abbreviation of his name). He was born on 8 September 1965 at the same New York hospital, Mount Sinai, as his sister.

By now I felt I had been wrong in my misgivings about Joan marrying Tony Newley. She had settled down at last to a comfortable, stable private life and was happy, which made me happy too. She and Tony had brought two nice children into the world and Joan was proving a perfect mother.

However, I still could not bring myself to feel genuine warmth in my own relationship with Newley.

Once, when he came to London on business and Joan was in Los Angeles he stayed at the flat with me. When he saw the bedroom I was offering him, actually Joan's old room, he sniffed disdainfully. 'Um . . . so you're putting me into a little back room. It's rather dark in here.' Tony could have seen for himself that as our home at Harley House was a semi-basement flat we did not get much sun in any of the rooms.

Still, I tried to be as friendly as I could and invited him to come with me to a football match.

'Football match?' Tony frowned. 'Oh, no thank you. Not my kind of thing at all.'

Tony Newley was no ideal house guest. I don't know why he had objected to a dark bedroom, because he did not seem to care for the sun anyway. He would stay in his room during daylight hours with the curtains drawn, a habit I considered very weird. He was untidy too: he had an irritating way of coming out of the bathroom with his wet towels over his arms and dumping them all over the flat.

When I had party guests, instead of moving from one group to another Newley would retire to a corner and stay there, not talking to anyone. I consider this bad manners.

Tony's great friends, his collaborator Leslie Bricusse and his wife Yvonne, I found much jollier, more communicative people. You could have a laugh with them. Tony I considered a peculiar personality. There was not a bit of fun in him; he was withdrawn, an introvert who always seemed to be thinking deep thoughts. He would walk past visitors to my home without even greeting them, so preoccupied I don't suppose he even saw them.

Yet, despite his odd personal behaviour, I still appreciated Tony as a wonderful artiste and, even more important, he had a proper sense of responsibility towards his wife and children.

During his marriage to Joan the Newley-Bricusse song 'What Kind of Fool Am I?' from *Stop the World . . .* became one of the biggest hits of the decade. The Sammy Davis Jr version sold more than a million records and cabaret singers everywhere included it in their repertoire. Tony was pleased about all this not just for his own sake, but for the sake of Joan and their children too, for it would provide a continuing source of income.

Although Joan, occupied with rearing two young children, had slowed down on her acting commitments, Tony was always busy. After *Stop the World . . .*, he launched into another musical, *The Roar of the Greasepaint, the Smell of the Crowd*, and he made one film after another.

'I'm so wrapped up in my work it's a wonder my wife keeps her patience with me,' he admitted to me once. 'But she's strong and intelligent, and she's understanding.'

Then came ominous words, though to me not unexpected ones. 'I'm afraid, though, Joan is a much more sociable being than I am, so sometimes we clash.'

Soon after Newley's revealing words, he and Joan started work on a film he had co-written and was directing: *Can Hieronymus Merkins Ever Forget Mercy Humppe and Find True Happiness?* As this, I think, was supposed to be a comedy, I hoped it might give Joan a chance to show a facet of her talents which the film producers had neglected.

In 1958, teamed with the very likeable Hollywood couple Paul Newman and Joanne Woodward, who became Joan's good friends, she had made a film called *Rally Round the Flag, Boys* about the effect on an American community when a rocket site is built on their territory. In her role as a bright young thing tied to a dull husband Joan had shown such a subtle sense of fun I thought the powers-that-be in Hollywood would put her into more films in this light vein. However, the studio bosses continued to cast her in dramas.

When her film with Newley, *Can Heironymus . . .,* came out I was very disappointed. Like the title, I found it obscure rather than funny and it did nothing to advance Joan as a sophisticated comedienne. Not until years later did she get a chance to show she could make the public laugh, through the award-winning television commercials for the aperitif Cinzano, made with Leonard Rossiter.

The producer had intended to make a series of tele-ads teaming Rossiter with different actresses, and Joan was engaged originally only for the first of these commercials. However, the Collins-Rossiter double act worked so well she was booked for the whole lot.

Those ads, which usually ended with clumsy Rossiter spilling his drink on Joan, were in the best tradition of farce. The characters, the over-eager Mr Everyman played by Rossiter and the super-chic Melissa (Joan), were delightful. The disdainful lift to Joan's eyebrow conveyed more than a whole page of dialogue. As a stern critic of my daughter's work I was delighted with her performance.

These ads, of course, were in the future. Back in the late 'sixties during the filming of the clever-clever *Can Hieronymus . . .* I realized that Joan's marriage to Newley was no longer bringing her happiness. One of the pearls of philosophy he dropped indicated plainly how *he* felt.

'A married man is like a snail with a shell on his back. Wherever he goes he has to hump his wife and family and nannies with him.'

Joan did not confide in me, but I soon knew what was going on. Tony had found female interests elsewhere, and Joan was

Joan with her first husband,
Maxwell Reed, on their wedding day
in 1952.

Joan and second husband
Anthony Newley
on their wedding day.

Joan with Peter Holm, her present
husband.

Bringing 81st-birthday greetings to Joe
Collins – a stripogram girl.

Joe and some of the women in his life, in the
late 'sixties: left to right, new wife Irene, Joe's
sister Pauline Marks and daughter Joan.

Little Natasha Collins with the family 'treasure', Doris 'Dodo' Hugill.

Joan with her aunt, Joe's sister Lalla Godfrey.

Celebrating Joe's 80th birthday: back row, left to right, Ron Kass (Joan's husband at the time), Joe's wife Irene, Joan, Joan's son Sacha Newley, her daughter Tara Newley, Joe's sister Pauline Marks, Joe's son Bill Collins; front row, left to right, Bill Collins' wife Hazel, Jackie Collins' daughter Tracy Lerman, Joan's daughter Katy Kass, Joe and Natasha – Joe's youngest daughter.

Bring on the girls: pictured left to right, Joe's daughter Jackie, sister Pauline, daughter Joan and daughter-in-law Hazel.

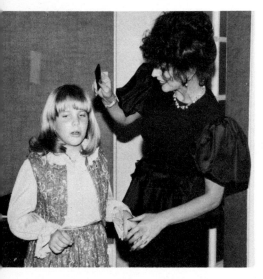

Joan with her daughter Katy Kass, aged ten.

Natasha's honorary grandmother Suttie (Mrs Vera Sutton) and her honorary uncle, singer Roger Whittaker.

Joan with her son Sacha Newley.

Joe with daughters Natasha (left) and Joan (right).

Jackie as a teenager, playing the bongo drums.

Joan Collins and
daughter Katy Kass
being presented to the
Queen and Prince
Philip at a charity
event.

Joe with daughter
Jackie.

Joe with daughter
Natasha.

Natasha Collins
recapturing the era of
her grandma Hettie
Collins.

Joe and his wife Irene on their way to a party.

Joan Collins, *Dynasty* siren.

back on the Hollywood party circuit again, no longer escorted by her husband.

When Joan and Newley announced they were ending their marriage it came as no surprise.

Newley made a public statement: 'Joanie and I are terribly conscious of what we've done and will probably spend the rest of our lives making sure the children go short of nothing in the way of respect and love.'

I approved his principles in expressing consideration for the children.

One evening, when we were sitting at the little bar just inside the entrance to the Harley House flat, I gently took Joan to task, saying she and Tony should have tried harder to make the marriage work.

'Daddy, it was impossible!' she replied. 'Tony and I could simply not have gone through the rest of our lives always suspecting each other of infidelity.'

There was nothing more I could say. Today I am still convinced that break-up was more Newley's fault than my daughter's. His reclusive temperament, his wandering eye for other girls, were more than she could handle.

Tony Newley and I never quarrelled or argued. There was never a cross word between us. We did not dislike each other; we simply did not particularly like each other. He never treated me as a friend, or as a father-in-law. Even so, to this day I still have my regrets that Joan and Tony ended their marriage, depriving two nice children of the joy of growing up in a secure family environment.

The second wedding of the 'sixties in the Collins family was my daughter Jackie's marriage, in 1966, to Oscar Lerman. I am pleased to say she made a fine choice, and they are enduringly happy together.

Oscar, an American from Philadelphia who was a few years older than Jackie, had come to Britain on a business trip and, feeling in tune with the ambience and energy of swinging 'sixties London, he stayed on. Jackie first met him in a discotheque, which turned out to be appropriate, as these noisy haunts have been second homes to both of them ever since. Discos are Oscar's chief business interest. In 1964 he opened the Ad Lib Club, where the young Princess Anne, not to mention show-business names like the Beatles, the Rolling Stones and Michael Caine, were among the patrons.

Oscar later had an interest in another club, Dolly's, again being patronized by highly paid young executives, advertising folk, models, photographers, star footballers and everyone who was anyone in the field of entertainment. Then, in 1969, Oscar and his partner Johnny Gold opened Tramp in Jermyn Street, their best-known club of all. Beatle Ringo Starr proposed to his first wife, Maureen Cox, at the Ad Lib and later courted his present wife, the actress Barbara Bach, at Tramp. No other disco anywhere can match Tramp's long reputation as an in-crowd playground. The name has become so famous that there is now a second Tramp, in Los Angeles.

From the start, I liked and respected Oscar. He is a reticent, stable, steady kind of man, very cool and calm, never bad-tempered. I would have preferred it if he had learned to share my passion for soccer matches, but as he's an American I excuse him! Instead we shared an interest in boxing matches.

Jackie and Oscar held their wedding ceremony in California, at Joan and Tony Newley's home. I wasn't there. I did not know the romance had developed as far as marriage until Jackie telephoned me on her wedding eve.

I was relieved that Jackie had not expected me to fly out to Los Angeles to give her away, because I don't like long flights, and she and Oscar were in any case due to return to London soon.

Jackie has taken on an astounding load of activities. She is incredibly well organized and competent. In the early days of her marriage to Oscar she was spending about five evenings a week at her husband's clubs, and at the same time caring for Tracy, her daughter by her first marriage, running her home to perfection and cooking excellent dinners for guests.

When Jackie and Oscar produced two sisters for Tracy – Tiffany in 1967 and Rory Samantha in 1969 – Jackie was always at home and on hand during her daughters' waking hours while continuing her disco-going at night.

Considering she had a full round of domestic activities as well as her club life I don't know how Jackie found time to write the novels which have made her internationally celebrated and probably more wealthy than Joan.

I have Oscar to thank for supporting Jackie in an area where Elsa and I, through lack of perception, had failed her. Oscar appreciated Jackie's urge to prove herself as a writer. Until she had a book published she would always be restless, starting to write a novel, then giving up because no one else cared. Oscar encouraged Jackie and had faith in her talent.

I remember a time when Jackie said she wanted to be a writer of children's books. So I was quite startled when, in 1968, she gave me a copy of her newly published first novel *The World Is Full of Married Men*. I settled down in bed that night and read the first few pages, about an advertising man cheating on his wife and having an affair with a nubile young model. Jackie's racy style was altogether too much for me. This was nothing like a children's book! I could read no further.

My reaction to all Jackie's subsequent books has been rather similar. When visitors to my home spot the signed copy of Jackie's latest book lying on our grand piano they have literally stood over me, cajoling me to read it, but I won't.

Jackie herself has learned to live with my attitude. At first she gave me her books with loving inscriptions, but when she came to realize I was not reading her novels the inscriptions changed.

On the flyleaf of *Lovehead*, the one about 'three exotic women with a common cause and vengeance in their hearts', so the blurb says, Jackie wrote, 'I know you won't read this one but it *is* a good book.'

With my copy of *Hollywood Wives* came the message 'To Irene and Daddy. Irene, for goodness' sake don't let him read this one.'

I have tried to analyse my resistance to Jackie's novels. I am not a prude: I'm thick-skinned and broad-minded and hard to shock. I am not put out when I see Joan on television in bed with some actor. So why don't I follow Jackie's work too?

Firstly, for me, reading any book is a chore. The second reason is more subtle. An author creates a more personal relationship with the reader than an entertainer creates with an individual person in the audience. I feel it distasteful for a father to read his daughter's descriptions of sex.

I prefer to think of my daughter Jackie in quite different terms. The Jackie I know is a straightforward, proper woman. Like that of her own mother, my first wife Elsa, Jackie's first priority is the welfare of her husband and children. She is a most protective mother. I cannot reconcile her own lifestyle with that portrayed in her books though, goodness knows, I don't need to be told that she is a gifted, imaginative storyteller, with a flair for titillating situations and dialogue, whose novels have given pleasure to millions.

Though I don't read Jackie's books I must say I have been intrigued to sit and watch her when she is gathering her material. At Oscar's club Tramp, I would join Jackie's table, just inside the door, where she sat like a queen holding court, listening to the chit-chat of the trendies. If Joan and Bill were also there with their friends, when I appeared there'd be a whole chorus of 'Hello, Daddy! Hello, Daddy!' – then they'd all go back to their previous conversations.

These new-style discos, I find, are no different in concept from the old nightclubs and bottle parties, my haunts of the 'thirties and 'forties. Their owners also seek to create an atmosphere of sensuality, intimacy and exclusivity.

I congratulate Oscar and his partner, Johnny Gold, on the professional way they have run Tramp, continuing to attract the smartest clientele, which is quite a feat, considering they have been going for so long.

Oscar has fitted into our family life very well. He and my son Bill, who have been business partners in a car-hire firm and also in an art gallery, are particularly good friends.

Jackie and Oscar complement each other ideally in personality and character. So long as they are in good health, I don't have any worries about the Lerman family.

The third marriage in the Collins family during the 'sixties was my own. My wife Irene and I had a register office ceremony on 26 January 1967, have lived happily since and been blessed by a wonderful daughter, Natasha Jane.

Unlike my eldest daughter Joan, I am no believer in astrology or the supernatural. However, it has to be significant that the day my beloved first wife Elsa died, 8 May 1962, was the very day Irene arrived in Britain from her native Germany to work in a show-business company.

Irene, 33 years younger than me, three years younger than my daughter Joan, is of a totally different background from my own. As a girl she knew so little about show business that when she wrote off for her first job in what was described as a theatrical agency she thought it was an agency selling theatre tickets. However, she caught up very quickly, and today Irene is the successful manager of top entertainer Roger Whittaker. I give her much credit for building him into a star.

Irene, a dainty blonde, was born Irene Korff in Essen, daughter of an engineer at the biggest coal mine in Germany. She had much more formal education than I did, going to school until she was 19, hoping to go on to university, but though her parents were prepared to back her if she studied medicine, law or teaching, when she confessed her ambition was journalism they refused. Still undecided about her future, Irene enrolled at a college to study foreign languages, a strategy which has proved most useful in her present work, for she has a better command of European languages than any other show-business agent in Britain.

As part of her English-language studies Irene first came to England as an *au pair* for a vicar's family in a rural parish in the Essex marshes. The vicar had an invalid wife and five children, so Irene's presence in the household was a boon, for she sewed dresses for the girls, knitted sweaters for the boys and, as the family seemed short of cash, bought food with the pocket money her father sent her.

Returning to Europe, Irene started her career, at last, in a job with a theatrical agency run, as it happened, by an Englishman, Allan Blackburn, who was booking acts to appear at the American bases in Germany.

Soon Irene was helping to engage big stars like Frank Sinatra, Sammy Davis Jr, Johnny Mathis, Guy Mitchell, Jerry Lee Lewis, all of them eager to go to Germany to entertain the American troops.

After a while Allan Blackburn decided to set up business in London, so Irene gladly came too. During her stay in Essex she had fallen in love with England.

I met Irene for the first time a few months after Elsa had died, when I called at Blackburn's office on business with my old chum, the entertainer Hal Monty.

Though Hal was married to a cousin of mine, Leah Levy, and had a steady girlfriend too of whom he was very fond, this irrepressible man still had an eye for other women. Hal immediately started chatting up Irene, as was his wont when confronted with a new, pretty face.

'How about coming to the Embassy Club tonight with Joe and me?'

I realized Irene was not wildly keen to accept Hal's invitation, but she did, basically because she was lonely: she knew very few people in London.

When we called for her that evening she had changed into a stunning dress made entirely of Paisley silk scarves, which showed off her slim figure.

'You look great!' Hal enthused.

I felt irritated with him, rushing in with a compliment I would like to have paid myself.

At the club we took a ringside seat and soon Hal led Irene on to the dance floor. Watching them, I felt embarrassed. Hal was giving Irene the big 'come-on', while she was attempting to rebuff him politely – a difficult process, considering the way he was clutching at her.

When they rejoined me at the table I kept quiet – and kept my distance. But after we had taken Irene back to her home I spoke up.

'What's the matter with you, Hal? Why did you start that heavy flirting? Couldn't you see she didn't like it?'

'Habit. Sheer habit.' Hal was unruffled. 'Anyway, what did *you* think of Irene?'

182

'She's a very nice girl. Very nice indeed. Very intelligent.'

I did not give much more thought to that outing with Irene. Elsa's death was still too fresh for me to think seriously about any other woman. I was living the life of a typical widower. In my line of business there are always plenty of girls around, and I was never short of female company, if I wanted it. But I did not want to get too close to anyone.

In November 1962, when my birthday came round, my first without Elsa, I felt desolate. Not wishing to spend that particular day alone with my memories, on impulse I telephoned Irene at her office.

'Do you remember me, Joe Collins?'

'Yes, of course. I've known your name for some time. When we book artistes through your agency I deal with the paperwork.'

I felt very bashful, but I asked her if she would spend the day with me.

Irene and I had a lovely day out together, my happiest of 1962. My housekeeper packed a picnic lunch and we motored down to Brighton. It happened to be the same day as the annual vintage car rally.

I found Irene's company very compatible. Apart from the normal human attraction, the fact that she was also in the agency business, and making a go of it, appealed to me too. We spoke the same language.

I stopped the car in a side road and produced a bottle of champagne from my lunch hamper.

'Today we're celebrating. It's my sixtieth birthday.'

'Don't be ridiculous – you're kidding! You can't possibly be 60. You look at least ten years younger.'

I don't know if Irene was just being tactful, but I was pleased to hear her compliment!

Despite those pleasant hours together that day, I felt it was still early days for me to start a new relationship. A full two years passed before I resumed my friendship with Irene, and we started going out together regularly.

Irene, meantime, had been building her career. She left Allan Blackburn's business, worked for a while as a booker in my organization at Chandos House, then joined Brian Epstein's staff, with the job of setting up European tours for his artistes.

This proved difficult, for the Europeans were not interested in the Epstein stable of talent, except for his Beatles. So instead Irene booked continental tours for other British attractions, including the Who, the Kinks and Shirley Bassey.

Though now settled in Britain, Irene was still uneasy about her future, the big worry being her relationship with me. 'I'm spending more time with you at Harley House than in my own flat, and I'm really not cut out to be a mistress,' she told me bluntly. 'I'd like to get married.'

'Do you mean marry *me*? How ridiculous! I'm too old for you. We got together because we were both lonely. But I feel you ought to meet someone else, someone younger. Surely you don't want to marry an old man?'

'Why not?'

'It's wrong. Believe me, I'm only concerned about *you*. I'm fed up with a succession of housekeepers, and I'd rather have *you* running my home. Actually, I'm in love with you. But marriage wouldn't be right.'

Many similar dialogues went on between us, until Irene's career forced a decision. We were dining at Antoine's, the smart fish restaurant in Charlotte Street, when she said something which made my blood run cold.

'Look, Joe. Herb Alpert, the band-leader, has offered me a job in America with his company, the second job in the US I've been offered in the past two weeks. If we don't get married I shall accept one of these offers.'

I didn't argue. I simply made up my mind very quickly. Two days later I telephoned Irene at the Epstein office in Argyll Street, near the London Palladium.

'Can you be available next Thursday at 11 am?'

'Sure, what do you want to discuss?'

I could tell from Irene's brisk tone of voice she thought I was suggesting a business appointment.

'I'll tell you what I want: we're going to get married. I've already fixed it with the registrar.'

Our wedding day was certainly not conventional. My son Bill

and Ziggy Winters, wife of comedian Bernie Winters, were witnesses at our marriage ceremony, and almost immediately afterwards Irene hurried back to the Epstein office while I returned to Harley House.

That evening my bride arrived on my doorstep, now *our* doorstep, with three bottles of champagne and another man. She introduced him as Jeff Patterson, an Australian show-business promoter.

Irene and I had a hasty confab in the kitchen. 'I had to ask him back here. I had an appointment to see him at the office this morning, and he just sat there waiting for me not knowing I was out getting married. I'm supposed to be fixing up with him about a Fats Domino tour and we haven't discussed the details yet.'

I don't recall any business being discussed that evening, but Jeff Patterson was in no hurry to leave: he stayed with my bride and me at Harley House, talking and drinking till 5 the next morning. Neither Irene nor I has ever seen him since!

Patterson apart, our wedding was altogether a very low-key event. Irene's widowed mother, Elizabeth Korff, had already voiced her objections to the match because of the difference in our ages. As for my own family, Bill had been very understanding, but I had hesitated to tell my good news to Jackie and Joan. I did not tell them anything until after the ceremony.

I don't think the girls were at all happy to hear I had got married. Their reaction was instinctive: they were so close to their late mother, they thought it wrong I should love anyone else. It took quite some time before their feelings towards Irene became as friendly as they are now, and so appreciative of everything she has done for me.

I am delighted to say that Joan, Jackie and Bill have asked me to put on record their feelings concerning Irene.

Jackie is their spokeswoman. 'You've got to say, Daddy, that we all think Irene is a fabulous lady.'

13

And Baby Makes Three

Soon after we married Irene and I had drinks with Joan and Anthony Newley, her husband of the time, at Dolly's, one of my son-in-law Oscar Lerman's clubs.

I decided to put Joan's mind at rest on a point I felt might be troubling her and my other children.

'I'm going to tell you, Joan, that Irene and I will not be having any children. You'll agree, I'm sure, that at my age' (I was then 64) 'it would be utterly ridiculous to contemplate such a thing.'

To my surprise Joan stared at me, shocked. She turned to Irene. 'Is that what you've *both* decided? Do you think Daddy is right? Don't you want to have a baby?'

'No, she doesn't!' I snapped before Irene could answer. 'We agreed before we got married there would be no children under any circumstances.'

'Well, that's not exactly the situation, is it Joe?' Irene spoke up, hesitantly. 'You made the decision for both of us. Actually, the truth is, if you should go and I am left, I would have liked a child to remember you by.'

'There you go! Daddy, you're being selfish,' Joan remonstrated. 'Irene, you *must* have a baby!'

'Joan, stop being so bloody stupid.' I began to get annoyed. 'Irene and I have made up our minds, so don't interfere!'

I thought that this was the end of the matter. Shortly afterwards Irene and I left for a delayed honeymoon in Scotland, seeing the beauty spots and rushing around the village shops buying kilts and tam-o'-shanters for my grandchildren – and we never mentioned the subject again.

Around the following Christmas it dawned on me that Irene, a most healthy woman, seemed to be off-colour.

One night she woke me up.

'What's the matter?' I asked, half asleep.

'I'm not feeling very well.'

'You'd better see a doctor in the morning.'

'There's nothing wrong with me. It's only that . . . Joe, I didn't want to tell you, but I'm four months pregnant.'

My instinctive reaction astounded me. I was elated and thrilled to bits by Irene's announcement. At the age of 65 it seemed a great idea to be adding a fourth child, a child by Irene, to my family.

'That's wonderful!' I cried. 'Let's get up and open some champagne.' Irene's smile, so happy, and so relieved, was something I'll remember always.

Joan, Jackie and Bill were delighted by our news. Jackie, whose second daughter, Tiffany, was now a year old, gave Irene all her own maternity clothes and some baby clothes, and went shopping with her for more things she would need. My grandchildren were tickled about having a baby aunt or uncle.

On 4 May 1968, my new daughter was born at the Welbeck Street Nursing Home. Seeing her for the first time took my mind back 35 years to my first glimpse of newborn Joan. My latest baby too was just a scraggy bit of skin and bone. But I was enthralled with her.

My three eldest children came round to see their sister.

'What are you going to call her?' Joan asked.

'Natasha Jane.'

'But I was going to call *my* next daughter Natasha,' said Joan, frowning. 'Now I'll have to think up some other Russian name.'

I thank God that Irene disregarded my 'no children' ruling and produced Natasha. Today she is a fine young woman and bringing her up has been a most delightful experience.

Though I have had many years' experience of engaging domestic staff it is a field in which I cannot claim unfailing proficiency. From the early days of marriage to my first wife Elsa we always had live-in help, and we seemed to have a way of always picking the least suitable applicants. They were either kleptomaniacs or nyphomaniacs, as Jackie phrased it, and they usually stayed no longer than a week.

Later, during my five years as a widower I was still making

mistakes. The one person to save the day was my 'daily', Mrs Doris 'Dodo' Hugill, who was introduced to me by my sister Pauline, for whom she worked a couple of days a week. Dodo was a gentle, quietly-spoken lady, a widow from Bury, Lancashire, whose husband had been killed in the Second World War shortly before their son was born. She was absolutely the tops working for me, then for Irene and me, providing the necessary continuity between housekeepers.

Dodo was part of the family. Though shy when meeting our friends, she had no silly inhibitions when we were alone. She would bring me a cup of tea while I was taking a bath and earn my gratitude by staying to wash my back!

Apart from Dodo, most of my domestic staff reduced me to despair. My first live-in housekeeper of my widower years was the very grand Mrs A. She was well known in all the local pubs, where she called herself 'Lady Collins' and was treated with the deference due to a titled woman. She was perfect in her job at the start of the day, but by the end of the evening she was usually completely drunk.

Eventually I got so fed up with having to assist Lady Collins to her room when she came home barely able to stand on her feet I decided she must leave my employ.

Now wary of the 'lady' type of housekeeper, I engaged Mrs B. She had been a cook in a South London works canteen, she had no fancy airs and graces and I thought she would suit me fine. Her gentleman friend, an army batman, became a part-time member of the household too, and when he was on leave he would clean my car, clean the silver and polish my shoes until they glistened.

Unfortunately, despite these obvious advantages, there was a big drawback. Though Mrs B.'s simple meals suited me fine when I was alone, she had no idea of sophisticated entertaining for company.

The first time I invited Irene to have dinner at home with me I gave Mrs B. my instructions. 'I've got a nice lady coming here and I want to impress her. I'll tell you the menu. We'll have asparagus to start with, followed by veal cutlets and a selection of vegetables.'

I had intended to woo Irene with a fine meal, creating an atmosphere of well-being and relaxation. Instead we were both uncomfortable, trying to stop ourselves from laughing.

First Mrs B. served the asparagus: she had cut off the heads and cooked only the stalks.

Then she brought the main course: two dinner plates piled so high the food would have spilled over had it not been glued together with lashings of thick gavy.

Under the gravy coating were roast potatoes, chipped potatoes, baked potatoes, boiled potatoes, cabbage, sprouts and carrots. As Irene and I tried to dig our way down to the veal cutlets at the bottom of our plates we spattered gravy all over the table.

I apologized to Irene. Thinking I might have hurt Mrs B.'s feelings when I remonstrated with her about not using serving dishes, I apologized to Mrs B. too.

Next time I invited Irene home to dinner I decided it had better be a simple meal. I went out myself, to Mossie Marks' shop off Petticoat Lane, and bought the best-quality smoked salmon.

All Mrs B. had to do was put it on a plate . . . or so I thought!

As Irene and I drank our pre-dinner cocktails we wondered about the strange smell coming from the kitchen.

'Mrs B. must be frying some kippers,' I speculated. I was wrong. Mrs B. was frying our smoked salmon!

Since Irene and I married she too has proved how easy it is to make mistakes when taking on domestic staff.

One housekeeper she engaged was a secret sherry-drinker. We found this out when the wardrobe in her bedroom collapsed under the weight of bottles. Her successor was a lady we thought very practical and sensible, until she confided in us that she'd taken the job while on the run from the Secret Service who, she claimed, were persecuting her. Finally she absconded from our home in the middle of the night, never to return. (We did check that she was safe, and the Secret Service had not caught up with her.)

Among my many mistakes, I do take credit for engaging someone who really was the perfect housekeeper, Mrs Vera

Sutton. She was a widow, and with time on her hands she was seeking a job she considered useful.

Mrs Sutton ran the home when Irene and I were first married. When our baby daughter Natasha was born, 'Suttie' became Natasha's nanny – more like her grandmother, really.

Suttie did not intend to stay with us indefinitely, but she agreed to stay until Natasha was at least five years old and ready for school.

We are very, very grateful to her. With Irene so busy building her protégé Roger Whittaker's career, I don't know how we could ever have coped without Suttie. Though now it is some years since she left us, she and her daughter Barbara and all her family are still our close friends.

If Suttie was Natasha's adopted grandmother, Roger Whittaker was her honorary uncle. In her early childhood, when Irene and I were becoming more and more involved with Roger, he and his wife Natalie lived in an Essex cottage miles from town, and as Roger frequently needed to be in London we invited him to stay with us at our flat. Our spare room virtually became 'Roger's room'. Natasha adored him. She would listen fascinated as he talked about his early life in Kenya and the animals there. Before coming to Britain he had had a spell as a teacher, so he knew how to make his stories interesting to a small girl.

Irene was first introduced to Roger in 1965, when she worked for Brian Epstein. Roger, then 29, recently married and fresh out of Bangor University with a B.Sc. degree, had abandoned the idea of an academic life and was starting to make records. Now he needed a good agent for live work.

Epstein's chief executive, the former band-leader Vic Lewis, suggested Irene should take him on. Actually, she had enough on her plate already, with Epstein's continental business and with me (we had started seeing each other regularly), but Irene has a kind heart, so she agreed to meet Roger and watch his act.

Though impressed, before committing herself she wanted my approval – and she asked me to come with her to see this new singer-composer at Quaglino's, the restaurant off Jermyn Street where he was appearing in cabaret.

My first impression was shock. Roger, tall and gangling, lolloped on to the stage carrying his guitar and wearing clothes which looked as though he had slept in them for a week.

'Call that talent?' I muttered to Irene. 'The fellow hasn't even cleaned his shoes.'

By the time Roger had taken his bow, however, I had changed my mind. With his fresh pink cheeks and beard giving him a slightly professorial look, Roger presented a picture of innocence and friendly charm I found very appealing. His repertoire could not be slotted into any of the usual categories. He was not strictly 'folk' or 'pop' or even conventional 'middle-of-the-road. He just chose a cross-section of pleasant songs, performed with great enthusiasm.

Irene started off with Roger in a modest way, booking cabaret dates for him on behalf of the Epstein organization. Then, two years later, in 1967, when Brian Epstein organized a team of British entrants for the big Song Festival in Knokke, Belgium, intended as a showcase for his pop group Gerry and the Pacemakers, Irene suggested Roger should join the team too. Roger resisted at first, for the logical reason that it would mean working for two weeks without pay. But Irene had more foresight. She perceived that this festival could open up the European market for his records.

She was right: it was the start of everything. Both the songs Roger performed in the festival, his own composition 'Mexican Whistler' and 'If I Were a Rich Man', which I had suggested he should do, were instant hits when the records were issued, topping the charts in France, Belgium and Holland.

Roger himself was so elated about Irene's judgement that when she and I got married and she left Brian Epstein's office, he asked her to continue as his manager on an independent basis.

This was something we had not anticipated, but, as usual, Irene did not want to let Roger down. 'I'll take him on, Joe . . . but only if you'll back me up!'

How could I refuse? I had already experienced for myself the thrill of building a star, and I knew how rarely an agent found such promising talent. I would have been very mean indeed not to support Irene in her opportunity. Besides, I too liked Roger and wanted to help.

No sooner had I given her my blessing when my diligent wife wrote to Roger's record company, EMI, urging them to take note of his value in the European market. Ignoring the lesser people involved, she addressed her letter to the head of the company, Sir Joseph Lockwood.

Sir Joseph was obviously impressed, for EMI gave Roger's next release, his composition 'Durham Town', its fullest exploitation, and in November 1969 this record became his first hit in Britain, staying in the charts for a full three months.

Though most of the credit for getting Roger established goes to Irene, when he was starting to make his mark it was I who saw to it that he was adequately paid. My wife and her 'discovery' were not experienced enough to demand the best fees. I conducted the financial negotiations, knowing just when the time was right to ask £500 a week for Roger's services, and when this could be increased to £1,000 a week.

I could assess his audience-pulling power in relation to that of the other artistes I was booking. For instance, during one particular week in 1972 I fixed a fee of £700 for the comedy partners Mike and Bernie Winters for just one night's cabaret at the Hilton Hotel in Park Lane; £2,500 for singer Frankie Vaughan for six evenings' cabaret at Ringmer, Sussex; and £1,750 for Roger Whittaker for a week in cabaret at Dunstable, Bedfordshire. Today each of Roger's *backing* musicians earns almost that sum in a week!

Knowing the importance of keeping an artiste's name constantly before the public, I also engaged a top publicity agent for Roger, Clifford Elson, whom I had first met when I was booking my variety shows and pantomimes into the ABC cinemas and Clifford was the publicity director for the circuit. Clifford is now publicist for a roster of names including Bob Hope, Engelbert Humperdink, Des O'Connor, Jim Davidson, Mike Yarwood, Paul Daniels and Russ Abbot. If there is any chance of getting an artiste's name featured in a newspaper, Clifford will arrange it!

*

In those earlier years, to give Irene a break I would sometimes go on the road with Roger myself, for an artiste can be vulnerable and needs skilled protection from mishaps which might befall him.

This I realized all too well when I went with him to Scarborough, the East Yorkshire seaside resort, and we stayed at an hotel where a large coach party had been booked in for a lunch stop.

When Roger and I came down for our meal these coach travellers were standing outside the dining room, waiting patiently for the lunch bell to ring. Roger and I, as 'regular' guests, simply walked past them into the empty room, heading for our window table.

An irate waiter intercepted us. 'We're not ready for you yet!' he cried rudely. 'Go back and wait with the others.'

I started to explain. 'No, waiter, we're not with the coach party. We're in Scarborough on business and we'd like to eat quickly as we haven't got much time.'

The waiter wasn't listening. 'Never mind about that! Just get out of here and wait outside!'

The man's tone was so impudent I could not contain myself. Instinctively I brandished my fists at him. The man stepped back, tripped and fell.

At this point the restaurant manager rushed up, apologizing profusely. 'I'm sorry, Mr Whittaker, sorry, Mr Collins . . . It's just a misunderstanding . . .'

Hearing the man's contrite tone, my anger evaporated instantly. By the time we were seated I was actually laughing . . . at Roger. For throughout this little altercation with the waiter Roger, though twice my size and half my age, had stood beside me, glaring fiercely into space, but not saying a word or making the slightest move.

Now Roger was grinning. 'Good job he didn't hit you! I'd have had to defend you.'

'Good job you didn't!' I retorted. 'That would have meant bad publicity in the press, and we'd both have suffered.'

This was one of those situations when a star must think very quickly. A star must always stay aloof and let his manager take

193

the rap. The public does not care if a manager gets into a fight, but if a star loses his temper, it can lead to a damaging newspaper story.

When Roger became well known I was astounded at how many of my friends were ambitious to be songwriters. They saw a golden chance, for if you write a major hit the royalties can go on ticking up throughout your lifetime. Roger always listened to these compositions which my friends, and strangers, too, offered us.

One of my mates, the comedian Cardew 'The Cad' Robinson has struck lucky. One Saturday afternoon, when we were watching a football match – Arsenal playing at Highbury – Cardew handed me a scrap of paper with a lyric he had written. Irene and I thought it good enough to show to Roger, who worked out some chords on his guitar to fit the words. When he gave his verdict – 'Yes, Joe, you're right, this song has potential' – I was as pleased as if I'd written it myself.

I feel really delighted for Cardew that this song, Roger's tune and Cardew's lyric 'The First Hello, the Last Goodbye', has been on several of Roger's albums and is one of his most requested songs, especially in the US.

By 1970 it was clear to all of us that Roger had potential to be a star not only in Britain and Europe but throughout the world. Soon Irene was helping to open up markets for him in Australasia and Canada. In 1975, when his record 'The Last Farewell' (with lyrics by an amateur composer, Birmingham silversmith Ron Webster) became his biggest international hit to date, and one of the most popular songs of the decade, he was soon a big name in the US too.

This expansion meant much travelling for Irene. For me, my wife's involvement with her artiste's career, particularly in the 'seventies when it was all starting to happen, meant my parental role reversed from what it used to be.

During my first marriage, when Joan, Jackie and Bill were growing up, I was the busy agent, often away from home, while Elsa stayed with the children. After my marriage to Irene, I became the parent always on hand. I enjoyed the experience. It was my pleasure to give Natasha the security she needed when her mother was in some distant country. I had Suttie for back-up, of course, and I knew that should some crisis occur Irene would catch the next plane home. Irene used to chide me that I was ruining Natasha's teeth by feeding her too many sweets, but that was her only complaint about my child-rearing.

Roger, who is also a family man, understood our situation. He treats me as a father figure, and we are good friends. Roger has many qualities I admire: a genial personality, terrific appeal as a versatile performer, and I also appreciate his ability as a siffleur (that's the music-hall term for 'whistler').

I'm very fond of Roger's lively, pretty wife, Natalie, a great character in her own right, a very positive person. As his former recording manager's secretary Natalie has known Roger right from the first time he set foot in a sound studio.

Natalie has a fascinating lineage. Her late father, Toby O'Brien, was a public relations officer to, among others, Sir Winston Churchill, and she is descended from Turlogh, King of Munster and Principal King of Ireland. The family tree, including Roger's and Natalie's names, appears in Debrett's *Illustrated Peerage and Baronetage*.

Today the Whittakers live in grand style. Their main home is a country mansion in the heart of Essex, where portraits of Natalie's titled forebears, the Inchiquins, grace the stately walls. Even the indoor swimming-pool is very grand and imposing, a tribute to Roger's Kenya background, with mosaic walls depicting elephants and other African wildlife. This pool building also has a clock tower, with a bell that strikes so loudly the villagers have complained about it.

The people of the neighbourhood are not too pleased either that their peace is disturbed by the unearthly screeching of Roger's two black tropical birds he keeps in his aviary and feeds on a diet of rotting bananas.

I don't mind Roger's exotic birds, but I detest his dogs. The Whittakers' four bulldogs are so fierce I'm scared to go near them. On the whole I'm fond of dogs, and we have a little schnauzer, Max, as a much-loved pet. I can spend literally all day just throwing balls or sticks for him to retrieve. But I could never bring myself to pat any of Roger's dogs – I value my hands too highly!

Natalie and Roger have five children, each arrival heralded with a caviar-and-champagne party. The birth I remember most clearly, however, was that of Alexander, their youngest son and youngest child, born in 1978.

The pregnant Natalie, nearing her time, was staying at my home while Roger was on a concert tour in Germany and Irene was in America.

'Come along, Joe,' Natalie said jovially one evening. 'Let's go out! I'll treat you to an oyster supper.'

No sooner had we arrived at the Trattoria Pescatori, in Soho, when I heard an urgent voice behind me. 'Quick, Joe, we've got to get out of here. The baby's coming!'

I drove Natalie back to our house to be met at the door by my daughter Natasha and the Whittaker's eldest daughter, Emily. The girls, both ten years old, turned deadly white at the very sight of us.

'My things are in my room and packed,' cried Natalie. 'Bring them out and let's get going.'

After rushing Natalie to the nursing home I telephoned Roger in Germany to inform him his wife was in labour. He was given the message while still on stage. Immediately after the show Roger, a qualified pilot, boarded his own plane back to Britain and while in flight the news was relayed to him by an air-traffic controller that Alexander had now arrived, six weeks earlier than expected.

As far as I am concerned, this is not the end of the story. Natalie has unfinished business: I am still waiting for her to buy me my oyster supper!

Obviously, the involvement with Roger's career has brought increased prosperity to the Collins family too. My wife Irene has become a first-class businesswoman, regarded in the industry as a very high-powered lady. She heads several companies centred on Roger: she is his manager, agent, music publisher and record company chief.

Behind her professional image, however, she is still the sweet girl I married, impeccable in all her dealings, very feminine, compassionate, sincere. Natasha and I are both very proud of her.

Though I had given up my big offices to run my business from home, in the late 'sixties and 'seventies I was still very occupied with artistes other than Roger Whittaker.

In the late 'sixties I tried to build the career of a pretty brunette teenager, Susan Shirley, whose parents kept a pub in Liverpool. As she had a first-class singing voice, I fixed her up with club dates and a recording contract.

Susan was not earning big money yet, so I arranged for a wealthy London hotelier I knew, Meir Gareh, to rent her a room at a specially low price. From this point my efforts to make Susan a star were thwarted. She married the wealthy hotel-owner instead.

She did make a few records though, including one called 'True Love and Apple Pie'. The composers, Roger Cook and Roger Greenaway, were so pleased with the tune they later rewrote the lyric as a commercial for Coca-Cola. Released as a single by the New Seekers group, that composition became 'I'd Like to Teach the World to Sing', a mid-'seventies world hit, selling six million copies. If Susan, in turn, felt thwarted by this twist of fate it doesn't show. Susan and Meir are very happy in their marriage.

My special protégés of my days working from Harley House were the North London brothers Mike and Bernie Winters, breezy comics in pure music-hall tradition.

These boys had an adoring father, a bookmaker, who suggested gags for their act and watched them on stage in every theatre where they appeared. When he died the double act broke up, as I had anticipated. It was only their mutual respect for their dad which had kept them working together for as long as they did.

The basic trouble was that, as in many double acts, one partner was more enthusiastic than the other. Bernie, the big-toothed, funny younger brother, was very keen indeed. He would always be in his dressing-room an hour before a show began, worrying about the performance and preparing himself, but Mike, the 'straight-man', would not turn up until the last minute.

Mike eventually confessed he was tired of show business and wanted to quit. He is now a businessman and author.

As Bernie was continuing his comedy career I remained his agent, and he 'replaced' Mike as a stage partner with Schnorbitz, a St Bernard dog. This great lumbering creature was owned 50 per cent by Irene and me and 50 per cent by Mike and his wife Ziggy. So when Bernie left my agency, we had a problem: how could we divide up Schnorbitz?

As this was a job none of us was prepared to tackle, we thought it would be kinder if Bernie and Ziggy were to keep the whole dog.

14

Public Confessions, Private Pain

My wife Irene was not the only member of my family whose career blossomed with the 'seventies. This was the era when my daughter Jackie came into her own in a very big way. Those endless hours when she had shut herself off from other people, scribbling away in solitude, were at last proving to have been time well spent.

Her novel *The World Is Full of Married Men* was made into a film starring Carroll Baker and Anthony Franciosa, and Jackie produced a further string of potboilers. Her second book was *Sunday Simmons and Charlie Brick* (now re-titled *Sinners*), about two handsome Hollywood hopefuls, but the most publicized of her earlier output was *The Stud*, the tale of a randy nightclub host and the bed-hopping wife of an Arab millionaire.

As usual, after reading a few pages of this novel I decided it was not my cup of tea. And, as usual, I had a minor argument about it with Jackie. 'Daddy, I've never written anything I'm ashamed of and won't have it when you say my books aren't decent. They only take the readers so far and leave them to imagine the rest for themselves.'

'What will you do if your little daughters find your books and read them?'

'*Find them*? They don't have to *find* them. My books are right there on the bookshelves with all the others, not hidden away, like *you* used to conceal books!' Jackie fired back at me. 'Daddy, my daughters are *proud* of me.'

I had my last word. 'Well, I wish you'd write under your married name instead of "Collins".'

Despite my personal reaction to her works, I did feel delighted when it was brought home to me that other people enjoyed them. It was gratifying to see her photograph on the dust covers and read her name in the bestseller lists.

When she appeared on television, to be interviewed no longer as an actress but as a celebrity, I was even more thrilled, for I realized that her years in show business had not been wasted: she had confidence when facing a camera and an audience.

In the mid-'seventies Jackie, Oscar and their children moved from their flat in Victoria, near Buckingham Palace, to a bigger residence, a house in Hamilton Terrace, St John's Wood, one of London's most exclusive streets.

Once you had walked past the two stone dogs guarding the front gate and up the steps into the house, there was evidence everywhere of the occupants. Oscar is a talented painter (a gift my granddaughter Rory has inherited too) and his works were on display. Other walls were lined with bookshelves housing Oscar's collection of art manuals, as well as the works of writers in the same genre as Jackie, such as Harold Robbins and Jacqueline Susann.

Jackie and Joan have both copied their mother Elsa's practice of putting photographs of family and close friends on display. In Jackie's house there were pictures everywhere.

Jackie soon had another face to add to her gallery – quite a decorative face at that – belonging to her latest brother-in-law, Ron Kass. Joan had meet Kass, an American about a year her junior, when her marriage to Anthony Newley crumbled at the end of the 'sixties and Kass's own marriage was also in its final phase.

When Joan introduced me to Ron Kass he gave an instant impression of the archetypal American executive. He was good-looking, fair-haired, clean-cut and immaculately tailored. His manner was affable and easy, and I thought at once he was a reliable sort of chap, with nothing fly-by-night about him.

When he talked of his education and business background I was bowled over, what with his University of California B.Sc. degree in business studies and his arts degree in music and his qualifications as a Certified Public Accountant. Reassuringly, Ron had been a professional trombone-player, too, with Herb Alpert's Tijuana Brass.

Even before he told me all these things, what I already knew about Ron was reference enough. He was head of the Beatles' company, Apple Records, a job which Paul McCartney had offered him personally when Ron was working in Britain as European vice president of Liberty Records.

I think Paul must have chosen him not just for his ability, but to give a bit of conventional polish to the Apple image. At the time Ron joined their company the Beatles were in their late 'sixties hippy phase, and their office building in Savile Row was always thronged with weird and colourful people. Ron remained aloof. His office, with its all-white decor and the latest Danish office furniture, offered a restful setting in which to conduct serious business.

Joan and Ron had not known each other long when an upheaval shook Apple. The American record industry whizzkid, Allen Klein, who had now fulfilled his ambition to become the Beatles' manager, instigated a purge within the company. Several able people lost their jobs, most notably Ron. However, it was widely known within the record world that Ron had done a good job at Apple, and he was soon snapped up by another firm.

Whenever Ron was offered some new appointment, it was always right at the top. By the time Joan and Ron were married – in the US at the start of the 'seventies – he was heading MGM Records, and he and my daughter were catching transatlantic planes like other people catch buses.

Joan and Ron were in America when they telephoned me with the news that Joan was pregnant, and they would be coming back home so she could have the baby in London. On Irene's recommendation, Joan booked into the Welbeck Street nursing home, where our daughter Natasha was born.

Joan's new child arrived on 20 June 1972, a month after her mother's 39th birthday. I was not surprised she had given birth to a second daughter, for in the Collins family the chances are four to one that any new baby will be a girl. But for Ron, whose previous marriage had brought him three fine sons, a daughter was a special delight. As Ron agreed with Joan's choice of a Russian name for her, they opted for Katyana, but we always call her Katy.

The arrival of her daughter Katy did not mean Joan took a

rest from work, as she had done when she was married to Newley and Tara and Sacha were babies. She could not allow herself such a luxury. For all his good jobs, Ron Kass was not in the same financial league as Newley, and besides, Joan's career as an actress was looking dodgy.

One day at my local Greek restaurant I heard a young girl whisper to her escort, 'Did you say that man over there is the father of Joan Collins? Isn't she the one who was married to Anthony Newley?'

I realized that, for the first time since she was 18, there were some young people who had never heard of Joan, or couldn't quite place her.

Joan was never actually short of work offers. She was kept very busy, and though in the past I had attended the premieres of all her films, now I could no longer keep up with her output.

Few were major movies. Her new line was what I called 'horror films', and though some of them, such as *Tales from the Crypt* which also starred Sir Ralph Richardson, were well reviewed, they were a type of film I was never keen to see for myself.

'We've go to admit it, Daddy,' my daughter said cheerfully, 'Joan Collins is not the name she used to be.'

'But do you have to make *horror* films?'

'Daddy, do you mind! They're psychological thrillers. And they pay the bills. I'm sorry you don't like them, but it could be worse. In one film they wanted me to wear a transparent swimsuit. I refused partly because I didn't want to embarrass you.'

'Look, Joan, that's nonsense,' I said. 'If the role's good and you're asked to strip off, then do it. I know it's part of the job.'

Joan, it seems, took me at my word. For in her next movie, *Alfie, Darling*, in which she played one of a string of women having affairs with the title character (played by rock musician Alan Price), Joan did go topless.

Horror films and *Alfie, Darling* apart, some of Joan's work around this time was of very high calibre. She proved her strength as an actress in some very demanding roles.

In the television version of Noel Coward's *Fallen Angels*,

produced by her husband Ron, Joan and Susannah York were teamed as sharp-tongued sophisticated ladies drooling over a Frenchman (Sacha Distel). I was proud too when Joan co-starred on television with Sir John Gielgud in *Neck*, one of Roald Dahl's *Tales of the Unexpected*. Joan played a domineering titled woman, Lady Turton, who flaunts her lovers in front of her husband (Michael Aldridge). Gielgud was the butler who helped the husband plot his revenge.

In the 'seventies one incident of Joan's career brought me personal disappointment. She was to have had the lead in a stage play about Marilyn Monroe, but unfortunately the plans were cancelled. During her early days in Hollywood Joan had known Monroe slightly, for both were signed to 20th Century-Fox. Joan, I feel, had a very good insight into Marilyn Monroe's mind and motivation, and given a blonde wig could have portrayed her very well.

In general, assessing Joan's career with a professional eye, I was optimistic about her future.

'You're starting to be recognized as a very good actress. So why don't you make the most of it and forget about being a film star?' I asked her.

'Daddy, I know that's what I ought to do, but unfortunately good actresses rarely earn film-star salaries. And you know I've grown used to the film-star lifestyle. I've lived expensively since I was 21 and it's hard to lower one's standards.'

I was still ruminating on Joan's future when in 1975 Ron Kass landed an excellent job based on Los Angeles, running a new film and television company he was to set up for Edgar Bronfman of the Seagram distilleries empire.

I was sorry to see the Kass family leave London. For a long time now all my children and grandchildren had been living near my own home. Joan and Ron's Katy, now a pretty, bubbly 3-year-old, was often brought round to play with her 8-year-old Aunt Natasha, who kept toys specially for her.

At the Kass family farewell party, held at Tramp, I had a sense of foreboding. Irene, my sister Pauline and I shared a table with Sam and Pat Ford, an American couple who were taking up residence in Joan and Ron's lovely old-fashioned townhouse (a legacy of his Apple days) in South Street, Mayfair, while Joan and Ron occupied the Fords' Los Angeles home. I had a feeling that Joan and Ron would not be coming back to South Street.

As I sat watching Joan's trendy friends plonking extravagant farewell kisses on her cheeks, I recalled another party at Tramp, five years previously. It was a swinging affair with everyone dressed up as cowboys and Indians, given by Jackie and Oscar to celebrate Joan's return to Britain from the US after her split from her second husband, Anthony Newley.

I confided my gloomy thoughts to Jackie. 'I hope next time you give a party here for Joan she won't come back in Britain again without a husband!'

'Don't be silly, Daddy. Can't you see from the way Joan and Ron look at each other that they adore each other? Everything will be just fine.'

Sadly, at least part of my pessimism about Joan and Ron's future in the US turned out to be justified, for they hardly seemed to be settled there when Ron lost his wonderful job with Bronfman. And Joan, while making guest appearances on high-rating television series, was certainly not regarded as a major Hollywood name.

I don't know what would have happened next but for the intervention of good old Jackie. It was my novelist daughter who stepped in and saved the day for her sister.

Rightly or wrongly, I have always considered Jackie the more self-sufficient of my two eldest daughters. She has always been independent, a bit of a rebel, a bit of a loner. In her adult life Jackie has never turned to me for guidance. Like me, though, she is intuitive and can tune in very quickly to what goes on concerning Joan.

Jackie knew, even before I did, exactly how things were going for Joan and Ron, and she had a solution at her fingertips in the form of her first filmscript, based on her book *The Stud*.

'I want it to be a vehicle for Joan,' she told me. 'It's the least I can do to repay her for helping me when I was in my teens and she brought me out to Hollywood.'

Joan toted Jackie's script around herself, and by 1977 they had set up a production deal for *The Stud* to be made by the British Brent-Walker company. Not only were my two daughters involved, but their husbands, Oscar and Ron, were producers.

Of course, I still had not got round to reading the book on which it was based, but as the film was such a family affair I knew I must go to see it.

By the time I took my seat at the London film premiere in 1978, I had a pretty good idea what I was in for, and I was determined to put on my best smile even during the bits intended to shock.

I managed to keep smiling even though, frankly, I found the film distasteful. The 'Stud' himself, played by Oliver Tobias, and the ready-lay Fontaine, played by Joan, were authentic types, and the action portrayed a lifestyle I know does exist in certain circles. But it was not my idea of entertainment.

Still, I knew the film would have impact, and would no doubt do well at the box office, so at the celebration party after the screening I felt quite jaunty. The guests pointed me out as something of a curiosity: father of two successful queens of erotica. In these liberated times, that's quite a status!

The film *The Stud*, as I had anticipated, became a huge hit, as did the video version and the album of the soundtrack music. But for my daughters and their co-producer husbands the venture did not work out well financially at first. They did not get a very good deal with either *The Stud* or its sequel *The Bitch*, also scripted by Jackie, until they took legal action in 1986. However, these films did provide Joan with the career boost she needed in the late 'seventies.

Many Hollywood people connected with casting the television series *Dynasty* have claimed credit for 'spotting' Joan, but I am convinced myself that it was her performance as the sex-hungry, money-fixated woman-of-the-world Fontaine which convinced producer Aaron Spelling that Joan could take on Alexis.

The *Dynasty* boom did not happen until a few years later. Back in 1978 Joan and Ron had no immediate prospects in the

US. Resettled in London, they bought a solid Georgian house with white porticos off Maida Vale, in a picturesque area known as Little Venice. Their front windows overlooked a peaceful stretch of water with a weeping willow tree, bridges and ducks.

They furnished this house at great expense, though in my view it was all too theatrical. Joan is still in love with the silver screen, which I suppose is why silver is her favourite colour for decorating a room.

As they were living near me again, I would often drop by. Ron, a most hospitable son-in-law, was always ready to jump up and make me a cup of tea. He made me feel at home.

For all this pleasantness, however, I knew something was amiss. The money to support their lifestyle was no longer coming in as it did when Joan was a film star and Ron headed record companies. Joan was seeking income from what, to me, seemed strange sources for her, like cutting a keep-fit record album and writing books.

In her growing-up years Joan loved reading books as much as Jackie did, but I had not envisaged that she too would want to be an author. One particular book Joan wrote has dogged me ever since it was published in 1978. Today, when I see a particularly sly look come across someone's face when they are speaking to me about Joan I can guess they are going to ask me about her latest marriage or about her autobiography, *Past Imperfect*.

I just wish people would leave me alone about it. I am tired of having to recite my standard answer, 'Haven't got around to reading it yet.'

Now I'll tell you the truth. I never *will* read that book, for I do have an idea of the contents, and I don't want to find out more about my daughter's affairs – nor do I want to read anything she has said about me. That book is not relevant to my love for my daughter, or to her love for me. I am convinced she wrote it for the one and only reason that she was short of money . . . *her* kind of money.

I do own a copy of the autobiography, which Joan sent me. She has written on the flyleaf, 'For Daddy, with whom it all began', and she enclosed a little letter: 'I actually wrote this book with a lot of love for you – however, sometimes it does not appear that way because I *have* tried to be honest about my feelings towards men in general – and after all you were the first man in my life. I hope you like it and I hope you understand me more. All my love, Joan.'

I appreciate the letter. I am not interested in the book. Joan has since confessed to me that she wished she hadn't written it, so that is enough.

Though her spicy confessions have made money for her, when it first appeared Joan began to panic that this book, and her sexy films, might permanently damage her image. I don't think, with hindsight, that she was right, but that was how she felt at the time and she wanted to back-pedal.

One evening, while dining at our home with Irene and me, she started recalling her earlier years, before she became so involved with movies.

'I'd like to do some stage acting again,' she said. 'It's about time I had a go at Shakespeare.'

'How about Lady Macbeth?' I suggested, quick as a flash. I was not familiar with Shakespeare's *Macbeth*; I only mentioned the role because Lady Macbeth's sleep-walking soliloquy is a favourite audition piece for aspiring young actresses, but my suggestion brought a sharp look from Joan.

'No, Daddy. That's a part I'm not right for. But I could play Kate in *Taming of the Shrew*. She's a nice, fiery lady.'

Joan did return to the stage, but her choice of play bewildered me. It was one I'd actually seen myself in the 'twenties, when I was working in Liverpool: *The Last of Mrs Cheyney* by Frederick Lonsdale. I had thought the play was all right in its day, but it seemed a quite outlandish vehicle for Joan. The play was to be revived at the prestigious Chichester Arts Festival theatre in Sussex, bringing Joan into the company of Britain's most respected stage actors.

As Chichester is a leisurely country town, with its theatre set in a park, Irene and I felt that going to see Joan in this play would be a holiday occasion. We drove to Chichester, with Natasha, for the first night and thoroughly enjoyed ourselves. As we waited in the foyer before the play began, I could not help but be amused that the kind of genteel ladies who had 'tut-tutted' over Joan's recent films and her autobiography had turned up in full force to see what she looked like in person.

Joan and Jackie had never been enthusiastic about my own favourite form of entertainment, the music hall; I suppose I did not encourage them enough when they were younger. Equally, I had never been able to arouse much interest in their particular entertainment taste, straight theatre.

All the same, though straight theatre is not my forte I am qualified to make valid judgements, and my judgement of *The Last of Mrs Cheyney* was not too favourable.

It had some charm, but it was not brilliant, and I still could not work out why anyone would have taken the trouble to revive it. Joan, her leading man Simon Williams (a star of the television series *Upstairs, Downstairs*) and the rest of the cast had slender material to work on.

The title character, played by Joan, while a social-climbing jewel thief, has impeccable morals where sex is concerned. Joan made her very demure. She was neither saucy nor provocative and she didn't reveal as much as a bare midriff. You could not associate Mrs Cheyney with Joan's recent lusty, self-flaunting performances.

The Last of Mrs Cheyney, all in all, made a harmless outing for the 'matinee audience', especially when the weather was warm enough for people to linger in the park afterwards, and I am sure Joan's presence contributed to the fact that this play was the biggest hit at Chichester since Sir John Gielgud had played there 19 years previously.

Despite this tribute to Joan's drawing power, I was still surprised when the co-production team of Larry Parnes, Duncan Weldon and Ron Kass set up a deal to transfer the play to the Cambridge theatre in the West End. I doubted if this old-fashioned piece would fare well in competition with other shows, and besides, the Cambridge was London's fifth-largest theatre, with 1300 seats – a lot of tickets to sell!

The producers had decided that for the West End the production needed some extra 'dressing-up', so Joan, with Ron and her daughter Tara Newley, left Paris, to meet the designer

Erté, who was to create a completely new stage wardrobe for her.

They had been in Paris only one day when on 10 August 1980 the tragedy happened. Katy, my youngest grandchild, only eight years old, was badly injured in a road accident.

Irene and I had been down to the coast for the day with Natasha. We did not hear about the accident for several hours after it happened. The first member of our family to be told the bad news was Bill.

Katy had been staying with a friend's family at Ascot, and the two little girls, who were out playing, chased across a country lane right into the path of an approaching car. What happened next was not the fault of the driver.

Katy's friend, Georgina, was hurt by the impact, but fortunately not severely. Katy, who got the worst of it, was almost killed. Thrown against the concrete curb, she suffered a fractured skull and was taken, unconscious, to hospital.

Bill had no idea where he could contact Joan and Ron. They had not left their Paris telephone number with any of the family. Methodically, Bill started phoning every major hotel in Paris until, at last, in the early hours of the following morning, he tracked them down.

When I spoke to Joan she was frantic. 'Daddy, we've got to get back to Katy and there isn't another plane for seven hours. Can you think of anything, please, Daddy?'

At that moment I thanked God that Roger Whittaker has a pilot's licence and owns an aeroplane. I rang Roger, who was asleep in bed. Again I had cause to be thankful: Roger, I knew, was always calm and quick-thinking whatever the crisis. He immediately promised to fly to Paris and fetch them.

After Roger had bought them back to London, Joan and Ron went straight to the Central Middlesex Hospital, where Katy was in intensive care. Then my daughter came home to me; ironically this was the first time Joan had spent a night with Irene and me at our beautiful new house in Regent's Park.

The next day plans were made. Ron and Joan, having resolved to stay by Katy's side throughout all their waking hours, were to be accommodated in a caravan in the hospital grounds.

I made daily visits to the hospital myself.

I asked the surgeon, Robin Illingworth, what her chances were. 'Sixty per cent chance of survival,' came the grim reply.

'And if she does survive, will she recover completely?'

Mr Illingworth could not answer.

For weeks Joan and Ron devoted themselves to striving for Katy's recovery, rarely leaving her bedside, rarely changing their clothes or even taking a bath.

In those days of tension I developed an enormous admiration for Ron.

He does not have the stamina of the Collins bloodline. Iron strength like ours is a very rare thing. I realized his struggle to pull Katy through was taking a great toll on him, emotionally and mentally. But he never wavered in his immediate objective of helping Katy's recovery. I admired Joan too in her single-mindedness. She talked to Katy for hours on end, hoping the sound of her voice would pull the little girl back to consciousness – a difficult thing to do, when you see your child lying in that state.

I too did my best, though I was continually fighting tears. That little figure covered in all kinds of tubes looked so still, so bloodless, so corpse-like.

Six weeks after the accident Joan and Ron gave me the wonderful news that Katy would make a complete recovery, though it would take many months.

Katy did recover, thanks to the impeccable medical care, her parents and her own strength of will. I feel that the effort of fighting for her life has left her a more subdued person than she used to be, but she is now medically and mentally well again.

15

Destined for *Dynasty*

Joan is a trouper. After Katy's accident she would have been justified in backing out of the West End *Last of Mrs Cheyney* production, but she didn't. When Katy was out of danger, the play opened in October 1980 and ran for four months. It was not a financial success, one of the casualties of a London theatre recession. It seemed to me quite the wrong move when Joan agreed to star in another play for one of the co-producers, Duncan Weldon and his company Triumph Productions.

The new project was a thriller, *Murder in Mind*, which was to tour the British provinces with the possibility of a West End run to follow. Before rehearsals started the Kass family went off for a holiday in Marbella, Spain, where Joan at one time owned a villa.

The day they returned Ron Kass telephoned me in a dreadful state.

'This is terrible! Joan's been offered a leading role in that American television series *Dynasty* – you know, it's one of those series about very rich people, like *Dallas*. But she can't take it. She's contracted to tour in that play for Triumph Productions. They won't agree to release her.'

I felt the blood rush to my face. I shouted, 'Do you want Joan to go round the provinces in some bloody stinking play that may not even draw audiences when she could be seen all over the world on television? You must be off your head!'

'But don't you understand, the situation is impossible!' Ron went on. 'Joan has offered to do two plays for Triumph as soon as her work on *Dynasty* ends, but they won't hear of it. We've even offered them money to let her go. Yet they're still threatening to sue us if she takes up the television offer.'

I cut Ron short. I just could not listen to him accepting defeat. I asked to speak to Joan. My instructions were brief. 'Now look here, Daughter. You get over to my place and we'll thrash this thing out. I know all about the situation you're in and I know how to deal with it! You *are* going into *Dynasty*, understand that!'

'All right, Daddy,' Joan said quietly. 'We'll come over right now.'

I put down the telephone. For the first time since she was 17 I was about to play a part in Joan's career. I knew that by getting into this expensively mounted American series Joan could be on the ladder again to where she wanted – and deserved – to be. Yet even I, in my optimism, could not have anticipated it would turn Joan from a star-on-the-slide to the most popular television personality in the world.

From the time Joan went up for her first film job I knew I could not run her career myself. Being primarily a man of the variety theatre, unfamiliar with the 'legit' side, I would not have made the right decisions. Yet in contractual matters, as Joan has always known, no show-business father could be better equipped than I to give sound advice to an actress daughter.

When Joan was offered her role in *Dynasty* I saw clearly that she could not legally be compelled to tour the British provinces in a play which might not even reach the West End when she could be starring in an American television series drawing millions of viewers.

I have had much experience of this type of situation. I am an ex-vice president and treasurer of the Theatrical Agents' Association (not to mention their most senior active member) and a member of the Council of Arbitration for theatre bodies. I have sat in judgement on many such cases of this kind.

I was aware that both the company producing *Murder in Mind* and the owners of the theatres where Joan had been scheduled to appear might well lose not just finance, but credibility for the future, if she broke her contract. The management's case, however, was weak because it still had plenty of time to find someone else to fill Joan's role, and it was open to question whether my daughter's name, at the time, would pull in larger audiences than that of some other good, well-known actress.

An arbitration panel would also give Joan's viewpoint sympathetic consideration. They would understand her wish to boost a flagging career, and the *Dynasty* series was a much better offer than the play.

However, the fact which I am sure would finally have settled judgement in favour of Joan was her wish to build up the health of her daughter Katy, for whom the warm California climate would be beneficial.

When my tearful daughter and her distressed husband arrived at our home in Regent's Park I sat them down side by side on the pink settee in our drawing room and asked them to tell me about it.

'Triumph Productions are being very tough,' Ron began. 'They say if Joan goes off to California and breaks her contract they'll make darned sure she never works in Britain again.'

'They say they've asked Equity to stop me working in the States.' Joan was crying. 'I've been told that if I go there I'm signing my own death warrant.'

'Well, stop worrying about all that,' I said firmly. 'Forget about being barred or banned or placating people. Just do what I say. Take Katy, get on a plane, fly out to America and start work on *Dynasty*. Katy will be better off in California, so you take her there – just go! Let the rest take its course.'

My daughter and son-in-law left our home that evening reassured and relieved. I had taken a load off their minds. But now, for the first time since Ron had told me about the *Dynasty* offer, I began to have doubts. Was I right to have interfered?

Irene had taken no part in the summit conference with Joan and Ron, for though she is a top-grade businesswoman, her good manners and tact had kept her silent while I was giving fatherly advice. But as Joan and Ron's footsteps faded away outside the house I asked her if I had said the right thing.

'Of course you did,' Irene responded instantly. 'No question of it!'

In the end, despite my counselling, Joan and Ron did make an out-of-court financial settlement concerning the broken contract for her theatre tour. I still think that had the case gone to arbitration this would not have been necessary.

A curious twist to this tale is that I myself was the original owner of Triumph Productions, but I had long ceased to operate the company and the present users of the title probably don't know it was ever used by me.

Before Joan went off to start work on *Dynasty* I was not very interested in that particular series. The only television soap opera I watch regularly is the British series *Crossroads*. I've followed the fortunes of the characters since it first started back in 1964, and I don't like to miss a single instalment, so on the three evenings a week it is screened I make a point of being at home: I don't want to wait to see it on video.

I like *Crossroads* because it is homely and true to life as I know it, which *Dynasty* is not. I am not attracted by the wealth on display, the fashion parades or the story lines of *Dynasty*.

Even though my daughter is now in the cast, I still don't watch *Dynasty* regularly, but I have to admit from the time Joan made her first entrance – I remember it was a courtroom scene, filmed in August 1981 – I realized that the character of Alexis suited her perfectly.

Once Joan was seen in *Dynasty*, and the series shot to the top of the American ratings, the producers must have been patting themselves on the back for having given her the role after Sophia Loren and Raquel Welch had turned it down. I don't think either of these women would have played it as well as Joan does.

Two American critics, quite early on, expressed what I was thinking better than I could express it myself: 'Joan Collins is the power plant which makes the show run. She gives it bite and much of its dramatic interest.' The second critic said: 'Alexis is the bitch goddess who is totally amoral and seems to enjoy every minute of it.'

It's a bit overwhelming, as Joan's father, to see her playing the outrageous Alexis, for though this character might seem to be a projection of Joan herself, it is a black, distorted projection.

Joan is intelligent, elegant, bold and ambitious, but she is not, like Alexis, vicious and devious by nature. Even when she has tried to be hard, for business reasons, she has not succeeded very well.

Joan does not seek personal power either, and I could not see her behind a desk heading a business empire. She is too traditionally feminine for that: she prefers some man to be in charge of her business affairs, even when her common-sense tells her she is smarter and more experienced than he is.

Joan's relationships with men have often left me astonished at her naiveté. She has never manipulated any man, nor played off one man against another. In this respect, Alexis would despise Joan as a stupid little ninny.

I shouldn't complain too much about the character Alexis. After all, Joan's portrayal of this vivid person brought her from the brink of being a 'has-been' to the most talked-about star in the world.

While Joan was back where she wanted to be, professionally, her husband Ron was in a pitiable state. He no longer had his old drive and confidence. He seemed to be going to pieces, incapable of making decisions or even handling domestic finances.

He and I still had a good relationship. When he came to Britain on business while Joan was filming her series in Los Angeles he stayed with Irene and me at Regent's Park. He would ask Irene to make him her special chicken soup, talk to Natasha about her school work and show concern for the rest of the family. Yet though he tried to give an impression that all was well, he had patently developed some peculiar ways.

Sometimes he would stay in his room nearly all day.

'I can't make Mr Kass's bed. He hasn't got up yet!' our housekeeper would report.

Sure enough, when I checked, Ron would be lying asleep with his unopened mail all over the bedclothes and the telephone on his chest: he had fallen asleep while making his through-the-night calls. I dreaded to think about the bills his calls were running up . . . or whether those piles of letters would ever be answered.

My son-in-law, once so slim, keen and able, was now overeating and overweight. Joan had never approved of people allowing themselves to run to fat, and I wondered whether she had taken him to task about it. Probably this was the least of their worries. I knew there were many tensions in the marriage caused by Ron's much-changed behaviour pattern.

I reached the conclusion that, but for their mutal love of Katy, Ron and Joan would have parted by now. As neither of them wanted to make any move which might prove a setback to their child so soon after her recovery from her accident, they were still trying to pretend all was well.

I was upset to see Ron in such a bad state. Irene and I talked over the problem but we were still unable to come up with constructive ideas to help him.

Soon there was to be another big event in our circle. As my 80th birthday approached – 3 November 1982 – Irene and Natasha started to plan a big celebration.

We knew that part of the family would be missing. Jackie and Oscar had sold their house in St John's Wood and with their younger daughters, Tiffany and Rory, had moved to Jackie's beloved California, where Oscar was to open another Tramp discotheque. As Jackie detests flying she only comes to Britain when she has vital business to attend, so it was unlikely that any Lerman except Tracy would be with me on my big day. But all my other loved ones would be there, to help me blow out the candles on my cake.

There was an extra dimension of excitement. Coinciding with my birthday and the release of her latest big-screen movie, *Nutcracker* (in which she played the head of a dubious ballet school), Joan was to be the subject of British television's *This Is Your Life*. We all kidded Joan into coming over from America for the programme by telling her it was to be a tribute to *me*.

It was a very odd experience. Everyone taking part in the show, including Joan's former headmistress at Francis Holland School, Miss Joslin, now in her nineties, was ready and waiting at the Thames Television Studios by the river at Teddington, Middlesex. Joan was to be driven straight to the studio from Heathrow Airport, as soon as she arrived from America.

Half an hour before the show was due to start, I took up my place with the presenter Eamonn Andrews in the street outside the studio, preparing to welcome my daughter and listening to radio messages informing us of her progress along the route from the airport.

When she was there at last, stepping out of her limousine, she came straight over to me and gave me a kiss. 'Happy birthday, Daddy. So this is your life.' The cameras came into position. We were on the air. 'No, Joan,' Eamonn announced. 'We've switched. This is not your daddy's programme. Joan Collins, this is *your* life!'

For just a second Joan looked startled. Then she beamed. From that point on she loved every minute of the programme.

As soon as the public appearance was over, we drove back to my home in Regent's Park for *my* tribute, my birthday party. Sharing this milestone with me were my sister Pauline, my son Bill and his new wife, the stunning model Hazel, Joan with Ron and her children Tara, Sacha and Katy, Jackie's eldest daughter Tracy, who lives in London, Roger and Natalie Whittaker and many, many good friends.

My youngest daughter Natasha had excelled herself. She had baked and iced a huge birthday cake all by herself, a great achievement for a 14-year-old.

Joan, as usual, was the most fashionably dressed woman in the gathering, in her glittery outfit of black chiffon and sequins, pearls round her neck and a cute little hat. The birthday gift she and Ron brought me was a bottle of Cartier cologne in a smart container. (I have kept this present ever since to show off to visitors, but to this day I have never actually used any of the cologne.)

At the party everyone who could pick out a tune with one finger had a shot at playing 'Happy Birthday to You' on our grand piano. Everyone had brought their cameras. Ron and Irene clicked away recording everything and capturing some very good shots, which was as well, as the professional photographer we had engaged later had his camera and film stolen from his car.

Someone dared to ask Joan and Ron about press reports that their marriage was on the rocks.

'Absolute bunkum!' Joan smiled. 'We're a very happy family.'

'These rumours are so cruel. We're very upset about the stupid things people say,' Ron insisted.

I hoped the Kasses would weather the storm. That year Joan and Ron spent Christmas with their children at their London house in Little Venice. Joan cooked the Christmas dinner herself. She burned her hand when taking the turkey out of the oven, but I gave her full marks for effort.

Then, early in 1983, the charade was over. Ron and Joan parted. When it happened no one was surprised.

Looking back on Joan's third marriage, I have to say I have no personal grievance against Ron Kass. He was not a bad fellow. Though all the eleven years he was Joan's husband he was an attentive son-in-law and fitted in well with all the family. He is still an adoring father to Katy. I am only sorry that things went so wrong for him . . . and for him and my daughter.

Once again Joan's private life was causing me anxiety. I could now see a pattern: Joan never seemed to find her match. She always had more strength, more resilience than any of the husbands she chose. After the break-up with Ron, I told her, as I had been doing for years, that she ought to show a bit of sense and find a husband who could look after her. But, of course, it was superfluous for me to tell someone as mature and successful as my daughter about how she should run her life. It is part of her pattern that she works hard, she can take knocks which might shatter other people, and at the end of it all she still has the vigour to enjoy herself.

Whenever I think of it, it still strikes me as an amazing twist of fate that Joan got a part in *Dynasty* and went on to new pinnacles professionally. This just goes to show how your luck can change if you get the right break.

During 1984 she was so busy I did not see a lot of Joan, but she did come home to London for Christmas and on Christmas Day she entertained my sister Pauline, Bill and Hazel, Irene, Natasha and me, as well as her children and some friends, to a festive dinner at Claridge's Hotel. She was full of *joie de vivre* and sparkling away like a teenager. She hasn't changed.

I was not very happy to see her paying a bill of £500 for the meal. I don't approve of such extravagance. So I guess I haven't changed either.

Since she went into *Dynasty* Joan has been presented to the Queen and Prince Philip several times, and on one royal occasion my granddaughter Katy had the honour of presenting Her Majesty with a bouquet.

Actually, though, one of my biggest personal thrills since my daughter achieved her present status came in July 1985, when I attended the unveiling of her model for Madame Tussaud's waxworks – just down the road from Harley House, our old family home.

That summer I braved the queues round Madame Tussaud's and went to take another look at the wax figure of Joan. It was a sentimental occasion, for I recalled the time I had taken Joan and Jackie on an outing to Madame Tussaud's when they were children.

'It's very boring here!' Joan had complained. 'They haven't got enough film stars.'

None of us could have dreamed that Joan herself would help repair this omission.

My daughter Jackie's path has been much smoother than Joan's. She is settled in her marriage to Oscar and has her family well organized. She's a great wife, great mother, great cook . . . a strong, matriarchal woman. In her career as a novelist, Jackie has gone from strength to strength. Her sales figures are staggering: I did not know there were so many people in the world who actually bought books. Even non-readers are familiar with her tales, for most of them have been filmed, either for the big screen or for television.

I sometimes re-run the video she sent me of the television mini-series *Hollywood Wives*, based on her bestseller. I like to watch it for the lovely ladies in it, all expensively dressed and undressed: Candice Bergen, Angie Dickinson, Stefanie Powers, Mary Crosby, to name but a few. Even though I don't pay much attention to the dialogue and the plot, I enjoy the scenery!

I'd still rather watch Jackie herself interviewed on television than see the films of her books, for she's a great talker, and always has something fresh to say. My daughter Jackie is an interesting personality.

'Daddy, you know I'm not in this for the money,' Jackie has assured me. 'I've been writing since I was a child and it is now my way of life. I'll go on writing till I'm 95!'

'Well, perhaps by that time you'll have written some book which *I* might enjoy,' I retort.

I have to say that with Joan and Jackie in the newspapers every day it's costing me a small fortune in postage, for I cut out all the stories about them, whether large or small, and send off a package to each of them every week. They, in turn, send me cuttings about themselves from the American papers.

I think it amuses them both that I read about my daughters even more avidly than I read the football results!

My 83rd birthday, 3 November 1985, was celebrated quietly: Irene, Natasha and I had dinner at our home with my sister Pauline, my son Bill and daughter-in-law Hazel.

During the evening Jackie telephoned from California and I also spoke to Oscar and the girls. But not a word from Joan. She did not call up till two days later. She was speaking from her studio dressing-room. After belatedly wishing me happy birthday, she then went on chattering at length, telling me she had been invited to switch on the Christmas illuminations in Regent Street (an honour usually reserved for royalty), that she was due to take part in the annual Royal Variety Performance and was going to record an appearance on Des O'Connor's television show. She talked for so long I had a feeling there was something else on her mind she wanted to say. But she never came to the point and our conversation ended abruptly when she was called back to the *Dynasty* set.

Two days later I answered a telephone call from a *Daily Mail* reporter. 'We've been told that Joan and Peter Holm got married last night in Las Vegas. Can you confirm that this is true?'

'I'm sorry, I can't. I don't know anything about it,' I answered truthfully.

I telephoned Bill. I telephoned Pauline. Neither of them had heard anything. I was beginning to think the wedding story was just a rumour when the *Daily Express* rang up with the same story. Within the next hour every newspaper in the country was trying to get through to me.

Still wondering what had happened, but by now pretty sure the marriage must have taken place, I continued as usual with my regular Thursday routine. I went to the post office to collect my pension, took Max for a walk and on the way back home stopped at a café for a cup of tea and some chocolate cake.

By the time I arrived back home it was late afternoon, and I knew that on the American west coast it would now be morning: people would be starting their day.

At 8 am Los Angeles time Irene answered the telephone again: a person-to-person call for me. The caller was Joan.

'Daddy, I've got some news for you. Peter and I were married last night. We kept it a secret.'

'Yes, I've heard about it . . . the newspapers have been on to me. Congratulations. I wish you every happiness.'

Joan told me briefly about the wedding, we arranged she would now telephone her Auntie Pauline and brother Bill, to tell them the news personally, and we would meet in London in a couple of weeks' time.

So Joan had entered on her fourth marriage. At this stage her Swedish-born husband Peter Holm is virtually a stranger to me. Though I have met him a few times now, I have not yet had the chance of a serious talk with him. I don't suppose this matters so long as he continues to make my daughter happy.

16

The Past Revisited

With Natasha, my youngest daughter, I have been a very attentive father. I've spent my whole life with her since she was born. By the time she arrived, in 1968, I had cut down on my outside commitments and was working from my home: her nursery was within shouting distance of the room I used as an office and I saw her even during business hours.

In the 35 years between the births of my eldest child and my youngest ideas about rearing children have changed. Trying to be a modern parent, I have a more open, easy-going relationship with Natasha than I had with the children of my first marriage when they were growing up.

My basic character hasn't changed. There are times when I shout at Natasha as I shouted at my other children. When very roused I still throw crockery. None of the Collins family bottle up wrath, and giving voluble vent to rage is a family trait. However, my standards are undoubtedly not as strict as they used to be.

Joan, Jackie and Bill were brought up by Elsa and me to be obedient. One word from me, and they did as they were told! But Natasha, typical of her generation, just gives me a silly smile which cuts me short when I try to dictate to her or, even worse, she shouts back at me.

One day, when Jackie was visiting us, I remonstrated with Natasha over some minor misdemeanour and my youngest daughter gave me a cheeky back-answer. Jackie went pale with apprehension, anticipating I would hit the roof. Instead, I simply grinned.

'You wouldn't have dared talk to me like that, would you, Jackie? But Natasha's grown so big I can't argue with her any more.'

My daughter, the writer of sizzling bestsellers, was shocked.

'I was a tall child too, Daddy,' she reminded me. 'But I still would not have dared talk back to you. I can't get over how you've mellowed.'

Once when Joan was visiting us, Natasha, then 14, in honour of her glamorous sister came downstairs with make-up on her face. It was the first time she'd used cosmetics and she wasn't very skilled, but knowing she'd made an effort to look nice I did not want to discourage her.

'You look lovely, dear . . . but it's only for this evening, isn't it?'

Joan was astounded. 'Is that all you've got to say, Daddy?' she cried. 'The first time *I* put make-up on I was older than Natasha, and you went into an absolute fury! You yelled at me to go and wash it off!'

Analysing this change of reaction, I realize I have discarded the idea, prevalent in my youth, that when a young girl puts make-up on her face she's doing it to make boys notice her and goodness knows what nasty things will happen when they do! I had shouted at Joan and Jackie because I could not handle this sign that they were growing up, and could not express what was really on my mind.

When I knew that my daughters had started going out on dates – a time came when I couldn't stop them – I would say darkly, 'Don't you ever do anything you might regret', but an open discussion would have been taboo. I simply hoped that they knew what I was referring to.

My first wife, Elsa, also grew up in the early part of the century when 'nice' people did not talk about sex to their children, even in clinical terms. I still recall my embarrassment when Joan as a child asked me innocently to tell her the 'facts of life'. I don't think at that stage she even knew the meaning of the phrase, or she would have asked her mother, not me. I was so confused I could only blurt out, 'The facts of life? Well, they're to do with the difference between you and little Georgie.' (Georgie was the son of Elsa's sister Renee.)

I don't know what conclusion Joan drew from that.

Irene, Natasha's mother, belongs to a different, more enlightened generation. She has answered all Natasha's questions concerning human reproduction, and as a result, knowing how

223

sensible she is about it all, I have never been scared about Natasha losing her head over a boy. She's as vulnerable about falling in love as any normal girl should be, she does have boyfriends, but she's not boy-crazy.

Joan and Jackie, now rearing daughters of their own, have been influenced by my earlier attitudes and those of Elsa, for they are surprised that since Natasha was 16 Irene and I have allowed her to go to discotheques – or anywhere she wants to go. We give her her freedom knowing she has a level head on her shoulders and we trust her completely.

Natasha has found pet causes to support, managing a school tuckshop in aid of Cancer Research, running a bring-and-buy sale for the World Wildlife Fund and doing done innumerable sponsored walks, and as a natural organizer has involved all her friends too in her fund-raising activities.

Natasha has grown up in a world of easy travel. At the age of six she flew unaccompanied to Ireland to stay with her honorary grandmother, Suttie, and at 12 she flew the Atlantic on Concorde to join Irene in the US, all without any of the fuss which happened when Joan and Jackie made their first flights to America.

Natasha was six years old when she got her first stage role, playing a goat in a biblical epic, *Noah's Ark*, at her local state primary school. Obviously her acting talent was recognized, for when she was ten her teacher gave her the title role in a simplified version of Shakespeare's *Hamlet*.

Since then, after she went on to Francis Holland, an all-girls' school, Natasha has never played a woman on stage. Despite a good figure, a pretty face and long, beautiful legs, she is also 5 feet 8 inches tall. Being taller than most of her contemporaries, this means in school productions she must always play a boy.

When she was younger, and doing well in her drama and ballet classes, I took it as a matter of course that Natasha would come into show business. I thought if she did not become an actress she would be a dancer, for she and Emily Whittaker, Roger and Natalie's eldest daughter, put on concerts for the family devising some terrific dance routines.

But when she was 15 years old Natasha told me quite firmly, 'Daddy, I will never make this my profession. I wouldn't be a performer for all the tea in China! I might *fancy* myself as a star, but it's just a fantasy. I've no intention of trying to make it reality.

'I've already learned enough about what goes on, and it's too difficult. I don't want to go through life always worrying about things like having the right image, and what my next job will be, and whether I'm getting too much publicity or not enough.'

I appreciated Natasha's opinion. I didn't argue.

Though they have been brought up differently in other ways, I have made sure that certain special skills should be passed down through the generations of the Collins family.

They are very special skills. I have taught all my children how to put a piece of string through horse chestnuts to use as 'conkers'. I've taught them card tricks. Thanks to me, each of them knows that the correct way to fillet a piece of fish is to remove the tail first. That's a tip handed down from our fishmonger forebears!

Each of my children knows my favourite music-hall songs which I learned in my youth. We make a great cats' chorus singing 'When Father Papered the Parlour', 'Let's All Go Down the Strand' and 'It's the Wrong Way to Tickle Mary' (which is my own special version of 'It's a Long Way to Tipperary').

I've insisted that each of my children learn to make pots of tea correctly. I overheard Natasha, when she was not yet ten years old, arguing with Jackie's daughter Tiffany about this vital matter. Tiffany had put tea bags into the cups with the milk and sugar and was about to pour in hot water.

'Didn't your mother tell you you must always make the tea in a pot and take the pot to the kettle, not the kettle to the pot?' remonstrated Natasha.

This incident made me aware for the first time that Natasha has a bossy streak in her nature, which was confirmed two years later when she started taking horse-riding lessons with Joan's 8-year-old daughter Katy Kass and 9-year-old Jade Jagger,

225

daughter of Mick and Bianca Jagger. Natasha would stand no nonsense from either of the two little girls. Though these children were usually self-assured, they were wary and obedient when Natasha was in charge.

Natasha's childish bossiness has now developed into a real gift for commanding obedience. She is a born leader and also has the team spirit. Unlike her older sisters, she is keen on sports and has captained the school hockey team. She is also of a more studious nature than my other children.

Once Natasha leaves Francis Holland School, in summer 1986, she hopes to go on to university to study history and politics. Then, if all goes well, she will train for the army at the Royal Military College at Sandhurst, the world's most famous military academy. She has already passed the demanding officer selection tests. My Natasha, I hope, will be an officer and a lady!

Natasha had considered other careers before she finally fixed on the army. She had contemplated becoming a doctor, or a journalist. Then, after attending a lecture on the army, she started taking a serious interest. As Irene and I, and my son Bill, had seen her reading the appropriate literature, Natasha's final decision to join the army came as no surprise to us. But when my older daughters came to visit from America and heard about her plans their reactions were hilarious to behold.

When Natasha told them she was going to 'join up', Joan seemed to be struck speechless. She sat gasping just one word, 'Why?'

As the Harts, Assenheims and Collins have all been either 'theatricals' or in some branch of commerce, when one of us chooses some other career it is bound to be a shock. We still haven't got over the fact that Jackie is a novelist, though this should not have seemed so odd because my father Will Collins wrote for *The Encore*, the theatrical newspaper, in his South Africa years.

But the army as a career . . . that was something else again!

When Natasha went off for her first army selection tests this was so totally outside my scope there was only one comment I could make: 'I hope their latrines have improved since *I* was in the Officers' Training Corps and you don't have to squat on a pole across a ditch!'

Actually, when she returned home I was pleased to learn that I had been of some help after all. I had taught my children the finer points of behaviour at table, and Natasha was able to satisfy the examiners that she knew the correct way to pass the port after dinner. (You pass it from the right to the left, sliding it along the table so that the sediment in the decanter or bottle is not disturbed.)

Now that we are all used to the idea that Natasha is joining the army, all the Collins family are jubilant that she has been accepted for Sandhurst, for it was only in 1984 that it opened its doors to Women's Royal Army Corps cadets, for the first time in its 162-year history.

I have to admit I was not sorry to learn that it is British army policy that girl soldiers, despite their gruelling assault-course training, will not be armed or go into combat units. They do other useful jobs.

Natasha, I feel, would be excellent in their public relations field. When she has talked on television about her army ambitions she has given a charming yet authoritative impression for one so young. I suddenly realized as I watched her that she is a woman.

Natasha has coped very well with having two celebrated sisters. 'Sometimes it's a nuisance, being in the spotlight because of someone else's achievements,' she has said. 'I feel uncomfortable when people start asking me questions about Joan and Jackie. But like you, Daddy, I'm getting used to handling it.' I am pleased to say, however, that Natasha has not allowed this reflected fame to swamp her own identity.

Only once do I remember Natasha using the names of her elder sisters to gain advantage. This was when she was 12 years old and wrote a fan letter to Lewis Collins (no relation), star of the television series *The Professionals*.

Natasha explained to her mother and me, 'I wrote that they were my sisters because I was asking Mr Collins for two autographed photographs, and he might have thought I was a bit cheeky.'

I would like to think that my youngest daughter may one day end up on the management side of show business, or on the recording side, for she knows so much about it through Irene and me. Meantime she always keeps in front of her a card sent by Joan with a message she knows well: 'ALL THE WORLD'S A STAGE . . . ONLY SOME OF US JUST GET BETTER PARTS!'

I am sure Natasha's role will be a leading one. She is already, very positively, her own woman.

It is now nearly a hundred years since my parents started the Collins line of show-business folk. My sisters and I continued the tradition and so did my daughters. Now I have to accept that some of my descendants have chosen other fields.

Apart from Bill and Natasha, my only grandson, Joan's son Sacha Newley, aspires to be a writer, and so does Joan's younger daughter Katy Kass. I don't know yet which way Jackie's daughters Tiffany and Rory are heading, for they are still studying.

However, Jackie's eldest daughter Tracy is a make-up artist and Joan's eldest daughter Tara is involved in video production, so it looks as though the family trade will not be totally abandoned.

My grandchildren, even my own children, are light years away from the East End background of their forebears. I don't think any of my offspring have ever set foot in that colourful section of the City of London whence the Collins dynasty sprang. Recently, trying to re-cap on family history, I went back to the East End. It was hard trying to find the old landmarks.

The place I knew best, the St James' Tavern in Creechurch Lane which I ran with my mother, is now the site of a hamburger business. No. 101 Middlesex Street, where my fishmonger great-grandfather Zalig Hart lived before moving to West London, has now been swallowed up by a huge marble-fronted office complex. The place where my mother spent her childhood, the dwellings in Stoney Lane that we called 'the buildings', no longer exists. The whole lane is occupied mainly by a block of flats.

The only landmark remaining is the Three Tuns pub, now

refurbished, but the house in Three Tuns Alley behind it – my grandmother Julia Phillips' home before her marriage to grandfather Zuesman Hart – has been demolished.

I once had dozens of cousins on my mother's side of the family who kept shops in Middlesex Street, the old Petticoat Lane, and the adjoining Wentworth Street. The Assenheims were pillars of local commerce, selling groceries, delicatessen items, green groceries and ice cream. These market streets where they traded are still the liveliest, and most colourful, in London, if not the entire world, with customers of every race. But my own relatives put up their shutters long ago.

Though I never had a Cockney accent, I am familiar enough with East Enders to join in their special Petticoat Lane brand of friendly patter. I am not regarded as a stranger in these streets.

On this nostalgic trip of mine I went up to an elderly shopkeeper, standing outside his clothing store.

'Seen any of the Assenheims, the hokey-pokey family, around here lately?' I asked casually.

The man stared. 'Seen any Assenheims?' he echoed. 'Not for about 40 years!'

The man (I saw from the sign above his shop that his name was Mo) tried to be helpful. 'Come to think of it, I did meet one of the Assenheim grandchildren quite recently, at Brighton Races,' he volunteered. 'That was Mickie Stewart, son of one of the Assenheim daughters. Mickie's always at the races. He's a tick-tack man' (a bookmaker's signalman).

'Yes, I know Mickie. He's my cousin.'

Mo stared at me again. 'Don't I recognize you? Aren't you Joe Collins, the Assenheim grandson who became a theatrical agent?'

'Yes, that's me.'

'Cor . . .' Mo sounded impressed. He shouted to a man who was passing by, wheeling a rail of clothing.

' 'Ere, Alf! Come over 'ere, there's someone I want you to meet! This is Joe Collins. He's one of the Assenheims. Remember them, don't you – the hokey-pokey family?'

Alf stopped in his tracks and nodded politely in my direction. '*You know who he is!*' Mo shouted again. 'He's the theatrical agent

. . . the father of Joan and Jackie Collins.'

Now Alf was really interested. He wheeled his rail to where we were standing. A second acquaintance of Mo who happened to be passing and had overheard our conversation also joined our group. They all began pressing me for family news.

'Are you still working?' 'Are your family religious?' (East Enders like to know these things!) 'Who did you marry?' 'Have you any other children, apart from Joan and Jackie?'

I told them about my first wife, Elsa; about my present wife, Irene; about Bill and Natasha.

'That youngest daughter of yours – is she a cracker like her sisters?' Mo wanted to know. 'Is she going into show business too?'

'She's a good-looking girl,' I answered, 'but she's not coming into show business. She's decided on the Kate Carney' (Cockney rhyming slang for army).

'I must say, Joe,' Mo reflected, 'your two older girls have done very well. Got right to the top, as you might say.'

Mo broke off to speak to a man who was examining a jacket in his shop window. 'Go right into the shop! They'll attend to you in there. I'll help you with the price and if you've got no money I'll give it to you!'

Mo turned back to me with a wink. 'Down 'ere that's how you talk to the customers. You got to know the right verbals!'

Then Mo said something which startled me. 'I knew your daughter Joan's first husband, Maxwell Reed. Used to meet him up the West End. Reed was a wrong 'un. See Joan's got another husband now. Hope it works out for her. Looks like I missed my chance!'

I continued my stroll around the East End, trying to reconstruct the chain of events which had taken my family so far from this part of London. Whenever I begin on this train of thought, I always start thinking about my father, and a mystery I have never yet solved.

While my mother stayed close to her roots and continued to observe her Jewish religion, my father, it seems to me, had wanted to make a total break from his origins. I don't know why he never talked to me about his parents or told me anything about his life before he went to South Africa. I have had to rely on his documents and his memorabilia to fill in the gaps.

One thing is for sure: he and my mother were swept into show business by the excitement of Victorian music hall, and he wanted me to grow up in that tradition. He also wanted me to grow up in upper-class British tradition, which was why he sent me off to preparatory school in Rottingdean.

This particular stretch of the Sussex coast around Brighton is, thanks to my father, where my heart belongs. I love it.

It was here I remember seeing the sea for the first time, from the back seat of my father's hired motor car. It was to Brighton, at the age of 17, that I headed when I made my first long-distance run in my own first car, a second-hand Lagonda.

In the recent years my happiest times have been spent in our flat overlooking the sea in Hove, the town that adjoins Brighton. I can't wait to get down there at weekends.

While Irene rests, or cooks, or walks the dog, and Natasha is in her room studying, I wander off alone, relishing the bracing air, enjoying nostalgic journeys around the area.

Not a lot here has changed since my childhood and youth. The Pavilion built by Prince Regent is still the outstanding local landmark, much more impressive than the modern Brighton Conference Centre. The Volks Electric Railway, the first electric railway in Britain, opened in 1883, is still operating along the seafront.

The Albion Hotel, where my father liked to take a dignified lunch, is still a great place for a good meal. Even the cinema where I used to grope my first girlfriend, Jeddy, as we watched Pearl White escape death on the railway line, is still in use.

The house my mother bought after my father's death in 1915, a grand house next to the Grand Hotel, is still standing and proud. I look up at the window of my old room. Then my eyes travel to the bedroom where my grandmother, Leah Assenheim, in her nineties, spent her last years sitting by her window gazing out to sea and no doubt thinking of the 19 children she bore, the last of whom, Annie and Hannah, also lived until their nineties.

Sometimes I go to Brighton cemetery where my mother now

rests. The names of Pauline, Lalla and me, her children, are on her gravestone, and an additional little stone heart mentions the names of her grandchildren, Joan, Jackie and Bill (Natasha, of course, was born long after my mother's death in 1957).

I linger at a seafront attraction, the aquarium and dolphinarium. Years ago my friend Reg Davis and I took a lease on this place, which was being run as a very staid exhibition, just the fish, dolphins, seals and sea-lions. The only excitement for patrons was watching the keeper feeding the sea-lions. Being a man of the theatre, a showman, I had wanted to bring a little more fun to the aquarium and dolphinarium, add a restaurant, sell ice cream, saucy postcards, paper hats, Brighton rock. But the local council, the governing body, insisted that the place must be kept as what it termed a '*respected* attraction', so as our venture was not destined to be profitable my partner and I soon surrendered our lease. Today the aquarium and dolphinarium is exactly as I had envisaged it should be, a lively marketplace for the latest in seaside fun and thrills, plus, of course, the aquatic life.

I motor along the cliffs towards the coastal village of Rotting-dean. Passing through the village of Ovingdean en route I pause at a certain spot in Ovingdean Road and I look out across the field, just behind the grass verge of the roadside. This was where I always used to take my first wife, Elsa, our little daughter Joan and baby Jackie to have a picnic . . . a nice open spot where we could breathe the pure air of the Sussex Downs.

Jackie was too young to remember this tranquil spot, but I do wonder if Joan, rushing around Los Angeles in her Rolls-Royce, ever looks back on this childhood treat.

I make a detour to call on the owner of Brighton's Theatre Royal, my chum David Land, the impresario who 'discovered' lyricist Tim Rice and composer Andrew Lloyd Webber. David and his wife Zara always welcome me. Their garden overlooks the playing fields of my old school, Rottingdean. Climbing over a stile, I am once again in those very orchards where, some 75 years ago, we boys would make our daring raids on the apple trees. I'm sorry I lost touch with these old pals.

Rottingdean School itself no longer exists: it is now the site of a smart housing development. But on the opposite side of the road I spot the country lane where we schoolboys would hunt with the beagles, following the dogs on foot as they chased after hares.

Dominating the village is St Margaret's, the Rottingdean parish church, dating back to Saxon times: probably built more than a century before the Norman Conquest of Britain.

Once again I walk beneath the archway with its text 'Blessed Are They That Hear the Word of God and Keep It'. I cross the area which used to be the choir stalls, where I sang at Matins and Evensong every Sunday. The collection plate, where I placed a silver threepenny piece at each church service, is still in its old place.

I can never leave Rottingdean without paying my respects to the Face in the Wall. The wall itself protects the houses on the opposite side of the road from the church, including the house where writer Rudyard Kipling lived from 1897 to 1903. The strange, half-human, rather ugly Face in the Wall, carved out of stone, fascinated me in my schooldays and still fascinates me today. I have never discovered who carved it, or why he placed it in the wall. I suppose I will never know the answer now.

I've had a good life, with no major illnesses and, apart from my first wife's death, no major disruptions. Altogether I have enjoyed some 50 years of contented married life. My present wife Irene has been very good to me. I couldn't wish for anyone better. She's a good woman.

I've had a finger in every aspect of show business except circus, and though in my career I was not the biggest thing that ever happened I was not the smallest either.

My children are healthy and have made their mark on the world. I think I can claim that almost every person, in every land, has had some form of entertainment, some pleasure, brought their way by one member or another of my family.

I was rather disappointed that Bill did not come into my firm, but he is making his way in his own business, and is settled in a smart little mews house in exclusive Belgravia. He and his wife Hazel, who comes from a professional family, from Guyana,

South America, have not yet produced any grandchildren for me.

My daughter Jackie had her frustrations earlier on, and does not enjoy looking back on her years in show business, but now she is fulfilled. Her books have made her a millionairess and she is sensible with her money.

Joan, my star actress, has done all right for herself from the start of her career. She is making plenty of money at the moment, but I have the feeling she manages to spend everything she earns.

My grandchildren are a quieter bunch than earlier generations of our family, but they all behave well, so I'm satisfied with them.

My hopes are now the ordinary ones of any family man.

I consider my youngest daughter, Natasha, a good catch, so I'd like to see her married to a husband worthy of her. I'd also like to know that Joan, in her personal life, is at last as settled and contented as her sister Jackie and brother Bill.

I'd like to live to see some great-grandchildren, who will probably be mostly girls, for the Collins line has produced only one son in each generation.

We Collins have our ups and downs. Because of the interest in anything to do with Joan and Jackie we see our opinions and criticisms of each other reported – and misreported – in newspapers, sometimes even before we've had a chance to talk things over among ourselves. But we are still a close-knit family, who care about one another.

I hope my record as the present head of the Collins bloodline has done us justice.

Index